THE ZEALOUS INTRUDERS

THE ZEALOUS INTRUDERS

The Western Rediscovery of Palestine,

NAOMI SHEPHERD

1817

HARPER & ROW, PUBLISHERS, SAN FRANCISCO

Cambridge, Hagerstown, New York, Philadelphia, Washington
London, Mexico City, São Paulo, Singapore, Sydney

William Collins Sons & Co. Ltd
London · Glasgow · Sydney · Auckland
Toronto · Johannesburg

Library of Congress Cataloging-in-Publication Data

Shepherd, Naomi.
    The Zealous Intruders.

    1. Palestine—Description and travel. 2. Visitors,
Foreign—Palestine—History—19th century. 3. Christian
pilgrims and pilgrimages—Palestine—History—
19th century. 4. Palestine—History—1799-1917.
5. Palestine—Foreign public opinion, Occidental
History—19th century.   I. Title.
DS107. S54   1988   956.94′03   87-17605

ISBN 0-06-067271-4

88 89 90 91 92 COL 10 9 8 7 6 5 4 3 2 1

First published in 1987
Copyright © Naomi Shepherd 1987

Map by Tamar Sofer

Photoset in Linotron Sabon at
The Spartan Press Ltd,
Lymington, Hants
Made and printed in Great Britain by
T. J. Press (Padstow) Ltd, Padstow, Cornwall

To Yehuda

CONTENTS

ILLUSTRATIONS

ACKNOWLEDGEMENTS

I should like to thank all those who made valuable suggestions for further reading and research during the preparation of this book, and in particular: Professor Yehoshua Ben Arieh; Dr André Chouraqui; Père Marcel Dubois; Professor Albert Hourani; Sarah Kochav; Dr Tudor Parfitt; Dr Ronni Reich; and Dr Mayir Vereté. Dr Amnon Cohen kindly allowed me to consult his unpublished thesis on Ahmed Djezzar Pasha; and Dr Ruth Kark allowed me to read her forthcoming study of the American consuls in Jerusalem in typescript.

I am deeply indebted to Mme Paula Lazard, in whose private collection of books on the subject I found many rare volumes; to another dedicated collector, Professor Yaakov Wahrman, who shared with me his encyclopaedic knowledge on the period literature; and to Martin Gilbert, for again giving me access to his Jerusalem library.

For expert help in the archives, I am particularly grateful to the following: Mme Marie Gallup, curator of the archives at the French Ministère de l'Extérieur, Quai d'Orsay; Dr Rupert Chapman, director of the Palestine Exploration Fund, London; and Edmund Swinglehurst, archivist at Thomas Cook, London, who kindly showed me holograph copies of letters exchanged by Thomas and John Cook on the subject of their Palestine tours. I should also like to thank the staff of the Public Record Office, Kew, London, and of the library of the Ben Zvi Institute, Jerusalem, for their exceptional helpfulness.

Rodney Searight kindly displayed for me a selection of paintings in his possession by artists working in the Near East during the nineteenth century, some of which appear in this book. Jane Martineau, Briony Llewellyn of the Victoria and Albert Museum, and Lady Delia Millar enabled me to track down paintings of Akil Aga and his tribe by Carl Haag.

Dr Aharon Kempinski suggested many additional sources and discussed with me the subject of nineteenth-century archaeologists in Palestine; he also read chapter VII in manuscript.

Yitzhak Tischler first suggested to me the subject of this book; I hope he will not be too disappointed with the result.

I should also like to recall the contribution of the late Bezalel Rabani, sometime inspector of antiquities in the Upper Galilee, at whose home in Tabgha, many years ago, I first read some of the works quoted in this study.

Stefan Mendelsohn read the entire manuscript and eliminated a number of stylistic and factual blunders. Any remaining errors are of course my own.

I am grateful to the Conservateur of the Library at the Institut de France for permission to consult and quote from the letters of Charles Clermont-Ganneau; to the Palestine Exploration Fund, for permission to quote from the Conder letters; to the Hebrew University of Jerusalem for permission to quote from Conder's private letters; to the Secretary of the Church's Mission to the Jews for permission to quote from the papers of the London Society (CMJ) deposited at the New Bodleian Library, Oxford; and to Penguin Books Ltd, for permission to quote from T. Carmi's prose translation of 'The Dirge of Moses Remos' in *The Penguin Book of Hebrew Verse*.

I am deeply grateful to Carol O'Brien, my editor at Collins, both for her initial encouragement and for the constructive criticism which determined the final shape of the book.

No list of acknowledgements would be complete without mention of the help of my family. Thanks, then, to Joshua, who provided liaison with libraries in London and Oxford; to Sarah and Isaac, for their practical help and patience; and to my husband, Yehuda Layish, to whom the book is dedicated.

JERUSALEM

TOMBS OF THE KINGS

OLD CITY WALLS

DAMASCUS GATE

MOSLEM QU.

ST. STEPHEN'S GATE

CHRISTIAN QU.

CHURCH of the HOLY SEPULCHRE

TEMPLE MT.

DOME of the ROCK

JEWISH QU.

Robinson Arch

AL AQSA

ABSALOM'S TOMB

JAFFA GATE

ARMENIAN QU.

DUNG GATE

ZION GATE

WARREN'S SHAFT

Tunnel

POOL OF SILOAM

SILOAM

MOUNT OF OLIVES

Kidron V.

Km

Mile

BEIRUT

SIDON

DAMASCUS

TYRE

MT. LEBANON

MT. HERMON

HAURAN

GALILEE

ACRE

SAFAD

SEA of GALILEE

HAIFA

TIBERIAS

GAMALA

GILEAD

NAZARETH

MI. CARMEL

ESDRAELON

AMT. TABOR

GADARA

Kishon

DECAPOLIS

JORDAN R.

CAESAREA

GERASA

NABLUS

W. Zerka

JAFFA

ES-SALT

JUDEA

JERICHO

PHILADELPHIA

ABU SHUSHEH

MEDITERRANEAN SEA

JERUSALEM

ASHKELON

BETHLEHEM

ARTAS

DEAD SEA

MOAB

GAZA

HEBRON

PORT SAID

KERAK

SUEZ CANAL (1869)

W. Zin

ISMAELIA

WILDERNESS OF ZIN

W. Musa

PETRA

EDOM

NAKHL

W. es-Sudr

S I N A I

AQABA

E G Y P T

GULF OF SUEZ

W. Mukatb

GULF OF AQABA

A R A B I A N

D E S E R T

ST. CATHERINE'S MONASTERY

∴ RUINS

0   50   100 KM

0   50   100 MILES

RED SEA

T. SOFFER

CHAPTER I

———◆•◆———

The Rediscovery of Palestine,
1799–1831

IN THE YEAR 1801, a painting of one of the first British victories of the Napoleonic Wars went on show at the Lyceum in the London Strand. The Lyceum was a place of popular entertainment, where magic lantern 'phantasmagoria' of storms and shipwrecks alternated with displays of 'historical paintings' which were essays in propaganda. Sir Robert Ker Porter's 'The Siege of Acre' was an illustration of the defence of the Palestinian sea town against Napoleon by British and Turkish forces in 1799. But its message was that Sir Sidney Smith, the British admiral, had won the battle on his own. Smith appears in the painting standing alone in the breach, flourishing his drawn sabre, while turbaned figures crouch apprehensively in the smoke behind him.

All the contemporary records indicate that the dominant figure in the defence of Acre was Ahmed Djezzar, the town's Bosnian governor, dubbed 'the butcher of Acre', who, though in his sixties, had personally led his mercenary soldiers into battle against Napoleon. Smith's offshore bombardment and the logistic help he provided, together with the assault force he finally led, were important: but Napoleon could not have been defeated had not Djezzar bravely held the town against the French throughout a siege which lasted two months. The French launched not one, but fourteen attempts to breach the walls. Djezzar and his men repelled them all, venturing out frequently against Europe's most formidable army, and blocking each attempt at a breakthrough with barrels of gunpowder and bales of cotton.

In 1804, Baron Antoine Gros' painting 'The Pest House in Jaffa' was unveiled at the Paris Salon. This painting represented an earlier event in Napoleon's disastrous Syrian campaign, when, after a lightning advance up the sea coast, his army was halted by the plague.

Gros portrayed Napoleon on an errand of mercy to his soldiers, and his outstretched hand, touching the breast of one stricken man, echoes the gesture of Christ the healer familiar from Renaissance art. The success of this painting underlined the fact that Napoleon had converted the military defeat in Syria into political victory in Paris. But Gros' healer was not the Napoleon who had ordered the massacre in Jaffa of four thousand helpless Turkish prisoners, nor the impatient general said to have prescribed lethal doses of opium to those soldiers too sick to be moved (an event Ker Porter celebrated in his cartoons). According to one eyewitness of Napoleon's visit to the pesthouse, he actually pushed aside a suffering soldier with the toe of his boot.

So little inclined was Napoleon to be regarded as Gros' Christian warrior that in Egypt he had ordered his men to respect Moslem sensibilities, assuring the sceptical populace that the French were at heart 'true Moslems' who had overthrown Islam's enemy, the Pope. During the Syrian campaign he made no effort to visit Jerusalem, arguing that the Holy City was 'not within his line of operations' as he had no wish to encounter the warlike clans in the Judean hills. Though Smith referred to himself as a 'Christian knight' in his local bulletins, and staged a march to Jerusalem to reassure the local Christian minority, he had courted the other ethnic groups as well – and British policy was to preserve Moslem rule, not to destroy it. In Palestine, as elsewhere in Asia, the Ottoman Turks were Britain's allies.

But both Ker Porter and Gros recognized that Palestine was most vividly associated in the mind of Europe with the theme of Christian chivalry and the memory of the Crusades. When Napoleon took his troops, fresh from the conquest of Egypt, into Palestine in the spring of 1799 he led the first European campaign in the Holy Land since the Crusades; Acre itself was famous as the place of the last stand of the Crusaders. Since that time, and until Napoleon's campaign, in Gibbon's words, 'a mournful and solitary silence prevailed along the coast which had so long resounded to the WORLD'S DEBATE'.

By the beginning of the nineteenth century, moreover, the West was disposed to renew that debate. The rationalist attacks on the Crusaders by Voltaire and Diderot were already being tempered by contemporaries like Heeren, who regarded the excesses of the Crusaders, their massacres of Moslems and Jews, as deplorable symptoms of the 'heroic adolescence' of Christianity. Romantic writers celebrated medieval Christianity and antiquarians sought for classical remains in nearby Greece and Egypt. Threatened by revolution and war on the continent of Europe, Protestant England clung to Evangelicalism, and the cult of the Bible. All this favoured a revival of interest in the Holy Land. But the condition of the country itself did not.

* * *

Palestine, at the end of the eighteenth century, had been almost *terra incognita*. It had no political frontiers but the shifting historical tidelines of biblical, Roman and medieval conquest. In political terms it was merely a part of the Ottoman province of Syria, administered by the governors of Acre and Damascus. European traders frequented the ports, but the interior of the country, save for Nazareth, Jerusalem and Bethlehem, was scarcely visited. Blake's poetry might invoke a heavenly Jerusalem, but in his contemporary Pinkerton's *Modern Geography* while Aleppo and Damascus, well-known Syrian trading centres, were mentioned, the earthly Jerusalem was not.

Palestine was not even familiar as a place of pilgrimage. By Napoleon's time the tradition of Catholic pilgrimage was moribund. Only a handful of Europeans were to be seen in Jerusalem during Easter Week, vastly outnumbered by pilgrims from the Eastern churches – Greek Orthodox, Armenian, Copt, and others. These were merchants and peasants from the Balkans, Russia and the Near East, many of whose rituals were as alien to the European as those of pilgrims of other faiths: Moslems for whom the *ziyara* to Jerusalem and the supposed tomb of the Prophet Moses was the sequel to the *Haj* to Mecca, and Jews from the rabbinical seminaries of Eastern Europe.

Many travellers from Europe at this period came as scientists and secular explorers: the most influential was the Count François de Volney, the French writer whose pioneering work on Egypt and Syria, first published in 1787, was according to Napoleon's General Berthier, the only reliable guide to the region for the entire French army. Napoleon himself studied and annotated it carefully and it was one of the books which he took into exile later.

Educated in a Jansenist seminary, but by temperament a freethinker (his adopted surname was a combination of the names of Voltaire and his estate at Ferney), Volney prepared himself to report on the Holy Land, its people and its customs, in a spirit utterly remote from the antiquarian and religious travellers who had preceded him. His purpose, as he later explained, was to compare great cultures in decline with those now flourishing in the West, but not to denigrate Islam or to patronize Moslems or Jews. He attributed the decline of Egypt and Palestine to despotic government and the unchallenged rule of religion; not, like so many of his predecessors and even his contemporaries, to the climate of the East or the inferiority of Islam to Christianity. Palestine interested him in particular, as the country which had produced the ideas 'which had so powerfully influenced our public and individual morality, our laws, and our entire social condition'.

The paradox that Palestine was at one and the same time glorious and obscure, mighty and fallen, had been a commonplace of Christian belief for centuries. The desolation and poverty of Palestine, as travellers saw it – and which they often exaggerated – was the punishment for the crime of deicide. While by the late eighteenth century this paradox had lost its literal force for all but the most devout, few visitors to Palestine after Napoleon failed to mention the divine curse on the land and its causes, if only to speculate on Palestine's alleged prosperity in biblical times and the cause of its present desolation. Volney took the most practical view. Unlike many visitors, he had not followed the pilgrim routes (Jerusalem had short shrift from Volney) and had noted the difference between the industrious – and rebellious – people of the hill towns and the more vulnerable

14

peasantry in the lowlands. He noted that the Ottoman system of taxation in kind, enforced by the local sheikhs who acted as tax farmers, backed up by the Ottoman soldiery, had deprived the peasants in the plains of the motive to grow other than subsistence crops, particularly since they were exposed, in addition, to raids by the invading Bedouin of the surrounding deserts.

For Volney, Palestine was a prime example of how despotic and corrupt regimes, and the passivity encouraged by an authoritarian religion, could wreck a potentially fertile and productive country. Those who followed him, whether soldiers, scholars or clergymen, compared early accounts of fertility with present evidence of neglect. They measured distances, calculated temperatures, and speculated about possible climatic changes over the centuries. They poked around in rock tombs and copied inscriptions in churches and monasteries, searching for confirmation of accounts by the early historians and the works of travelling chaplains in Syrian embassies. They 'borrowed' manuscripts from the Greek Orthodox clergy for Western libraries. They collected samples of water from the Jordan and scraped up soil from the shores of the Dead Sea, not for baptism or burial rites, but for analysis in European laboratories. They theorized on the curse as a metaphor for economic decline. Within a few years their reports had established the image of Palestine as a land desperately in need of Western enterprise and where the West, for historic reasons, had a special mission to perform 'a crusade', as the French historian Michaud put it, 'of philosophy and knowledge which would permanently reunite the East and the West'.

It was this idea of a secular mission which alone redeemed Napoleon's military failure in Egypt. Napoleon's decision to attack British interests in the East rather than in Europe had three main sources: he had hoped to secure his reputation far from the conflicts in Paris under the Directory; to establish a new French colony; and to block Britain's route to India. But Nelson's defeat of the French fleet, leaving Napoleon prisoner in Egypt, and Djezzar's refusal to parley, followed by the Syrian campaign and the defeat of France at Acre, ended Napoleon's hopes of dominion in the East.

Instead, he brought back the great *Description de l'Egypte*, a compendium of research by the French scholars and scientists who had accompanied Napoleon's army. Some of these men followed him to Syria; but in Palestine, multiple disasters prevented the extension of the *Description* to the Holy Land. The resistance Napoleon encountered, and his savage retribution, meant that by the time the French army retreated little was left of the modest landmarks of Jaffa and Acre: what Volney had described as 'a bazaar not inferior to that of Aleppo' and 'a public fountain which surpasses in elegance those of Damascus'. The French fired the stores of grain they had amassed in the Galilee, and the ashes of their fires still smouldered, it was reported, two years later. Napoleon systematically destroyed every village he suspected of having aided Djezzar. The Druse rebels had been encouraged by Smith; rumours had been spread that Napoleon intended to restore the Jewish nation to Palestine – and all Christians were naturally suspect. After the Europeans departed, the non-Moslem minorities, to whom both Napoleon and Smith had appealed for logistic support and to whom they had made promises, were left to defend themselves as best they could against accusations of disloyalty. It was a grim consummation of Volney's humanist vision.

What the Napoleonic campaign had done, however, was to remind the West of the physical reality of the Holy Land. As the wars continued, the privileged class whose passion for travel was little affected by war skirted the battlefields of Europe and began to explore this neglected corner of the Levant. 'European policies have directed the observation of enlightened travellers to regions they probably would not otherwise have noticed,' wrote Edward Clarke, one of the most assiduous of world travellers, in 1801; '. . . the harvest has begun.'

Palestine was now to be rescued from obscurity and made the focus of romantic and religious expectations. It was also, however, to be subjected to the analytical scrutiny inherited from the eighteenth century. This in itself was sufficient to make the visit to the Holy Land an ambivalent experience. What complicated matters still further was that much as visitors from the West resented the domination of Palestine, the Holy Land, by the

Moslem Turks, they were deeply disturbed by what they saw of the traditions, the practices and the very presence of the Eastern churches – the reminder that what was now a Western religion had originated and survived in the alien and hostile country which they were now discovering for the first time.

* * *

Volney was heir to a fortune, and a legacy enabled him to travel to the East. Edward Clarke, who at the turn of the century was just thirty, came from a family of scholars and clerics. Such men were dependent on patronage. Clarke's father was chaplain to Lord Bristol, while Clarke himself could only travel abroad as tutor or companion to the aristocracy.

He was an eager, eclectic scholar who as an adolescent had written on the comparative antiquity of the Egyptians and the Jews, did scientific experiments and explored caves and mountains in his early youth, and eventually became a Cambridge professor of mineralogy, most celebrated for having invented a gas blowpipe for use in laboratories. When he finally reached Palestine he explained that he 'came not in an age of credulity, though sufficiently a believer': not prepared to accept ancient traditions without submitting them to enquiry, yet devout enough to want to explore every historical site related to the life of Christ.

But it took years for him to find a patron to finance the journey. The travelling elite, with its retinue of scholars, physicians and bodyguards, had touched at Beirut en route for Egypt since the mid-eighteenth century, with no more than a passing glance at the Holy Land. The discovery of Graeco-Roman ruins at Palmyra had drawn visitors to northern Syria, but there was nothing to attract them to Palestine. It had no great monuments to rival the Parthenon or the Pyramids, no ruins to compare with Philae or Baalbeck, nor a single bazaar to match those of Alexandria, Cairo or Damascus.

Moreover, Palestine had to compete with a powerful rival: its own image in European art and literature. Painters since the Renaissance had set their Christian scenes in the familiar landscapes of their native Umbria, France or Spain, or in imaginary landscapes inspired by sources as diverse as Gothic architecture and Byzantine iconography. In Antonello da Messina's 'Crucifixion', Jerusalem overlooks not the desert, as in reality, but the sea; in Claude's 'Flight into Egypt', the Holy Family rests in the well-watered landscape of the Roman Campagna, and in El Greco's 'Mount Sinai', the twisted spouts of rock belong to a medieval vision of hell, not an observed desert. Scenes like these flashed upon the inward eye of every educated European as he heard or read the biblical narrative.

The Holy Land of Western painting had long been severed from its Levantine moorings, and the recognition of its real environment came as a shock. When travellers were confronted with the low and featureless coastline, the valleys empty of rivers and the hills despoiled of their forests, the wide stretches of uncultivated plain and the bare hills of Judea exposed to the white glare of the desert sun, they were almost invariably disappointed. When one traveller exclaimed, on seeing Jerusalem: 'Where was the Temple of Solomon . . . and Mount Zion, the glory of the whole earth?' he knew that the Herodian Temple had been razed by Roman legionaries in the first century after Christ. But somewhere in the back of his mind was the image of a Giorgione temple, marble beneath cypresses, and not 'plain embattled walls in the midst of a barren mountain tract . . . no palaces, arches, fountains, porticos, to announce its former military greatness or commercial opulence, but rude masonry and dull uniformity'.

From the time of the Mystery Plays and Luther's Bible, moreover, the patriarchs and the Holy Family had spoken the languages of Europe. Milton's *Paradise Lost*, Tasso's *Gerusalemme Liberata*, Racine's biblical dramas were derived from classical models so remote from any Levantine association that nineteenth-century travellers in the real Palestine quoted them with puzzled resentment. Milton's famous opening invocation of 'Siloa's Brook that flow'd/Fast by the oracle of God' suggested a Delphic stream; but the Abbé Desmazures, an early visitor to the site who traced the brook underground to its source, emerged covered with mud to find peasant women doing their washing. Tasso's Jerusalem was an eastern Ferrara: 'Where morning gilds

the city's eastern side/The Sacred Jordan pours its gentle tide.'
This scarcely prepared travellers for the steep descent from the
high, dry city to the rocky stream fiercely flooded at Easter. The
site of the Temple in Racine's *Athalie*, which French travellers
read aloud on Judean mountain tops, was occupied by Moslem
domes and minarets.

Edward Clarke eventually found his rich young travelling
companion and extended his journey through Europe, Scan-
dinavia, Russia and Asia Minor to Palestine. He arrived at Acre
in 1801 on a British naval vessel, whose captain had been
charged to collect a supply of bullocks to provision the forces
besieging Napoleon's army in Egypt.

The quickest way to reach Palestine, at the turn of the century,
was by sea, whether from Greece, Turkey or Egypt. To follow the
desert route from the south meant travelling by Bedouin caravan
through the territory of rival tribes. The route through the
mountainous north of Syria lay between mutually hostile
Turkoman and Kurdish tribes as well as among the Druse, the
Metawali (Shiite) Moslems and the Maronite Christians.

But to land on the Palestine sea coast was a hit or miss affair.
There was not a single harbour where a sailing ship could
anchor; the coast was studded with rocks and swept with fierce
currents. Before Sidney Smith could begin his bombardment of
Acre in the spring of 1799 one of his ships had to 'ride out the
equinoctial gales by being anchored in the undertow' while the
others 'clawed offshore by dint of carrying sail'. The Anglo-
Turkish force which occupied Palestine after Napoleon's retreat
only set sail from Constantinople after soothsayers had given
their approval, and the Turkish pilots, too nervous to chance
their luck in the open sea, guided the ships dangerously close to
the rocky shore.

Many ships foundered and, as contemporary prints show,
their skeletons littered the beaches. But Djezzar threatened to
execute any port officer who allowed a ship belonging to his allies
to run ashore; it was thus that Clarke reported that when one
British ship was brought into Acre, the pilot, though extremely
old, stripped, dived under the vessel's keel, and found exactly
four feet of water between the ship and the anchoring ground.

Clarke's first task on landing in Palestine was to pay his compliments to Djezzar with the ship's captain, and obtain the old tyrant's permission for their excursion. Djezzar was by this time a bogeyman in European eyes, the figure who embodied the image of the cruel Turk, Shakespeare's 'barbarous Scythian,/Or he that makes his generation messes/To gorge his appetite'.

Clarke witnessed the evidence of his barbarity: the grotesquely mutilated victims of the Pasha's displeasure, some without eyes, some without noses; Djezzar's banker and adviser, the Jewish Haim Farhi, wore a black taffeta patch over his disfigured nose, but continued to demonstrate his fidelity. He was later to be strangled and thrown into the sea on the orders of Djezzar's successor. Clarke himself experienced Djezzar's methods. Re-embarking one night by boat from Acre, the Englishmen were stoned by soldiers guarding the port. When Clarke went to complain to Djezzar next day, he immediately ordered the offending officer's execution, and it took all the Englishmen's pleas for the sentence to be commuted to mere demotion and exile.

Yet Clarke was too intelligent an observer not to see that Djezzar was an able ruler, whose power rested on his control of the agricultural trade of Palestine, 'the granary of Syria'; Clarke and his companions found it difficult to defend Sidney Smith against Djezzar's accusation that he had stirred up trouble among the Druse, and Clarke described him as a shrewd negotiator, contemptuous of sycophants and ceremony, who sat cutting out paper flowers as a distraction for his guests while assessing their intentions. The Turks were notorious for their venality, but Clarke put it on record that Djezzar at no time took payment from England for his services, save for some outdated pieces of artillery taken from the French.

Clarke's company now set out to explore Palestine with an escort of soldiers provided by Djezzar – something only accorded to important travellers. An escort was essential as Palestine had no roads, and maps were unreliable – the first modern map of Palestine, drawn by Napoleon's cartographer Jacotin, became available only after the wars. Neither bedding, food nor firearms could be purchased in the countryside, so that everything was carried by pack animals – camels, or donkeys, for horses were scarce. In Palestine, as throughout the Levant, there was not a single wheeled vehicle, and the party travelled holding umbrellas against the blazing sun. But Djezzar's soldiers at least protected the party from the ubiquitous marauders.

Though highwaymen and bandits still infested the wilder parts of Europe like the Apennines, most travellers felt that once they left the coastal towns of Palestine they stepped back into the Middle Ages. The gates of the main towns were locked at night – the governors of Acre and Damascus were intermittently at war – and the decay of Ottoman rule had strengthened the power of the local sheikhs and the frequency of tribal battles. Djezzar himself was a potential rebel against his masters in Constantinople, kept in check only by local rivals. Ancient quarrels dating back to the feuds of the Qays and Yemen factions of Arabia set the inhabitants of many towns and villages against one another, and the notorious Abu Ghosh clan, from a village astride the route from Jaffa to Jerusalem, demanded a toll fee from every non-Moslem. Reports of this situation encouraged the belief in the West that only an eventual change of government and reforms on a Western pattern would restore prosperity to the Holy Land.

If the first danger threatening travellers was banditry, the second was disease. Clarke fell ill with a malarial fever half way through his visit, and few visitors left without contracting either malaria or dysentery. The plague, which had attacked both Napoleon's army and the Anglo-Turkish forces, reappeared with terrifying and unpredictable frequency. The bodies of those massacred in Jaffa were only superficially buried under the shifting sands (their skeletons were still visible on the dunes up to thirty years later) and the sea breezes brought dangerous effluvia from the open drains of the coastal towns to those camped nearby. William Wittman, surgeon to the British military mission, attributed thousands of deaths from the plague to the 'superstitious prejudices and culpable neglect of the rulers'. He had attempted unsuccessfully to convince the Turkish Vizier that the troops camped near Jaffa should be moved, but the Vizier refused to budge, sceptical not only of Wittman's warnings but of the British General Koehler's information that the earth was round and moved around the sun.

Local fear of the plague often barred travellers from the Holy Places, where the monks shut themselves up, fumigated every *firman* – the Turkish letter of accreditation – before examining it, and were nervous of admitting sufferers seeking miraculous cures, such as those Clarke observed 'rubbing their bodies with hangings in the sanctuary' at the Church of the Annunciation in Nazareth.

Yet despite the lawlessness and the disease, Clarke observed like Volney that Palestine was a far more productive country than was then believed in the West. Its natural fertility reappeared every spring: the Sea of Galilee abounded in fish, though only one boat, formerly used by Djezzar's soldiers to bring wood from the eastern side of the lake, lay abandoned on its shores, and fishermen cast their nets only from its margins. There was an abundance of game; pheasant flew so low in the Galilee that they could be knocked down by a man with a stick. The grapes and figs of the Hebron area in Judea compared favourably with those of Europe, though the Moslem farmers made raisins and a sweet drink, *dibs*, of the surplus, not wine. In the hills, olive groves produced an oil and soap, the indigo plants near the Jordan yielded a primitive dye, and fine cotton was grown in the north.

Clarke's verdict, echoed by scores of other travellers, was that punitive taxation, by a distant government which did nothing for its subjects, was responsible for the neglect by the local people of the country's resources. Peasants could be seen working one side of a field of corn while their camels fed on the other, preferring this waste to giving the surplus up to the tax collectors. A French veterinary surgeon who visited the country to buy stallions was shocked to find splendid animals with their tails and ears cropped. This mutilation, he was told, was to discourage the Turks from confiscating the horses for their own use.

Clarke, whose travels in Asia Minor had trained him to identify the remains of ancient structures, noted the ruins of reservoirs, cisterns and wells, showing that the streams and winter rains had once been better exploited. His testimony, like that of other travellers, was included in the first guide book to

Palestine, published in 1825, to show that in what the editor called 'the most favoured and the most guilty land under heaven', European enterprise – roads, bridges, drainage, irrigation and afforestation – might reclaim the Holy Land and restore it to prosperity.

But the physical state of the country was not Clarke's only concern. What preoccupied him most was the discovery of the 'degrading superstitions which pollute the Holy Land': not the Moslem domination of Palestine, but the beliefs of the local Catholic and Greek Orthodox communities. Visiting Acre, Clarke observed that the Saracens had been far more enlightened than the Crusader invaders and that Moslem historians would surely make out a devastating indictment of the Christians. Contemporary rituals in the Holy Places of Nazareth, Jerusalem and Bethlehem disturbed him more profoundly still.

Like most travellers, Clarke lodged at the monasteries and hospices of the Catholics and was introduced to the Christian shrines by their traditional guardians, the Franciscans. For an 'enlightened' Protestant like Clarke, the preservation of relics and tangible objects of worship such as 'the place where the head of Adam was found, the rock on which the martyr Stephen was stoned and the place of the withered fig tree – the milk of the Virgin Mary and some of the bitter tears that St Peter wept' were degrading superstitions, 'mummery' or 'pious frauds', as so many Protestants called them, whether encountered in Rome, Naples or Nazareth. Still more repellent to Clarke was the glibness with which the Franciscans reeled off the pedigree of every supposedly holy site, 'with little reference to either history or common sense'. Clarke cast bitter scorn on Helena, mother of the Emperor Constantine, who had located all the shrines sacred to Christianity by imperial fiat fifteen centuries earlier. The body of legend and custom that had grown up around them was bound to infuriate those who respected only the text of the Bible. He made no allowance for the fact that the Franciscans, who according to the rules of their order might spend a dozen years of their lives in Palestine, were usually of poor Spanish and Italian families and often semi-literate. All the paraphernalia of Catholic pilgrimage displeased Clarke, and by the time he reached

Jerusalem his revulsion against the Catholic and the Greek Orthodox clergy and the shrines they shared led him to cast doubt even on the identity of the sites most sacred to Christianity, in the Holy City itself.

*   *   *

Looking down at Jerusalem from the Mount of Olives, Clarke described it as 'a flourishing and stately metropolis, presenting a magnificent assemblage of domes, towers, churches and monasteries'. Like other travellers, Clarke's enthusiasm waned as he entered the city streets; only the most passionate pilgrim could ignore what he saw. 'The streets of it are narrow and deserted, the houses dirty and ragged, the shops few and forsaken, and throughout the whole there is not one symptom of either commerce, comfort or happiness,' wrote a traveller newly arrived from the desert. 'The most sinful city in the world given over to idolatry,' proclaimed a missionary. 'A cemetery in the middle of the desert' was the verdict of a French man of letters. So it continued. 'The Jerusalem of sacred history is no more. Nothing remains of David's and Solomon's cities. The walls are changed, the boundaries doubtful.' 'A city of a singular and gloomy magnificence, scarcely possessed by any other city in the world.' 'I found Jerusalem a much handsomer city than I had expected – but to those who visit it for any other reason than that of devotion, it must be a tiresome and dull place.' 'The distant view is all.'

In brilliant sunshine, looking down from the Mount of Olives, east of the city, Jerusalem might well have appeared to Clarke as an assemblage of domes and towers – but these were mosques and minarets, not church domes and belltowers; Christians, at this period in Palestine, were not allowed to ring bells, and all the churches save the Holy Sepulchre were concealed from the view from the Mount of Olives, and the monasteries built like fortresses to protect their vulnerable inhabitants. The Holy Sepulchre itself lay too deep within the streets of the city for more than its dome to be visible, and in many early prints its size is exaggerated, so that it appears to rival the Moslem Dome of the Rock, far more prominent on the Temple Mount.

Only a Protestant missionary could have thought Jerusalem sinful, for it had no temptations for the sinner: not a single place of entertainment or inn, its bazaars among the poorest in the country, selling, for most of the year, nothing but the produce of the local farmers. The city was indeed a necropolis; its walls were surrounded by cemeteries and its rocks pitted with ancient burial caves, its chief monuments tombs, and its most renowned sites, for Christians and Jews respectively, the Holy Sepulchre and the Wailing Wall. At nightfall the four great gates in use were closed against marauders and no one ventured out into the unlit streets. All surveying and digging in the city was forbidden. The Temple Mount, the assumed site of Solomon's Temple, known to the Moslems as the Haram esh Sharif or Noble Sanctuary, whose magnificent proportions were visible from the east, was out of bounds to all non-Moslems.

The visit to the Holy Sepulchre was an ordeal for the Christian traveller, who had first to pass the city's tannery, where freshly skinned carcasses lay slippery underfoot. As the Turkish governors feared Christian riots every Easter, a huge stone partially blocked the entrance to the one low door which provided access to the church. An entrance fee was charged to worshippers, and Turkish soldiers lolled on a platform just inside the church, smoking and playing cards.

But what shocked Clarke and other visitors, both Protestant and Catholic, to the greatest of Christian shrines, was the chaotic rivalry between the Christian sects who shared the church between them. Catholic visitors were bombarded with complaints from the Latin priests, who shared the church with the Greek Orthodox, of harassment by their richer and more powerful rivals. The Latin situation became even weaker after a fire which broke out in 1808 and destroyed most of the interior of the building, whose repair was financed by the Orthodox. When the different sects celebrated their rites in close sequence, fights broke out, and warring priests sometimes damaged or removed their rivals' carpets, candlesticks, paintings or altars; sometimes they attacked one another with candelabra and incense burners. The Latin Superior complained bitterly to Ambroise Firmin Didot, the famous French master printer, that 'there is no church more sacred and yet more profaned than the Holy Sepulchre. The Greeks and the Armenians come here to discuss business, the women to see their lovers; it is in fact a real brothel.'

Clarke objected to the Holy Sepulchre both on aesthetic grounds and because he thought it an actual obstacle to historical research. 'The absurdity of hewing the rocks of Mount Calvary into gilded chapels, and disguising the Holy Sepulchre by coverings of marble and painted domes, has so effectually removed or concealed all that might have born witness to the history of the crucifixion, that a visit to Jerusalem has often weakened, instead of fortifying, the faith of pilgrims.' It was not enough for him to declare the shrines inauthentic – he himself used the few days he spent in Jerusalem in an attempt to locate the real sites, as he believed, of the events described in the Gospels, inspecting rock tombs and deciphering inscriptions.

Clarke was as hasty and mistaken in his substitute proposals for Calvary and the Sepulchre as he had been in discovering what he thought were the real tombs of Alexander and Euclid in Greece (there was more than one Euclid). But the idea of a critical appraisal of the traditional Holy Places caught the imagination of Protestant scholars throughout the West. Moreover, Protestant visitors after Clarke often shared his revulsion at the 'pious frauds' practised in the Holy City. Many fled Jerusalem and literally took to the hills, finding the experience they sought in the open air or in the desert. On the Mount of Olives, outside the city, they felt nearest to the source of Christianity; in Sinai, with its bare, lowering crags they thought they recognized the natural birthplace of the monotheistic faith.

*   *   *

Clarke was the first nineteenth-century critic of Palestine. The French writer Chateaubriand, who arrived in Palestine five years after Clarke, romanticized the country, maintaining that he was the last Frenchman to visit the Holy Land 'like a pilgrim of old'. The huge success of his *Itinéraire à Jérusalem*, probably the most widely read book on Palestine in the early years of the century (it went into twelve editions by 1814 and paid all its author's debts) and the most parodied (a surer index of success), was a tribute to the deliberate archaism of his approach. Clarke called the *Itinéraire* 'that entertaining narrative . . . wherein the chivalrous and bigoted spirit of the eleventh century seems singularly associated with the taste, the genius and the literature of the nineteenth'.

Chateaubriand praised the Crusaders, saw Napoleon's army as their heirs, and reasserted the theme of the primeval curse in the shape of a romantic melancholy and decay which enshrouded the Holy Land. His Palestine was a country peopled by martyred, noble monks, Bedouin fallen from a former civilized state, and Jews patiently awaiting their Messiah. Chateaubriand transformed all the symbols of pilgrimage into a literary cult of self: his vow was not the old pilgrim's vow to God, but one made to himself, to explore the Orient as a sequel to his American travels. He assumed the pilgrim's robe not out of humility, but for self-preservation – and his passage through the wilderness near the Dead Sea inspired him less with the fear of God than with a renewed confidence in his own creative spirit.

'Barbarism begins at Trieste,' he wrote, and his attack on Islam and its dominion was also deliberately archaic, written at the time when the serious study of Islam as a religion and a civilization was already under way. Yet between the great rhetorical passages there are intriguing glimpses of Chateaubriand's version of the new, analytical view of Palestine. His long passage on the history of Jerusalem, intended to look like scholarship, was lifted from a manuscript by the seventeenth-century Flemish divine, Quaresmius, which he found in the library of the monastery where he stayed in Jerusalem. His refutation of the eighteenth-century attacks on the Crusaders led him into the modern argument that the Crusaders saved Europe from revolution by funnelling off 'the excess population which sooner or later ruins states' – something which might have amused Clarke, a friend of Malthus – and in a small gesture to the spirit of scientific enquiry, he kept four Dead Sea fruit and a vial of Dead Sea water in which he intended to submerge a few French goldfish on his return to Paris.

Chateaubriand's 'pilgrimage' was the record of a personal experience; it also taught his readers how poorly Christians fared in their Holy Land. When, in a state of euphoric excitement,

Chateaubriand arrived offshore at Jaffa, he was disconcerted to see his servant, Julien, carried ashore in state by the porters who served the travellers, while he himself was dumped in the surf. The reason was that Julien wore white, the colour for Moslems, while Chateaubriand wore a Christian shade of blue. Later he was warned that travelling to Jerusalem in European clothing would expose him to assault and robbery, and for this reason he disguised himself; in Jerusalem he was relieved to resume the robes of a French chevalier. The local people tended to resent any foreigner wearing green (emblem of the Moslem's visit to the *Haj*) and considered European dress not only odd but indecent – in particular the men's tight silk breeches.

Like many of his Catholic contemporaries, Chateaubriand saw the priests of Palestine in the role of early Christian martyrs. As the Count de Forbin said of the Franciscan fathers in Jaffa, 'They come with trembling steps to hear the mass in a small vaulted subterraneous and obscure chapel which brings to mind the worship of the primitive Christians in the catacombs.' Throughout the first thirty years of the century the Christians were indeed a despised minority in the Holy Land, subject like the Jews to various punitive taxes, unable to practise their faith without fear of persecution, and continually under suspicion as the allies of Islam's enemies in Europe. During the Napoleonic Wars it was chiefly the Latin priests and the Jews who were suspected of collaborating with Napoleon; from the time of the Greek uprising in 1823 the Greek Orthodox community was consistently harassed by Turkish soldiers who entered the monasteries, seized the weapons the monks kept for self-defence against the Bedouin, and incited the local Moslem peasants against them.

Clarke and Chateaubriand both praised the Bedouin of Palestine as 'noble and unselfish' – in Clarke's words; Chateaubriand compared them favourably with the Indians of North America – not savages, but heirs to a half-forgotten civilization. The mystique of Bedouin gallantry had been current, particularly in France, ever since Laurent d'Arvieux, Louis XVI's commercial envoy to the Levant in the eighteenth century, had been hospitably received by a friendly sheikh on Mount Carmel in

1718; Gibbon, in the famous fiftieth chapter of *Decline and Fall*, had perpetuated the myth and the British diplomat Terrick Hamilton's translation of the Arabic epic *Antar*, the picaresque tale of the bastard son of an Arabian prince, who in translation emerged possessed of a combination of Herculean strength and Arthurian chivalry, had reinforced it. It was all very well for Clarke to praise the Bedouin since he travelled everywhere with an armed escort, and Chateaubriand, who enjoyed dramatizing his own adventures (somewhat deflated by Julien's account), also therefore had to praise Bedouin valour.

But such accounts were contradicted by every traveller in Palestine who had actually encountered a Bedouin – whether as guide, blackmailer or marauder. The Bedouin played a double role in the southern and eastern parts of the country: they were escorts and aggressors, guides and raiders. Recorded attacks on foreign travellers were rare, but it was enough for any guide from the towns to hear a rumour of their approach for him to turn back or raise the price of the journey. Travellers soon learned that the best escort was the very tribe which – had they been unescorted – would have attacked them.

For anyone who ventured east of Jerusalem or near the Dead Sea, or into the wadis near Hebron (a place of sanctuary for criminals since biblical times), found a patchwork of territories under the control of different Bedouin tribes. Bedouin escorts frequently renegotiated the price as they went and it took courage to make a Bedouin stick to his bargain – those travellers who threw their money about, like Lady Hester Stanhope and later the antiquarian de Saulcy, were notorious for spoiling the market, 'building a bridge of gold' as one traveller put it, to districts which were then priced beyond the pocket of the less affluent.

It was fatal to resist a Bedouin attack, as this would turn the encounter into a blood feud. If assailants thought a party of travellers vulnerable, they would attack, strip them of all their possessions and clothing, and leave them literally naked by the roadside. The spoils were often resold in Gaza, the Bedouin's favourite market town, nearest the escape route to the desert. This was what happened to Sir Frederick Henniker, who nearly lost his life on the notorious Jericho road in 1826. Henniker had taken the desert route from Egypt, on which he had managed to outwit several treacherous Bedouin guides despite their efforts to lead him off course and substitute sand for gunpowder in his pistols. He set out for Jericho with only one armed guard and his Maltese servant. When they were ambushed in one of the narrow passes, the guard made the mistake of fighting back, then panicked and left Henniker on the path alone. He was slashed about the head, stripped and left for dead, while vultures hovered over him. His servant, who had hidden himself, lent him a shirt and carried him to Jericho, where only one kind woman dared help a despised Christian. Eventually, Henniker recovered his clothes and other effects which the Bedouin had put on sale in Gaza – minus a green frill on one of his shirts. Other travellers were abandoned by Bedouin guides, seized for ransom or as hostages, or blackmailed mercilessly.

So Western travellers in Palestine rarely idealized the noble Arab of the desert, particularly as they were seen not only as treacherous guides but as predators of the Holy Land. The devastation the tribes had created in the plains was obvious. The Turks kept their soldiers in fixed garrisons, and when they did ride out, it was to enforce tax collection or wage private wars but not to repel the raiders, whose home ground was in the desert to the east and south and who came across the Jordan or from the south to plunder the villagers in the central and coastal plains at harvest time. Every traveller who passed through these regions during the early part of the century noticed how few villages stood exposed in open country. They were tucked into the hillsides, surrounded by thick hedges of cactus and prickly pear, which, with their tough thorns and succulent thick leaves, were impassable for horsemen. But it was a pathetic enough defence against the Bedouin horsemen who snatched crops and livestock in the fields far beyond the villages. Only the hill towns were relatively secure, not only because their inhabitants were notoriously tough, but because it was harder for the Bedouin cavalry to ride horses up the steep terraces than to sweep into the valleys leading from the Jordan to the plains.

Chateaubriand's picture of the Jews as exotic descendants of the patriarchs was only one side of the traveller's view of the ancient inhabitants of the Holy Land. In the early nineteenth century the romantic view of the Jews was distant and idealized; moreover, as travellers noticed, Christians and Jews in Moslem Palestine had similar disabilities in their relations with the Turkish authorities –as well as being constantly open to persecution by the criminals looking for easy prey, for it was difficult for them to obtain justice in the Moslem courts. It was thus that Chateaubriand could call both Christians and Jews in Palestine 'two abandoned peoples'.

Visiting priests, clergymen and missionaries, however, took a very different view of the local Jews – that of an unregenerate people who shared deservedly in the curse that had fallen on the Holy Land. And the observed condition of the Jews of Palestine confirmed both views.

The Jews of Palestine inhabited the four holy cities of Safed and Tiberias in the Galilee, Jerusalem and Hebron in the Judean hills. The older communities were Sefardi Jews from Turkey and all of Syria who, early in the century, were joined by Jews from the Barbary States of North Africa. These resembled their Moslem neighbours more closely and were less easily identified than the newcomers – the Ashkenazi or European Jews, most from the Russian or Eastern European states, whose dress, language and habits were distinctively foreign. Confined to the poorer quarters of the cities, living mainly off charity sent from abroad – like the priests – victims of poverty, overcrowding and disease, hated by the Greek Orthodox, bullied by the authorities, and suspected by the Moslems, they presented an unrelieved picture of human misery and decline.

Chateaubriand saw himself rightly as one of the last of an endangered species, the Western pilgrims. But, like Clarke, he did not visit Jerusalem at Easter and thus could not witness the vitality of Eastern pilgrimage, which no Western traveller arriving in the spring failed to record, whether with horror or amazement, and whose manifestations were soon as familiar to Western readers as the disillusion with the Holy Places.

As many as fourteen thousand Eastern pilgrims might visit Jerusalem in the spring – devoutly credulous, noisy crowds who, to the consternation of the Western travellers, turned the Holy Sepulchre into an Oriental market place.

Thousands of men, women and children jostled in the Holy Sepulchre for the Greek Orthodox ceremony of the Holy Fire, during which flames were mysteriously produced inside the Sepulchre itself, a ceremony for which travellers found various scientific explanations and about which they interrogated the Greek Orthodox priests. The pilgrims rushed forward in a mad rout to light their tapers, later to be taken back to Russia and elsewhere and used as tokens of absolution on their deathbeds, or melted down to harden their shrouds.

A young British diplomat, William Turner, arrived from Constantinople in 1816 on a mission to the financially hard-pressed Franciscans, enabling them to draw on British credit at the Porte. He carried a firman enabling him to enter the church 'without molestation or extortion' and there saw what he described as 'the most extraordinary scene I have ever beheld during the 22 years of my life'.

A janissary with a leather whip opened the way into the church for seven thousand pilgrims. Within the church itself were stalls selling bread, fruit, vegetables, beads and crucifixes, and the pilgrims, 'hallooing, shouting and singing', struggled for a good vantage point near the Sepulchre while the Turkish soldiers drove them back with their whips. One man, Turner observed, had his right ear torn off, while some pilgrims rode on others' shoulders.

The Greek and Armenian bishops, meanwhile, had been shut up in the Sepulchre – a small chamber in the heart of the church – for two hours with a Turkish soldier, and the Holy Fire appeared promptly at a sign from the Turkish governor, who was seated in one of the galleries above the crowd under a green canopy which showed his Moslem faith. Few visitors failed to comment disgustedly on the fact that the Christian miracle always occurred on the signal from the Moslem governor.

The crowd lit tapers, then extinguished them, leaving the church full of smoke, as the pilgrims, feeling their way forward in the haze, left through the one, narrow entrance. This was not the only ceremony which in its sound and fury (many compared it to ancient Greek rites at Ephesus) shocked the Western Christians: they also found blasphemous the Latin priests' ceremony in which a wooden or waxen effigy of Christ was carried in procession, crucified and entombed. But it was the Holy Fire which was most notorious, and Turner's account was one of the first of many. In 1834 Robert Curzon, touring Eastern monasteries, described a stampede during which hundreds of pilgrims were killed, either trodden underfoot or bayoneted by Turkish soldiers who mistook the panic for a Christian riot. Such reports created deep concern in the West over the custody of the Holy Places by the Eastern churches and contributed, among other things, to the rise of violent anti-Russian feeling in the mid-century.

Similar scenes of mass religious hysteria took place when the Russian pilgrims visited the Jordan and the Dead Sea for baptism rituals. Those on the fringes of the great crowds were sometimes swept away in the spring currents and drowned, or killed by the Turkish soldiers when they strayed from their tents at night, or fell and died by the wayside from hunger and exhaustion.

While some European Catholics tried to regard the Orthodox ceremonies indulgently – as the Trappist monk Géramb observed, 'harmonizing with the spirit of the Orientals, and examples of which we find only in the missions in Asia, which probably borrowed them from the practices adopted in Palestine' – the Protestants saw them as sheer blasphemy. In fact they were demonstrations of religious emotion unknown in Europe since the Middle Ages, and as such embarrassing to Western travellers who compared them unfavourably with what they saw as the austerity and dignity of Moslem worship.

While Catholic pilgrims from Europe would go through the motions of pilgrimage, receiving their certificates from the superiors officiating in the Holy Sepulchre, the entire exercise was regarded sceptically in Protestant England during the period early in the century, when the monarchy was in disrepute and church attendance most popular with fervent Evangelists.

In 1816 Caroline of Brunswick, the English Prince Regent's discarded wife, arrived in Jaffa on her way to Jerusalem, brushing aside the protocol which demanded that she obtain her escort from the governor of Acre. She was obliged to return to Acre for her firman, but this was not the only indignity this chronically undignified woman suffered in Palestine. Her jewellery was stolen by the muleteers with whom she travelled. In Jerusalem she was lodged in a convent cell bare of everything but bed and chair, and when an armed escort was provided for her pilgrimage to the Jordan, as her lady-in-waiting noted, 'its chief, as we were fortunately not till afterwards informed, had been condemned to death but a year before for having headed a band of robbers, and his followers . . . all had the air of fugitives from the galleys, or something even more horrible.'

The pilgrimage had no immediate publicity. But in 1821, when Caroline's husband became king, she returned to England to claim her place beside him on the throne. George IV, as he now was, promptly sued for divorce, and the subsequent battle divided England.

George was a notorious rake, Caroline scarcely better, and her pilgrimage to Jerusalem was used by supporters and detractors alike. A painting was displayed in Pall Mall showing Caroline's entry into Jerusalem riding on a donkey (the sycophantic account of her travels had compared this journey to that of 'her Saviour') and accompanied by her aide-de-camp and lover, Bergami. While the radical cartoonist Cruikshank portrayed the King as an oriental voluptuary, the satirists of the King's party responded with a blast at Caroline:

> Hear the crowd with jibs and jeerings
> Mark the pilgrims as they pass
> Laugh at Bergy's ruff and earrings
> And the Queen of England's Ass.

* * *

If the visit to the Holy Sepulchre was almost invariably a disappointment, what really excited Europe were the attempts to penetrate the visible mystery at the heart of Jerusalem: the Moslem shrines on the Temple Mount or, as it was increasingly well known in the West, the Haram esh Sharif or Noble Sanctuary.

Two sites of Moslem pilgrimage stood on the Sanctuary. One

was the Al Aqsa (the Furthest) mosque, third most sacred site in Islam after Mecca and Medina; the other was the Dome of the Rock, the seventh-century shrine – not a mosque – built over the site where Abraham was said to have offered up Isaac, and from which Mohammed was supposed to have ascended to heaven.

For Moslems, the Sanctuary was the visible proof of the fact that it was Islam which had inherited the very heart of Christianity and of Judaism before it – as much a source of pride for Moslems as of gall to Christians and Jews. Popular feeling among the Moslem citizens of Jerusalem, rather than any religious law, forbade access to the Sanctuary to those of any other but the Moslem faith, and it was rumoured that any trespasser would, if apprehended, be forced to convert to Islam or lose his life. Muscular Nubian guards patrolled the Sanctuary and sometimes manhandled the unfortunate stranger who, accidentally straying down an alley in the Moslem quarter, might set foot in the precincts.

No European knew what the interior of the Sanctuary looked like until the appearance of the only popular book to describe Palestine as a Moslem country. Its author approached Palestine not from the sea but after crossing the deserts of North Africa, where he had spent several months, and he wrote that Palestine appeared to him not as barren and deprived, but as overcivilized. 'On entering this country, bounded by private property, a man's heart shrinks and contracts. I cannot turn my gaze, I cannot take one step without immediately being brought up by a hedge which tells me: stop there, do not pass . . . I seem to be no longer the same Ali Bey, this Arab who full of energy and fire charged forward in the deserts of Africa and Arabia . . . all one gains [here] in security and peace, one loses in energy.'

This was, however, a European idea of Arab sentiments. Ali Bey el Abbassi was no Arab, but a Spanish nobleman, Domingo Badia y Leblich, though his real identity was revealed only after his death. All his readers believed him to be an Arab, and when Chateaubriand met him in Alexandria he did not penetrate his disguise. He may well have become a Moslem; he managed to convince the robber chiefs at Abu Ghosh by reciting the Koran that he was no Christian. It was rumoured in Palestine that he was the son of a Moroccan prince, and he gained entry without difficulty to the Sanctuary, where he worshipped. In Jerusalem he made the five obligatory visits to mosques and shrines, but compared the city unfavourably with Mecca (which no European had yet seen) as lacking wide streets and great public squares. Unlike other visitors, he thought it natural that the ancient capital should have been located so far from the sea, on the old trade route between Arabia, Egypt and Syria.

Moslem or no, Ali Bey was the only European to get beyond the entrance to the Noble Sanctuary before 1818. Many travellers had been allowed to look down into the Sanctuary from the terrace of the Turkish governor's headquarters nearby. But the 'Capo Verde' – the green-turbaned Moslem Kadi in charge of the Sanctuary – allowed them no further. In 1818, however, he developed a minor eye infection and it so happened that there was a Scottish physician in town who treated him. Wherever they went, Europeans were considered to be doctors of sorts, and those known to be professional physicians were offered 'every pulse in town' or a crowd of invalids stretching miles beyond it; the most prevalent problems were found to be dyspepsia, the hypochondria of wives so safely immured that only their hands might be extended from behind a door for examination, 'fistulous sores from neglected gunshot wounds' – and the eye infections endemic to the area.

The physician who tended the Kadi was Robert Richardson, a Scotsman in the entourage of the Earl of Belmore, who was touring the Levant on his private yacht. Richardson was able to spend much time with the 'Omar Effendi', as the Kadi was also known, and eventually persuaded him to smuggle Richardson into the Sanctuary by night, covered in a black cape borrowed from his patient.

Richardson's first impression was indistinct. The sacred rock within the octagonal Dome of the Rock lay beneath a dusty canopy, a slab of marble pierced by eighteen magical nails marked the spot where Solomon was supposedly buried – so he was told – and a looming Nubian guard shouted a challenge as Richardson crossed the platform of the Sanctuary on his return. He emerged unharmed – and the Omar Effendi, whose pride in the beauty of the Sanctuary overcame his misgivings, sent the doctor back next day for a closer look.

A great taboo had been shattered. Later the same year, Mrs Belzoni, the wife of an Italian architect who had restored some of the antique sites of Egypt, managed to get herself smuggled into the precincts of the Sanctuary in the disguise of a Turk. She blundered around the Dome of the Rock a couple of times and finally entered the Al Aqsa mosque where, detected by an alert bystander, she made her escape by a back entrance leading down from the walls of the Mount, leaving her shoes behind.

From this time forward, trying to get into the Noble Sanctuary became a new kind of European sport, attempted by every traveller of enterprise, an elegant revenge on the Moslems who ruled Jerusalem; or perhaps a voyeurist exercise of which, subsequently, the intruder could boast.

* * *

In 1817 a committee report of the Church Missionary Society of England complained: 'The Classic, the Painter, the Statuary, the Antiquarian, the Naturalist, the Merchant, the Patriot and the Soldier . . .' all had their reporters in the Holy Land. 'But no one details to us the number of characters of Christians; no one has opened to us channels of communication with such men; no one names the men who are there perhaps in retirement, sighing over the moral condition of the country and calling, as Europe once called to Asia – come over and help us.'

Until this date, the scientific explorers and the romantic travellers had dominated Western interest in Palestine. The pioneers of militant Protestant activity, which was to become the most important Western influence in the country, began only in 1823, with the arrival of the first English and American missionaries. The earlier recommendations for Western enterprise, economic reforms and development were not taken up by entrepreneurs or bankers or politicians, save in the most general context of diplomatic relations with the Porte and the administrative changes in the Ottoman empire urged on Turkey by the West. The few institutions for local change – schools, experimental farms, medical services and welfare, and the rest, were introduced by men and women whose main aim was to change the religion of the inhabitants.

William Jowett was the first Anglican clergyman to volunteer for mission work abroad for the CMS, and the first Protestant 'reporter' to spy out the Levant. He was one of a small company of missionaries who had worked out of Malta since 1815, and produced a pioneer field survey for his sponsors which faithfully reflected its views of the chances for the conversion of the Moslem population by the local churches. Jowett himself shared all the familiar doctrinal arguments against both Islam and Judaism, as well as most of the veteran Western prejudices against the 'vices of warm countries'. But the first sight of religious practices in the Holy Land shook his confidence in the Eastern churches and provided him with a new explanation to the old question of why Christianity, with its self-evident and superior truths, had not yet prevailed over the heresy of Islam:

> The conflicts of the Christian pilgrims at Jerusalem for the possession of the Holy Sepulchre exhibit, to this day, a scene sufficient of itself to rivet the infidelity of the commanding Turk. 'Look upon Zion, the city of our solemnities,' we can exclaim only with a sigh of self-reproach. We have indeed shewn Mahometans what professing Christians are – but not what is Christianity.

The answer was clearly to introduce the sobriety, the decorum and the simplicity of Protestant worship and the beneficent presence of the Mission. Jowett laid down what were to be the guidelines for subsequent action: the preaching of the Gospels in the local vernacular, with readings and discussions; the distribution of bibles and tracts in translation; the promotion of the status of women, beginning with their education; and education and welfare projects for all prospective converts.

The missionaries were quite aware that Ottoman rule in Palestine rested on a very delicate balance between the ethnic and religious communities which might well be disturbed by such intervention. Jowett recognized that each religious group was 'exclusive, intolerant, compact and self-attached' but this was no deterrent.

In Acre, in February 1823, the first Protestant service in Palestine was held in the local consul's home in Acre. Those taking part, apart from the consul and his dragoman, were some Catholic and Greek Orthodox residents of the town and a solitary local Jew. It was to prove a prophetic meeting; for almost all the converts made by both Protestant and Catholic missionaries from the West during the century were members of other Christian sects. For any Moslem to renounce his religion in Ottoman territory at this period meant risking the death penalty, though by the mid-century this was rarely enforced; but in any case the Moslems were as little inclined as the Jews to renounce their faith.

Even the attempt to begin the Mission's work earned Jowett the hostility of the other Christian sects. When he first attempted to distribute bibles in Nazareth, the Latin priests accused him of playing politics and threatened to burn his tracts. While the heads of the Greek Orthodox Church were far more friendly, Jowett found in Jenin that the local Greek Christians, 'sitting on the ground, playing a game of chance . . . seemed to regard our visit as a troublesome intrusion'.

Only the most strongly motivated missionary was likely to man a 'station' in Jerusalem, which Jowett called 'the metropolis of lucrative will worship'. The sole previous volunteer, a Swiss missionary, had given up and retreated to Beirut.

It was the New England Congregationalists, with their puritanical ethos and fundamentalist energy who were to provide the Protestant vanguard. Their zeal was at least in part the result of almost total ignorance of the conditions in which they were to work. The sermons preached by the first couple of young missionaries, Pliny Fisk and Levi Parsons, before their departure for Palestine in 1819, indicate that they believed that half the population of the Holy Land was already Christian (the correct figure was less than ten per cent). They also believed that, because of a shared belief in monotheism, the 'heathen' Moslems would prove more amenable to conversion than the Indian Hindus or the African Hottentots. They were at heart romantics, believing that 'caravans' would take the word of God everywhere in the East from their centre in Jerusalem.

Four years later, a dispirited Pliny Fisk, sitting in heavy disguise in a mosque in Acre and surveying the Moslem prayers, asked himself whether even Christ could have prevailed against such odds and in such circumstances. Nevertheless, he and his companions soldiered on in the Holy City for months, translating the Bible into Arabic with the help of Greek priests and distributing copies secretly among the local Christians and Jews. They had already learned that to do so among Moslems was to risk their lives to no purpose.

Arrested by the Turkish authorities along with other missionaries, and his books confiscated, a little later – he believed he had been informed on by the local Latin priests – Fisk expected, and even longed for, the fate of an early Christian martyr. But his end was slightly less dramatic. With the help of British and American agents in Jaffa and Beirut, the missionaries were freed, and set off after seven months in Jerusalem to the more secure missionary colony in Beirut, where Fisk died of an infection contracted during the journey.

Such fiascos convinced the missionary organizations in England and America that all thought of converting the Moslems of Palestine should be set aside, and mission energies were henceforth concentrated on the local Arab Christians – most of whom were Greek Orthodox – and the Jews.

*   *   *

With the exception of the monks who gave them hospitality and dubious accounts of the local Christian shrines, the Jews were the most accessible of all local communities to the Western traveller. Europeans had few contacts with Moslem notables, save for the rare meeting with a local potentate or official, but many of the European consuls, agents and merchants were Jews. They welcomed visitors, served as guides and interpreters, admitted foreigners to their synagogues, and were even prepared, as Jowett noted, to accept copies of the New Testament: 'I was especially struck', he noted on a visit to Tiberias, 'to see the readiness with which one youth shewed to another, at once, the 20th verse of the first chapter of St Matthew [the Annunciation] which he read with an air of scorn and threw the book down.'

Rabbis were quite often prepared to enter into theological discussions.

Towards the mid-century this attitude changed completely. But during the early years, when there were so few missionaries and they appeared to be so innocuous, the Jews scarcely took their proselytizing activities seriously. They saw travellers as useful go-betweens to take messages from the Jews of Jerusalem and Hebron, who rarely ventured on to the roads where they were vulnerable and conspicuous, to the consuls and agents in the coastal region.

This did not mean, however, that the Jews were likely to nourish the fantasies which brought many Protestant clergymen to Palestine in an enquiring mood looking for signs of patriotism and 'national feeling'. For, from the last decades of the eighteenth century the conversion and return of the Jews to Palestine was the subject of intense controversy in England and America. The French Revolution had triggered the revival of belief that such an apocalyptic event might prefigure the Jewish remnant's return, the Millenium and the Second Coming of Christ. 'The feelings of many devout Christians are, in the present day, wound up to the highest pitch in favour of the Jews. Prophecy is explored, history is carefully collated, conjecture catches at every probability.' Jowett's experiences in Palestine argued that 'visions of Millenial glory should not blind Christians to the fact that the Jews had not yet accepted that Jesus was the incarnation of God'. The restoration of the Jews, he concluded, was a matter for Providence, not man, and was not to be made the subject of 'commercial contracts or political expediency'.

John Carne, a famous traveller and raconteur who had taken Holy Orders but became a literary figure instead, also inspected the Jews of Palestine for indications of their forthcoming redemption. Carne, who had been kidnapped as a hostage by the Bedouin, dossed down in country caravanserai where he was shocked by local sodomy and slept in bales of merchandise in a bazaar in Ramle, was contemptuous of the Jews' obvious fear of the Turks and their attempts to placate both Turkish rulers and Moslem notables in Jerusalem; he saw the Jews as servile and

timorous, unworthy to be considered heirs to the biblical heroes.
He concluded that while the Jew 'will reason and converse with
the missionary in perfect good temper, and will in most cases give
him a very civil reception in his house', he would refuse
conversion; and that the Jews of Palestine 'lacked true patriotism' and 'had no taste for liberty as it was understood in Europe'.
Nor was Carne in the least disturbed that the redemption of
Palestine was thus not at hand; Palestine, he thought, should
remain barren: 'Take away its desolation, and you take from it
the chief charm.'

*   *   *

Travellers then looked in vain for signs of nationalism among
the traditional and pious Jews of the Holy Land. There was no
Jewish equivalent to Clarke or Chateaubriand. No Jewish
traveller or scholar tried to map or name the physical features of
the Holy Land between the time of the medieval traveller
Ashturi HaFarhi and Salomon Lowinsohn, whose geographical
lexicon of the Scriptures appeared in Vienna in 1819. Lowinsohn, though he did not visit Palestine, was the first
nineteenth-century Jew to try to explain the language of the
Bible with reference to its natural home. But he was an exception in every sense. Unlike almost every other observant Jew, he
had studied in a Capuchin monastery as well as in a Talmudic
seminary and was employed as proof reader in Hebrew in a
famous Viennese press.

The Jews of Palestine had not travelled there for adventure or
romance, or to renew the ancient homeland. Their patriotism
was that of history, not geography, and they carried with them,
as a snail its shell, all the paraphernalia of their lives in the
Diaspora, their Talmudic academies and kabbalistic sects, their
community institutions, their dress, and their perennial and
justified suspicion and wariness of their rulers. To live and die in
the Holy Land was a privilege, but not an end in itself, enabling
them to fulfil many of the Talmudic precepts inapplicable to the
Diaspora, but nonetheless less important than a life of piety.
They had little in common with the emancipated and more
prosperous Jews in the West with whom they were unfavourably

compared by many Western travellers. And the Holy Land was the last place where the Jews were likely to be converted to Christianity.

* * *

Palestine, first rediscovered as a battleground, was now to become the focus of Western energies all the more remarkable since until the last quarter of the century the country was negligible in the strategic sense and of no economic importance to the West. Nor was religious faith, in its simplest sense, the major factor which brought the West to the Holy Land.

For as long as the atmosphere of the country remained hostile to foreigners and non-Moslems – that is, until the Egyptian conquest of 1831 – it attracted mainly the adventurers, the most important of whom were explorers of Arabia and antiquarian collectors.

Later, under Egyptian rule, it attracted the 'scriptural geo-graphers' and a host of other scholars and clergymen bent on authenticating the text of the Bible. This was chiefly the result of the confrontation in the West between established religious beliefs and the latest discoveries in geology and human evolution. But Palestine provided no reassuring answers to their dilemma.

At the end of the 1830s, with the resumption of Turkish rule, Jerusalem once more became a centre of European political interest, though there was no attempt to challenge Ottoman control in order not to disturb the balance of power in Europe. Instead, the powers exerted indirect influence through the consuls and their non-Moslem protégés in Palestine. Here, too, the results were often unexpected.

When steamships made mass travel to the Holy Land feasible, what followed was a parody of the ancient pilgrimage, the stoical self-punishment of the earliest middle-class tourists.

From the 1860s onwards, more effort was to be invested in archaeological research of an unscientific kind in Palestine than in any other part of the world, though the harvest was meagre.

Throughout the second half of the century, moreover, large sums of money were poured into the Holy Land in the vain effort of the missions to convert the Jews to Christianity – an attempt which had as its most important consequence the involvement of the Jews of the West in the fate of their co-religionists in Palestine.

Rescued from neglect, the object of so many contemporary interests, fantasies and anxieties in Europe and America, Palestine became a country which defied and resisted the West as strongly as it obsessed and challenged it.

CHAPTER II

---•••---

The Baroque in the Desert

PALESTINE WAS SO SMALL A COUNTRY and so near Europe that it now seems absurd that it should have been one of the targets of great explorers. Yet in 1804 a Palestine Association was set up in London on the model of the great Africa Association which had sent James Bruce on his voyages of exploration to Abyssinia in the late eighteenth century, and Mungo Park up the Niger. Sir William Hamilton, president of the new association, explained its foundation in historical, not geographical terms: 'America, Siberia and the deserts of Africa are penetrated by modern hardihood and curiosity – yet the land which might be called the oldest part of the globe, or concerning which at least the oldest authentic history exists, is completely unknown.'

The first explorers of Palestine were less valiant than Bruce or Park: they turned back at Malta when they heard of disturbances in Palestine following Djezzar Pasha's death in 1808. The difficulty with Palestine, moreoever, was that explorers of the Holy Land needed more than the hardihood or curiosity of the men who opened up Africa. Biblical scholarship, the command of Oriental languages and a classical education were all necessary for the journey into the areas still uncharted: the sites recorded by historians of antiquity but as yet unseen by modern travellers. These included the Decapolis, the ten Graeco-Roman cities colonized during the first centuries after Christ, most of which lay in Bedouin territory east of the Jordan river; and Petra, capital of biblical Edom, the Nabatean caravan city whose existence had last been recorded by the Crusaders but which lay hidden in a valley somewhere to the southeast of the Dead Sea.

The problem of identifying such ancient sites depended on understanding how one civilization had superseded another in the same region, rebuilding, renaming, or abandoning the original sites. This was intellectually as hazardous a task as the trek into Bedouin territory was a physical one, and it was a strangely matched group of explorers who ventured out beyond the pilgrim routes in the period between 1805 and 1820. Not one of them was motivated by religious faith.

The German Ulrich Seetzen and the Swiss Jean-Louis Burckhardt used Palestine as the nursery slope on which they trained for far more daring expeditions: Seetzen for Mecca and the Yemen, Burckhardt for Egypt, on his way to Africa, where his sponsors in London hoped that he would find a way into the interior from the east. Both were scholars of Arabic, finding their way by questioning the local peasants and the Bedouin with whom they travelled.

Behind Seetzen and Burckhardt were important patrons. Seetzen had undertaken to collect antiquities, geological specimens and plants, as well as to note inscriptions in ancient languages, for the Duke of Saxe Gotha and his museum – and later for Czar Alexander I. Burckhardt was the young protégé of the African Association, now headed by Sir Joseph Banks, the scientist best known for having sailed with Captain Cook to the Pacific, less famous for his professional writings on subjects like the various forms of blight and the habitat of merino sheep.

The successors of Seetzen and Burckhardt were four Englishmen: James Silk Buckingham, sailor, journalist and fighter for a number of liberal causes, in the service of a mercantile company in India; Clifford Leonard Irby and James Mangles, naval officers of independent means; and William Bankes, antiquarian and scholar. Bankes travelled first with Buckingham, and later with the two officers, providing that knowledge of ancient history and classical literature which was indispensable. Like Edward Clarke, the man who had first aroused antiquarian interest in the Holy Land, Bankes was an enthusiastic collector of antiquities. In 1815, just before he began his Levant travels, he had sent home an obelisk from Philae with instructions that it be set up in the grounds of his Dorsetshire estate.

Between them, these half dozen men opened up those parts of Palestine which until now had been hidden, and their writings stimulated a new interest in Palestine: not in its Jewish and Christian shrines and monasteries, its Islamic monuments or the reasons for its decline from biblical splendour, but in its classical ruins, on the one hand, and its native population on the other.

The little group were colleagues, but they were also rivals. At this time, explorers and antiquarians travelling in Asia Minor and the Levant collided regularly on their travels. Unlike the great African explorers, who travelled vast distances without meeting another European, and whose accounts were all the harder to challenge, the explorers of Palestine trod hard on one another's heels, meeting the same peasant communities and guided by the same Bedouin sheikhs as their predecessors. The fame of 'Sheikh Musa' (Seetzen) and 'Sheikh Ibrahim' (Burckhardt) lived after them in every village and encampment in the country.

The Europeans, moreover, according to the custom of the time, carved their names on every ruin and monastery door between the Pyramids and Palmyra. Seetzen left a pencilled message on the wall of St Catherine's monastery in Sinai 'notifying his having penetrated the country in a direct line between the Dead Sea and Mount Sinai, a route never before accomplished'. Burckhardt never caught up with Seetzen, but heard rumours everywhere of his progress. Buckingham, washed up in a shipwreck in Jeddah, was lent money by Burckhardt. When Irby and Mangles met Bankes in Aleppo, they exchanged information on regions they had travelled. 'We mutually gave each other all the information we possessed – Mr Bankes on Asia Minor and Greece, and we on Egypt and Nubia.' Burckhardt distributed notes and advice with the greatest liberality. These exchanges were useful, but they also confused the issue of who saw what first; who was the purveyor of knowledge, who the recipient. Seetzen and Burckhardt were both students of Islam, moreover, who seem to have been more concerned with the accuracy of their observation than the publication of their findings. Seetzen left little clue to his personality: he was said to have become a Moslem, and had become increasingly un-

European in his behaviour by the end of his life. Burckhardt was a less puzzling figure: his adoption of Arab dress and his familiarity with Arab codes of behaviour were more clearly a means to an end. But, like Seetzen, he never managed to publish his own findings, which remained in note form for years after his early death.

The Englishmen, on the other hand, were more obviously concerned with their reputation in the literary and social world in London, and with beating one another to the publishers. Buckingham was chronically hard up and Bankes wished to promote his reputation as a connoisseur of antiquities.

So it was scarcely surprising that when the time came for the memoirs of these explorers to be published, charges of plagiarism, bad faith and even outright theft were bandied about and lawsuits filed in London. As for Irby and Mangles, whose names are perpetually linked in the dusty literature of nineteenth-century Palestine exploration, they are mere extras to the drama, involved quite by chance in this story of rivalries.

*　　*　　*

The explorers of Palestine spent little time in monasteries or in the towns frequented by other European travellers. They were more likely to sleep in the *medhaf* or public room of a Syrian village, in Bedouin encampments, in Turkish garrisons, or even rolled up in their cloaks on the floor of a cave. They ate with the Bedouin, catching pieces of mutton tossed to them, scooping up *burghul* (cracked wheat) from a common bowl, rolling rice into balls between their fingers as their hosts did. Burckhardt wrote: 'I stop at the dirtiest caravanserai, use the floor as my mattress and my coat as a blanket, eat with camel drivers and brush my horse myself, but I see and hear things which remain unknown to him who travels in comfort.'

But they had one overriding problem: how to take notes. They were never out of sight of the watchful and suspicious eyes of the country people, for whom all foreigners were 'necromancers', and 'treasure hunters', whose use of compasses, note-taking, copying of inscriptions and sketching of ruins could have only one aim: to possess themselves of hidden riches which were not rightfully theirs. The explorers used every possible subterfuge, of which disguise was only the first. The most resourceful was Burckhardt, who, when travelling in Sinai, would leap from his camel, squat down as if to defecate, and make notes hurriedly under his robes.

'It is very unfortunate for European travellers', wrote Burckhardt, 'that the idea of treasure hidden in ancient edifices is strongly rooted in the minds of Arabs and Turks.' In Palestine the belief in hidden treasure was far from irrational. The country had been overrun so many times that there were hundreds of caches with property left by those who fled before rival clans or armies; every few years a 'treasure' of some kind would be accidentally uncovered. In a country so subject to volcanic tremors, and where houses were so badly built that it took little to bring them down, looting sprees in ruins were common. Even the peasants, who had little enough to hide, concealed coins, and surplus stocks of grain, in underground cisterns, sometimes roughly covered with branches, into which travellers' horses might suddenly plunge.

The peasants' belief in the magic of classical ruins, moreover, was deep-rooted. Lord Elgin's removal of the first of his marble trophies, the Boustrophedon inscription at Sigaeum, in Asia Minor, was bitterly opposed by the local Christians, who thought the letters possessed properties against disease. Among the equally superstitious Palestine Moslems, the idea of the 'spiritus loci' probably went back to pre-Moslem beliefs about spirits which took different shapes – great birds, monsters, ghosts. Even the most casual visitor to Palestine would notice rags fluttering from the branches of trees on hilltops and by springs, and little shrines in caves; but the ancient beliefs which underlay these practices were scarcely investigated at this time, though they were a serious obstacle to research. Anything the explorers did confirmed the local people's fears that they were spiriting away treasure and disturbing local gods.

Ironically enough, the only foreign visitor who lived up to the local people's expectations as a treasure hunter was Lady Hester Stanhope, who did dig in the hope of finding buried coins in Ashkelon in 1815. Her only discovery, a headless statue of

Hadrian, she promptly had smashed and thrown into the sea —
for by this time the removal of the Parthenon frieze by Lord Elgin
had been denounced as vandalism in England itself, and Lady
Hester did not wish to alienate the Turks. In the case of Palestine,
however, the removal of stone monuments by antiquarians
would certainly have been justified at this time, as the local
Pashas dismembered every ruin they could lay hands on, and
used pillars, marble and mosaics for the mosques and bathhouses
of Acre and Jaffa during rebuilding after the Napoleonic Wars,
without evoking protest. Caesaria, the capital of Roman
Palestine, described by one traveller as 'a fallen Crusader lying in
his armour', was regularly pillaged and its ruins used as a quarry;
only the fact that much of its structure lay hidden under the
shifting sands of the seashore saved it from total obliteration.

*   *   *

Ulrich Jasper Seetzen, the first scientific explorer of Palestine, was
a German physician who had studied Arabic and Islamic culture
for several years before arriving in Palestine. Intending to avoid
the usual pilgrim routes, he was not discouraged by rumours of
the dangers: 'I had too good an opinion of the nomad Arabs to
permit myself to be deterred by such reports.' On reaching
Damascus in the autumn of 1805, however, he could find no
local guide who shared his optimism; three cancelled their
agreements with him at the last moment. He finally left
Damascus in December, with an Armenian guide and a firman
from the Pasha of Damascus. The two men spent less than a week
riding through the Leja region of the Hauran, the mountainous
plateau northeast of the Jordan, past ruined villages and black
outcrops of basalt rock, 'which inspired the soul with a kind of
terror', noting down inscriptions and sketching columns at every
classical ruin. Then, after inspecting remains from the Byzantine
period, they were taken prisoner by ten Turkish horsemen and
held by a local army officer who accused them of carrying false
documents. After he released them, they were menaced by
Bedouin tribesmen and only escaped because of the guide's
presence of mind. Seetzen suspected that the Turkish officer had
set the Bedouin on him, and returned to Damascus.

The following month, carrying books, medicines and special paper in which to preserve his plant specimens, Seetzen set out again, disguised in the clothes of 'an Arab Sheikh of the second rank', accompanied by muleteers and a Greek Orthodox guide who had travelled widely among the Aneze, the great Bedouin confederation which dominated the northeastern borders of Palestine. This time, he succeeded in reaching one of the sources of the Jordan river, near the ruins of Caesarea Philippae (which the Arabs called Banias because of a shrine to the god Pan), and unseen by any European since the Crusades. Seetzen and his escorts travelled on south, following the river to the Huleh marshes, where at night he watched local hunters set fire to the rushes and reeds to flush out wild boar and other game. He eventually reached Tiberias on foot, intermittently deserted by nervous guides and fleeced by others. But this did not dissuade him from his plan of crossing the Jordan, and his ambition to discover the cities of the Decapolis.

These were the remains of what had once been the furthest outposts of Western civilization. Strung out in a line between Damascus, to the north, and Philadelphia, in the hills east of the Dead Sea, to the south, they had marked a flourishing trade route, defended the Syrian littoral against the incursions of the tribesmen of the desert, and sheltered a flourishing Hellenistic culture. Described by Pliny and Josephus, and familiar from the New Testament, their fate before Seetzen's time was uncertain. Whether the land surrounding them was fertile, as the historians had alleged; whether they now belonged to the desert, and whether or not they were totally ruined, was unknown. To cross into the territory of the Bedouin, for local guides, was to risk one's life to very little purpose.

'I put over my shirt an old *kombaz* or dressing gown, and above that an old blue and ragged shift; I covered my head with some shreds, and my feet with old slippers. An old tattered Abai [cloak] thrown over my shoulders protected me from the cold and rain, and a branch of a tree served me for a walking stick.' In this costume, that of a common beggar, Seetzen hoped to avoid the attention of Bedouin and other robbers. A few miles on, he found the slippers too uncomfortable, kicked them off, and went on barefoot through the mud on a rainy February day.

Thus Ulrich Seetzen, doctor of medicine and Oriental scholar, became the first European to identify the Graeco-Roman ruins of Gadara, Gerasa (Jerash) and Philadelphia (Amman), on his long winter trek along the eastern hills of the Jordan valley. He encountered no bandits; only wild, dishevelled but harmless peasant families living in caves beside and among the splendid ruins. He shared their food – wild herbs, gruel made of wheat, and rice – and slept in caves with their flocks of goats.

The first city he identified was Gadara – now an Arab village named Om Keis – because of its proximity to the hot springs recorded by the Roman historians. These same sulphurous waters were now used by the peasants to cure the mange which afflicted their camels. Exploring the ruins, he came upon the most feared of all the Bedouin tribes of the area – the Bene Sakhr – pasturing their flocks. Seetzen calmly offered their inquisitive chief a puff on his pipe, and they passed on. The peasants at first followed Seetzen everywhere, sure he would lead them to treasure in the ruins, but when they saw him collecting plants, desisted.

With most of his journey still before him, Seetzen had almost exhausted his funds; he abandoned his last precaution and sold his pistols to peasants he encountered by the way. Unarmed, finding escorts as and where he could, he crossed the hills of Gilead, still covered with snow in early March, to come upon Gerasa – Jerash – a perfect model of a Roman colonial town, with its Corinthian columns, three temples, amphitheatre and ruined palaces. 'It is impossible to explain', wrote Seetzen, 'how this place, formerly of such manifest celebrity, can have so long escaped the notice of all lovers of antiquity.'

As he travelled further south, he suffered hunger and fear. When he sheltered in a Christian village, he pretended to share the peasants' Greek Orthodox faith; thus he had nothing to eat but carob pods, as a fast had just commenced. When in a Bedouin camp, he pretended to be a Moslem; this did not save him from being robbed 'under pretence of exacting a toll'. But he was the first to note that Es Salt, the southernmost town of the valley, was surrounded by fertile agricultural land, and not by desert, as many Europeans believed; and before he returned to Jerusalem, he discovered his third great ruin, Philadelphia (Amman).

During the year that followed, 1807, he explored the Dead Sea, the first traveller to circle it completely. He found that most of the villages were in total ruin save for Es Salt and Kerak, the Crusader fort in the hills, 'the whole country being abandoned to the wandering Arabs [Bedouin]'. He corrected the maps in use, and his reports, brief as they were, discredited the stories of many travellers before him. There were no remnants of the Cities of the Plain, he maintained, no pillars of salt, no outline of Sodom and Gomorrah beneath the heavy, oily waters of the Dead Sea; the tales of floating iron, of birds dropping dead as they flew across the lake, were nonsense. Nor was it possible, he wrote, as lazier men had asserted, to see the entire contour of the Dead Sea from the safe heights of Jerusalem. Seetzen went on to cross Sinai – the note left on the wall of St Catherine's all that was known of his journey for years – and reached Cairo in the spring of 1807. For two years he remained in Egypt whence, disguised as a merchant physician, he travelled widely in the Nile valley, learned African languages from a slave trader, and prepared for the most dangerous of his journeys, the pilgrimage to Mecca, which he reached in October 1809. Though to sketch or portray the holy site was punishable by death, Seetzen succeeded in doing so without being detected.

But when he finally raised his guard, it was fatal. Seetzen met his death in the Yemen in 1811. For some time only rumours reached Europe; then, in July 1815, Burckhardt wrote to Edward Clarke from Egypt: 'I have had positive news from Mocha that Dr Seetzen was not killed in Africa as reported some years ago in the public prints, but poisoned in September 1811 by order of the Imam of Yemen, at Taes ... while he was just starting on a journey through the inland countries of Yemen to Makat and Bassora; his papers and baggage, which latter had principally attracted the cupidity of the government, being loaded upon seventeen camels (a circumstance hardly to be believed, but positively affirmed by the gentlemen of the East India factory, who saw Dr Seetzen only two days before his melancholy fate).'

Apart from a few brief notes published by the Palestine Association, little was known of his journey to the Decapolis cities; he had only whetted the appetite of other explorers.

* * *

Jean-Louis Burckhardt came from a distinguished Basle family whose proud and civilized life was ruined when Switzerland briefly lost its independence to France after the Revolution. His father, a Swiss patriot and liberal, was exiled; his elder brother, after a term of imprisonment, went mad. After completing his Oriental studies in Leipzig and Heidelberg, Burckhardt, with his hatred for both revolutionary and republican France, came to see England as his adopted country. He arrived there almost penniless, was taken up by Sir Joseph Banks, and studied under Edward Clarke, the mineralogist, at Cambridge. Burckhardt volunteered to undertake a journey of exploration in Africa, and left England in 1809 for Aleppo.

But he was never to reach the African interior; he became increasingly fascinated by the Arab East, and is best known as the first European to have brought back a detailed description of Mecca (which, like Seetzen, he visited in disguise), and as author of one of the first accounts of Bedouin life, *Notes on the Bedouin and Wahabis*. Despite the fact that during his own travels with the Bedouin he was repeatedly betrayed, humiliated and abandoned, he maintained that the true Bedouin, somewhere in the depths of Arabia, led a life of honour, patriotism and independence 'not inferior to any which ennobled the history of the Grecian or Helvetian republics'.

Burckhardt's training for his adventures began in Syria, where he thought all English travellers should practise explorations, as so many ancient sites and country districts were still uncharted. On one of his first long trips out of Aleppo, a visit to the banks of the Euphrates in 1811, his camel was killed, and Bedouin stripped him to the skin. It was probably this experience which convinced him that there were only two ways to travel in Syria: 'either in the Pasha's retinue', or alone 'and trust to the country people as a "poor devil"'. Half measures, he wrote to Clarke, were worst.

Riding from village to village, questioning and probing, Burckhardt studied the lives of the peasantry of northern Syria and Palestine as no traveller had done before him: the pilgrims on the *Haj* route harried by Turkish soldiery and Bedouin marauders alike; the Latin Christians of Nazareth, forgotten by their native countries but tolerated by their neighbours in this district – the monks went hunting in their European habits; the country fairs at Moslem shrines 'as pilgrimage in the east is generally coupled with mercantile speculations' (something the horrified observers of Jerusalem seemed to have forgotten).

No other visitor saw the results of Turkish misrule in more detail. Burckhardt noted that the peasants in the Hauran, many Druse and Christians, had been reduced to a semi-nomadic existence, moving from place to place to avoid the tax farmers, and thus planted neither orchards nor vegetable gardens. 'Shall I sow for strangers?' they answered when he asked why the land was not more densely cultivated. Each group preyed on the other; the Turks with their punitive taxes, the Bedouin taking tribute, the European agents profiteering ruthlessly on the produce which they sold, the Jews of Tiberias overcharging their pilgrims from Eastern Europe. Travellers resorted to bribery as the way out of trouble. 'A penknife worth two shillings overcomes the fanaticism of the peasant; increase the present and it will have an equal effect upon a townsman; make it a considerable sum and the Mufti himself will wave [sic] all religious scruples.'

Even liberal payment, however, was not sufficient to persuade Burckhardt's guides to linger among the ruins when he retraced Seetzen's journey along the eastern banks of the Jordan, where the sight of a horse's fresh footprint was enough to put any guide to flight.

Burckhardt made rapid but exact sketches of the ruins, and was the first to record all the Arab place names correctly. But he did not claim expertise as a classical scholar, and assumed that later travellers would assess the importance of the cities of the Decapolis more precisely. It was this which was to excite the ambitions of later, and less modest explorers.

As an Oriental scholar, Burckhardt knew that the Jordan

valley, or Ghor, had been a flourishing agricultural region at the time of the Mameluke rulers of the sixteenth century, confirming the biblical accounts of its fertility; and like Seetzen, he found the remaining farmers centred around Es Salt. However, the territory across the river was only nominally under Turkish rule, and while the peasants there were not subject to taxation, they were dominated by the Bedouin. Arriving at Kerak in the hills east of the Dead Sea, Burckhardt discovered that the Greek Orthodox and Moslem townspeople lived under the 'protection' of the semi-nomadic Bene Amr, with whom they had also intermarried. Learning that the Sheikh of Kerak was due to move south on what resembled a kind of magistrate's circuit – as *de facto* ruler of the region he also settled local disputes – Burckhardt decided to join the Sheikh's retinue as far as the plain south of the Dead Sea, whence he hoped the Howeytat Bedouin, whose territory began there, would take him to Cairo.

Burckhardt was confident by now that he had mastered the Bedouin code; but he was no match for the wily Sheikh, who managed to trick Burckhardt, on the journey, out of his fine Damascus saddle, while his adolescent son got hold of Burckhardt's stirrups. He was lucky to keep his mare, which he sold to the Howeytat for four goats and some corn. This was his advance payment to a family of peasants migrating to Egypt, with whom he hoped to travel. But before they had gone far, hostile Bedouin were sighted, and the guide not only cancelled the agreement with Burckhardt, but refused to return the goats. It was only after Burckhardt placed himself 'under the protection' of another local sheikh for arbitration that he managed to get his goats back, and promptly paid them over to a new guide as part payment for the journey to Cairo.

Burckhardt was now, he suspected, very near Wadi Musa, where Petra was rumoured to be situated. In order to persuade his guide to choose the route through the Wadi, he told him that he had vowed to sacrifice a goat at the tomb of Haroun (Aaron) which he knew overlooked the valley from the west. Fearing Haroun's anger should he prevent Burckhardt from carrying out a religious duty, the guide reluctantly agreed.

Together the two men entered the narrow, curving pass at the eastern end of the valley which led to the lost city; above them, hundreds of niches in the rock face signalled to Burckhardt that he had indeed stumbled on the necropolis which surrounded the city, and, as the valley widened, he caught his first glimpse of the ruins. As the temples and magnificent tombs hewn into the rock face came into view, on either side of the path through the valley, Burckhardt marvelled silently at the wonder of the caravan city, 'one of the most elegant remains of antiquity existing in Syria – a work of immense labour'. But with the guide at his side, he dared not show the slightest enthusiasm or interest, or even to slacken his pace. When he tried to leave the path and take a closer look at one of the nearer burial caves, the guide, who had been watching him narrowly, exclaimed: 'I see now clearly that you are an infidel, who has some particular business amongst the ruins of the city of your forefathers, but depend upon it, we shall not suffer you to take out one para [smallest coin] of the treasures hidden there, for they are in our territory, and belong to us.'

Burckhardt hastily denied any such intention. Though he had indeed discovered the city sought by all his fellow explorers – Seetzen had searched for Petra in vain – he feared that if he confirmed the guide's suspicions, he would be prevented from travelling on to Egypt. Moreover, he feared that his carefully concealed notes would be found and taken from him. His appearance and accent might be explained away – there were many European Moslems in the Ottoman empire; but an ardent interest in Hellenistic sculpture was not their distinguishing feature.

So at sunset, Burckhardt had to turn his back on Petra and wearily climb the western slope of Wadi Musa to the tomb of Haroun, too vexed even to examine the shrine, and carried out his 'sacrifice' under the eyes of his still suspicious guide. They then hastily cooked and ate the goat, the guide quickly dousing the flames of the fire, which he feared might be seen by nearby bandits – for the Wadi was a famous place of ambush. Future travellers, Burckhardt was to write later, needed an armed force if they wished to survey the antiquities of Syria.

Seetzen and Burckhardt's courage and enterprise had pinpointed some of the greatest ruins of Palestine; it was left to others, however, to reap the benefit. What they had also done was to show, by their careful noting of Arabic place names, that the traditions handed down by foreign colonists were often misleading. Though Burckhardt had been unable to identify any of the biblical sites by questioning the peasants, the principle that the ancient names had been preserved not by the historians but by the Moslem peasants was to guide the pioneers of historical geography, who began their work some twenty years later. It worked well until the 1870s – by which time the peasants, overfamiliar with the questions, and the answers, of the enquiring foreigners, had begun to repeat one geographer's theories to the next.

*   *   *

The voyages of Seetzen and Burckhardt took place at a time of war and instability, and Ottoman alliances changed accordingly; England's prospects in the Levant fell every time France's fortunes rose, and vice versa. In 1806, for instance, England found herself briefly at war with Turkey, and Sidney Smith's ships were bombarded in the Dardanelles. This period of unrest in the Levant, caused most directly by Turko-Russian conflicts, ended with the Treaty of Bucharest in 1812, which ensured that the Near East was little affected by European politics for several years. Finally the Battle of Waterloo, in 1815, put an end to the Napoleonic Wars. The Grand Tour resumed, and trading vessels and private yachts appeared in the Mediterranean once again, and with them, a different kind of explorer.

In 1817, Burckhardt died of dysentery in Cairo, leaving only unpublished notes. It took five years for his patrons in England to edit them. Seetzen had sent back hundreds of letters to Germany; but apart from the brief excerpt published by the Palestine Association in 1810, these were not collated and published until 1854. Thus very little was known at this time in Europe about the great pioneers' travels – with the important exception of those who had met them, or heard verbal accounts of their findings during their travels in the Levant.

It was for this reason that the sensational discovery of the classical ruins in the country to the east of the Jordan was first revealed to the public through the books of James Buckingham, whose *Travels in Palestine* was published in 1821 – a year ahead of Burckhardt's edited notes – and whose sequel, *Travels among the Arab Tribes* appeared in 1823. Burckhardt's written impressions of Petra, moreover, were necessarily so vague that the fame of the caravan city only began with the publication of Irby and Mangles's *Travels through Nubia, Palestine and Syria* in 1823, and even this, as will be seen, reached a limited audience. The appearance of Buckingham's *Travels* triggered a literary scandal whose echoes reverberated from London to Calcutta, and a series of legal proceedings which lasted for four years.

Throughout the nineteenth century, Buckingham had short shrift from professional scholars: 'greatly Burckhardt's inferior in the matter of sober, scientific observation,' wrote the American archaeologist Frederick Bliss in 1803, summing up nearly a century of disapproval. However, it was Buckingham who made Palestine exploration as exciting as Richard Burton was to make that of Arabia.

James Silk Buckingham was a sailor and journalist who attacked in his articles the restrictive practices of the East India Company (he was expelled from India in 1823 for his critical articles), the press-ganging of sailors and flogging in the armed services, and the official tolerance of drunkenness. A prolific writer, he never seems to have shared Burckhardt's feeling that 'it is a less fatiguing duty to perform travels than to write them down'.

Buckingham went to sea at the age of nine, in 1795, and was taken prisoner a year later and held by the French at Corunna, in Spain, for several months. He served on ships travelling to America, the Bahamas and the West Indies before finding employment with the merchant communities of Bombay and Calcutta. At a time when the overland route from Aleppo to the Persian Gulf was more popular than that through the Egyptian desert to the Red Sea – both led on to India – he tried to persuade Mohammed Ali, the Egyptian ruler, to trade with British merchants in India via the Red Sea. In order to plan this route, he learned Arabic, and disguised as an Egyptian peasant, crossed the desert of Suez and explored traces of the ancient canal which had once connected the Nile with the Arabian Gulf.

It was during these adventures that he first met Burckhardt, and heard of his travels in Palestine and elsewhere. Buckingham's ambitious offer to Mohammed Ali to restore the ancient canal was not taken up. In 1816, however, he was entrusted to deliver a commercial agreement signed by the Egyptian ruler and the British consul in Cairo to Briggs and Company, the merchants in whose employ he served in India.

But instead of returning to India via the Red Sea, as he had come, Buckingham made a detour through Palestine and Mesopotamia, thence to India via the Persian Gulf, arriving there a full year after he left Cairo. Buckingham was to argue that it was 'the prevailing winds from the south' which had made it impossible for him to take the Red Sea route, but it appears more likely that Burckhardt's stories had aroused his curiosity about Palestine, and whetted his literary appetite and ambitions; the Orientalist explorers' new discoveries to the east of the Jordan, he wrote, 'were scarcely known, even by name'.

Buckingham set out on a small boat from Alexandria in the winter of 1816. Marooned in a dead calm near the Egyptian shore, they made little progress till a brisk wind drove them all too rapidly northwards, almost drowning them off the dangerous Syrian coast when a storm blew up. Buckingham's skill as a sailor saved the boat, and he finally landed at Tyre. He then made his way south through Palestine, staying in villages where he helped the peasants sort the fibre from their cotton crops, fighting off Bedouin in an ambush in Galilee, and finally reaching Jerusalem, where he met the antiquarian, William Bankes.

The two men decided to travel across the Jordan together to explore and record the ruins Seetzen and Burckhardt had discovered. They were incongruous travelling companions, but their talents were complementary. Buckingham was resourceful, observant, and extremely tough; but he had no formal education. Bankes was cautious and pedantic by temperament, but immensely learned; he had been a college friend of Byron, and was a society figure in London. Buckingham was quick at languages; Bankes the kind of man who would speak no word of a language unless he knew it perfectly.

After purchasing horses and assuming their disguises – Bankes as a Turkish soldier, Buckingham as a Syrian Arab – they set out for the Jordan with a Bedouin guide, whose son Bankes had managed to get released from prison by personal intervention with the governor of Jerusalem. He also had an Albanian janissary as his personal bodyguard.

From Jericho they reached the Jordan through a dry ravine, thence across the river into what appeared to be 'the white and barren hills of Arabia'. Quite soon, however, they found that the land across the river was by no means barren. A short way inland, the territory known as biblical Gilead was revealed as 'a land of extraordinary richness . . . clothed with thick forest, varied with verdant slopes and possessing extensive plains of a fine red soil'. Near Zerka they found well-watered land 'thickly wooded with oleander and plane trees, with wild olives and wild almonds in blossom', a landscape cultivated by peasants with long beards and dressed in long white shirts 'looking like figures from the Old Masters'. These farmers, it appeared to Buckingham, lived a near idyllic life 'in complete independence of the Pashas', armed only against the Bedouin, in a land so fertile and freely available to the cultivator 'that the only claim to the possession of any particular spot is that of having ploughed and sown it'. Buckingham thought this region more beautiful than the Promised Land of western Palestine – which Western readers then believed was distressingly unproductive – and a vindication of everything which had been written in the histories of the ancient populousness of the country beyond the river.

Soon the travellers came to Gerasa, with its 'temples, colonnades, theatres, arched buildings with domes, detached groups of Ionic and Corinthian columns, bridges and aqueducts', and all in impeccable classical style. Despite the persistent harassment of the Englishmen by the local peasants, and a torrential spring downpour which left both men drenched to the skin, Bankes managed to sketch the city and Buckingham to make detailed notes. Bankes was as enthusiastic about the discovery of the Roman theatre as his temperament admitted: 'It occurred to Mr Bankes that, notwithstanding the ruin of some parts of this edifice, it was, perhaps, on the whole, the most perfect Roman theatre now remaining in the world. He had himself seen all those of Italy, and in Greece we knew how much they are destroyed, and he knew none so perfect as this, more particularly as to the stage and the scene.'

Both men realized that in Gerasa they had found a classical city of great importance with whose description they might make Bankes's reputation and Buckingham's fortune – to rival the reports of Robert Wood a century earlier on Palmyra and Baalbeck. However, the conditions under which they carried out their brief survey were not such as to ensure careful and scholarly assessment. Bankes was trying to remember a recent article in the *Gentleman's Magazine* on the exact specifications of Roman theatres, and, blinded by the pouring rain, he was not absolutely certain whether the lettering he had spotted on the ruins was in fact Greek or Latin. They were pestered by an old peasant in the ruins whom Buckingham told 'that they intended to take to the Sultan an account of one of his most wonderful possessions'. When they tried to write up their findings in a nearby village, the peasants were suspicious, though Buckingham explained that they were 'Turks writing prayers on the appearance of the new moon, after the manner of the faithful'.

Buckingham and Bankes continued northwards along the river bank and eventually reached the ruins Seetzen had named as those of Gadara; here they found ruins in a less perfect state of preservation, though still remarkable. Seetzen's account had made the briefest of identifications, with the mention of the famous hot springs but saying nothing of the theatres and temples. So Buckingham decided that this was in fact Gamala, a still undiscovered Decapolis city.

Buckingham was far more graphic than Seetzen had been about the peasant cave dwellers. He described them as shepherds and farmers, 'some inhabiting the ancient Roman tombs, some living in rude dwellings formed by a circle of broken sarcophagi and other large stones on the spot; some dwelling in conical huts of reed plastered on the outside with mud, like the Abyssinians, and other inhabitants of rainy climates, and others again reposing beneath tents woven from the hair and wool of their own flocks'. One of the ancient tombs was now used as a carpenter's shop, and another peasant used a sarcophagus as a

Strange allies: Sir Sidney Smith (centre), victor of the siege of Acre in 1799, and Ahmed Djezzar, the city's Bosnian defender, portrayed by a British naval surgeon (extreme right). Coloured stipple engraving from F.B. Spilsbury, *Picturesque Scenery in the Holy Land and Syria* (1803).

Napoleon Bonaparte as merciful healer; according to one eyewitness of this scene, however, he pushed aside a suffering soldier with the toe of his boot. 'The Pesthouse at Jaffa' ('Les Pestiférés à Jaffa') by Baron Antoine Gros (1804).

'View of Jerusalem from the Mount of Olives' by Luigi Mayer (1803). The seventh-century Moslem shrine of the Dome of the Rock is in the foreground, the Holy Sepulchre just behind it, the citadel on the horizon. The perspective is totally distorted in order to make the Moslem shrine appear smaller than the Christian church and the Turkish garrison fort (citadel), which dominates the whole.

'Good Friday in the Holy Sepulchre' by Sir John Leslie.
The Latin Patriarch and Franciscan fathers, with their flock, at an Easter ceremony in the Holy Sepulchre. The mannikin in the centre is a wax Christ figure which was carried in procession during the enaction of the Passion.

'Interior of the Dome of the Rock' by Carl Werner (*c.* 1860).
This shrine, first described by a nineteenth-century Western visitor (who entered in disguise) in 1818, was not open to non-Moslems until after the Crimean War – and for some time only by special dispensation.

Above right: Portrait of James Silk Buckingham and his wife; the adoption of local costume was often essential for reasons of safety.

Above left: Jean Louis Burckhardt as Sheikh Ibrahim from a sketch by H. Salt (1821).
'I stop at the dirtiest caravanserai, use the floor as my mattress and my coat as a blanket, eat with camel drivers and brush my horse myself, but I see and hear things which remain unknown to him who travels in comfort.'

Below: The Baroque in the desert. Western travellers who rediscovered Petra in the second decade of the century found it reminiscent of Borromini. 'El Deir Petra' by David Roberts (1839).

chest for corn 'so that this violated sepulchre of the dead had thus become a secure, a cool and a convenient retreat to the living of a different race'.

Near the Sea of Galilee the two men recrossed the Jordan. Here they had intended to part company – with Bankes going to Nazareth, Buckingham to Aleppo on his way to Persia. But Buckingham fell from his horse and sprained his ankle, compelling him to spend a few days' rest with Bankes at Nazareth. What happened during their stay there was to be angrily debated during the controversy that followed.

Shortly afterwards, the two men parted; Buckingham then retraced his entire journey along the east bank of the Jordan. His narrative explains this detour as an attempt to find a reliable guide to take him due south, but it seems more probable that he wanted to make additional notes and sketches of his own in the ruins the two had visited. On this solitary journey he had several times to shoot his way through ambushes. Having resurveyed Gerasa, he headed north again, then inland, and eventually arrived in India where he wrote up his adventures.

Travels in Palestine reached John Murray, the English publisher, at the end of 1818. Seetzen's notes were gathering dust in Germany; Burckhardt's were still unedited. But Murray hesitated. He had in his hands an exciting travel story (though padded with quotations from historical works Buckingham had found in mission libraries in India) and books on the Levant were selling well. But it also contained provocative material.

Buckingham, in his account of Jerusalem, had not limited himself to 'the discussion historical'. He had gone further towards debunking the Holy City than anyone who had written about Jerusalem at that time. He had taken issue with the most celebrated writers on Jerusalem of the period – Chateaubriand and Clarke. Chateaubriand had described the Latin friars, ten years earlier, as studious, dedicated and humble men; Buckingham, after talking to them, maintained that they 'never opened a book', were bored, depressed and homesick, sycophantic to the rich and uncharitable to the poor. He added that he had heard many reports of the friars keeping women in Bethlehem, and had himself visited a prostitute near the Holy Sepulchre, from whose home he had been forcibly 'rescued' by his friend, an Abyssinian prince named Musa.

Buckingham had read Clarke's strictures on the inauthenticity of the Holy Places; and plunging recklessly into the debate Clarke had started, took issue not only with Clarke but with the formidable literary review which had applauded his conclusions. Taking on the *Quarterly Review* was far more perilous than libelling the Catholic Church; and Buckingham not only argued that Clarke had not proven his case, and that Quaresmius had refuted all his objections centuries earlier, but, by implication, that the *Quarterly* ought to have known better than to have supported him.

Moreover, the portrait of Bankes himself was not entirely flattering. Buckingham described several excursions they had taken together, including a visit to some 'good-looking females' in an establishment near the Sepulchre. While he had dutifully quoted Bankes's expert opinions on the Decapolis ruins, he had managed to suggest in the narrative that the wealthy Bankes had enjoyed privileges *en route* not shared by his companion. When the two men returned, soaked, from Gerasa to their lodging in the nearby village, Buckingham wrote, Bankes had enjoyed 'dry covering' supplied by his bodyguard, while Buckingham 'got naked between straw mats'. Bankes's fine calico underwear, hung up to dry in the public room of a Moslem village, had attracted so much attention, Buckingham suggested, that it gave away the travellers' identity.

Murray did not cut the manuscript himself – though Buckingham, in sending it, had suggested that parts might perhaps be 'unfit for the public eye', leaving the matter to Murray's discretion. Instead, Murray asked Gifford, editor of the *Quarterly Review* (which Murray also published), for his opinion. When Gifford suggested docking forty pages, Murray gave up. The book was eventually published, in its entirety, by Longman's at the beginning of 1821. It was immediately a popular success, but not with the *Quarterly*, which tore into Buckingham with all the avidity of a Bedouin plundering his victim.

Buckingham was described as an ignorant, pretentious scribbler quoting from sources he did not understand and locating places which he had probably not seen. The *Quarterly* pinpointed more than forty errors in his text. Most of these corrections now look like deliberate misreadings of the text, or vindictive distortions, but the reviewer was clearly someone who was an authority on ancient history, while Buckingham, just as clearly, was not. (Contemporaries believed the review was written by Bankes himself.) The most damaging criticisms were those which undermined the very reason for the book's appearance: the detailed descriptions of Gerasa and Gadara – which Buckingham had persisted in identifying as Gamala, probably because Burckhardt had made the same mistake. The reviewer argued, moreover, that Buckingham had probably not seen the Roman ruins at Gerasa at all, but another, far less important ruin near the Jordan.

It was months before Buckingham saw the review, for the paper had to make its way by sea on the four-month journey round the Cape to India. Meanwhile, his silence was tantamount to an admission of ignorance and mendacity. In addition, Bankes had written his former travelling companion a venomous letter accusing him of outright theft and plagiarism. Buckingham, he said, had copied his notes and sketches, left on a window seat in the monastery in Nazareth, during the two men's stay there. These accusations now made the round of literary circles in London.

To cap everything, Buckingham was attacked from beyond the grave. As soon as Burckhardt had heard of Buckingham's journey to Palestine, he had written a violent attack on his fellow traveller, whom he accused of having boasted falsely of Burckhardt's friendship to smooth his way in the East, and of having abused the trust of his employers in making an unauthorized trip to Palestine.

Buckingham fought back. His answer to the *Quarterly* appeared in a lengthy appendix to his second book, *Travels among the Arab Tribes*, which appeared in 1823 and described in detail the circumstances of his return journey down the Jordan valley and second visit to Gerasa. He sued Bankes for libel, in a case which finally came to court in London in October 1826. It was long delayed while Bankes combed the Levant for his Albanian bodyguard, who he hoped would appear as witness for the defence. But to locate one Mahomet in the Orient was difficult.

Bankes now argued that Buckingham had been a mere servant, not a colleague, 'knowing less of science than the commonest mechanics even of that country'. Fortunately for Buckingham, though he had returned all Bankes's letters, as requested, much earlier, one had accidentally remained in his possession, stuck to the underside of his portmanteau by its sealing wax. This letter indicated that the two men had discussed architectural styles in great detail. Moreover, Bankes had written: 'I do not think you will be ashamed of having your name associated to what I may one day or another throw together into form.'

There was laughter in court when Bankes's famous 'notes' turned out to be twenty written pages in a notebook two inches square; as there was when Buckingham's counsel commented: 'I have heard of the jealousy of women, of the jealousy of Turks, of the jealousy of hare-brained projectors, and of the proverbial jealous irritability of poets; but their jealousy is nothing, it is placid and quiet compared with the jealousy of travellers.'

Buckingham won his case, and was awarded substantial damages. His two books sold well. By 1833 he was, like Bankes, a Member of Parliament, and during his term of office a Select Committee of the House of Commons recommended redress for his expulsion from India, and compensation in the form of a pension from the East India Company.

As for Bankes, by the time of his defeat by Buckingham in the law courts he had another cause of mortification. This was the private publication, in 1823, of an account of travels in the East by two young naval officers, Charles Irby and James Mangles. Once more, Bankes appeared in the role of learned bystander in a book he should have written himself.

*   *   *

After leaving Buckingham at Nazareth in 1816, Bankes had travelled to Aleppo, where he met Irby and Mangles at the house of the British consul-general, Barker. Where Burckhardt had found so much to interest him in the alleys and markets of Aleppo, the young officers were merely bored. 'There is a great sameness in all Turkish towns; and the absence of inns, theatres, museums, picture galleries, libraries, promenades, evening parties and the ever handy and comfortable café is a privation which an European must always feel.'

They met Bankes again in Tiberias, and this time elected to travel together. All three men had 'our poor friend Burckhardt's notes' of routes and places visited. They decided to follow in his footsteps, hoping to make a more detailed survey of Petra and its surroundings. They travelled first to Jerusalem, where at the Saint Saviour's monastery they met William Legh, 'one of the most enterprising travellers of the present age', just back from Russia, and Lord Belmore, who with a large entourage, travelling on his private yacht, had come up from Egypt. Legh was rather outclassed and wrote, 'all had been in Nubia and everyone except myself as far as the second cataract'.

While in Jerusalem the naval officers volunteered to act as guides to Lord and Lady Belmore. They went down to the Jordan with the Russian pilgrims, and staged a torchlight march to the river at two o'clock on a spring morning. Belmore had the ample escort of his sailors, and no ambushes were reported, though Legh was 'temporarily blinded' by the salty Dead Sea water during a swim.

Bankes, with Belmore's brother, Captain Corry, now organized what must have been the first of recorded nineteenth-century attempts to excavate the ruins of Jerusalem. He had for some time tried to get a firman from Constantinople to explore the rock tomb façade popularly known as the Tombs of the Kings — that is, the Kings of Judah. This was refused. The English party decided to do without the firman, privileged enough to trust that no great harm would come to them if discovered. Lord Belmore, however, prudently remained in the monastery.

Irby and Mangles reported: 'Late in the evening we quitted the town, singly, and from different gates, to avoid suspicion; and assembling at the rendezvous after dark, found that we mustered a party of ten persons, viz: Messrs Bankes and Legh, Captain Corry and ourselves, together with five servants, including two of

Lord Belmore's sailors whom his lordship had allowed to join us.' They worked all night long 'digging and clearing away the rubbish'.

> In the morning we had removed the rubbish to a depth of about 10 feet, when we came to an immense block of stone, apparently in the very spot where we expected to find the entrance to the tomb. As we were unable to move this mass, we returned to the city, pretty well fatigued, having been obliged, for want of spades, to clear away the rubbish with our hands. The next day Captain Corry, Mr Bankes, and Mahomet his janissary [the Albanian] acting on the suggestion of Lord Belmore, succeeded in breaking the stone by heating it, and then pouring cold vinegar on it; but, unfortunately, shortly after this was done, our proceedings were discovered by some Turks, and reported to the governor, who put a very effectual stop to our researches by ordering the whole of the portico to be walled in.

Every possible obstacle was subsequently put in the way of the English party's journey to Petra. The governors both of Jaffa and Jerusalem warned them against the journey; more than thirty Moslem pilgrims on their way back from Mecca had been murdered in Wadi Musa the previous year. This did not deter the travellers, and Irby and Mangles, Bankes and Legh, with their servants, set out for Hebron, all wearing Bedouin dress.

In Hebron, a Jewish moneylender acted as intermediary between the Englishmen and a local Bedouin chief. After the usual bargaining over the respective value of an English watch and danger money in Wadi Musa, the party took on a Bedouin escort, only to stop and start each time more money was demanded and the guides 'held pitched battles' over its division. Eventually, the party found itself in the care of the rascally Sheikh of Kerak who had outwitted Burckhardt some half dozen years earlier. The large English party was less susceptible to blackmail and all went well at first. But when they arrived at Wadi Musa, both the Englishmen and the Sheikh were confronted by a group of several tribes encamped at the entrance to the Wadi. Legh, who as an eager ethnographer was industriously taking notes on the behaviour of the Bedouin, noted how one sheikh placed himself 'under the protection' of another. 'If the Sheikh is in the company of strangers, ride straight through; if not, form a line, approach, then wheel around and reach the Sheikh from behind. A Bamboo spear with ostrich feathers is the sign of the Sheikh.'

Protocol was thus observed; but the Sheikh of Wadi Musa was not in the mood to admit foreigners to his territory. Though the Sheikh of Kerak displayed the various firmans in the party's possession, including even that of Legh's Tartar servant, who also had a firman from the Porte, the Sheikh of Wadi Musa brushed them all aside. The English, he said, had come to find out where the wells were located in the Wadi. When the English king learned where the wells were located, he would follow with his army. The Sheikh of Kerak protested that the English wished only to examine the old buildings, since in England there was nothing to compare with them. But the local Sheikh was adamant; the firmans were forgeries, he said, fabricated by the Jewish advisers to the Pashas of Acre and Damascus, and the Franks were nothing but necromancers and poisoners of wells. All the tribes were now poised for combat, and the Englishmen begged their escorts to retreat. But Bedouin honour was at stake.

At this critical moment, three Bedouin who had made the *Haj* to Mecca, and knew a genuine firman when they saw one, pronounced the documents authentic. The Sheikh of Wadi Musa gave the sign for the foreigners' admittance – as Legh noted, a white cotton waved on the end of a spear – but warned them to keep away from the wells. Bankes's expert inspection of Petra now began, incidentally fulfilling Burckhardt's wish that someone better qualified than himself in the knowledge of classical architecture should examine the site.

It was not Bankes however whose version of the experience was published, five years later, but that of Irby and Mangles. Their account of this first European visit to Petra frequently quotes what Bankes had to say, and the wealth of knowledge he brought to the survey. 'Although we are of the opinion that Mr Bankes could not have succeeded in accomplishing this journey without his junction with Mr Legh and ourselves, still he has the merit of being the first person travelling as a European who ever thought of extending his researches in that direction; and from his profound knowledge of ancient history, as well as his skill in drawing, he was by far the best calculated to go on such an expedition.' That suggests some conflict between the travellers, and Bankes's drawings did not adorn the officers' narrative. But their description combines their natural wonder and admiration at the splendid ruins in the desert, together with the admonitions of Bankes, as it were from offstage.

No sooner had the party entered the valley, and examined the first rock tombs, than a tomb face was described as 'in bad taste, with an infinity of broken lines and unnecessary angles and projections, and multiplied pediments and half pediments, and pedestals set upon columns which support nothing. It has more the air of a fantastical scene in a theatre than an architectural work in stone; and for unmeaning richness, and littleness of conception might, as Mr Bankes observed, have been the work of Borromini himself, whose style it exactly resembles, and carries to the extreme.'

'Theatrical' from Bankes was no compliment. Buckingham described him dismissing the Holy Sepulchre, too, as 'poor and paltry French theatre'. But Bankes was faithful to his time; the classical revival in Europe was at its zenith, and the Baroque in great disfavour – even in the desert.

It was Irby and Mangles, nonetheless, who managed to shake off Bankes's disapproval for long enough to compose the first account of Petra to capture the Western imagination:

> We proceeded along this narrow passage for nearly two miles, the sides increasing in height as the path continually descended, while the tops of the precipices retained an uniform level. Where they are at the highest, a beam of stronger light breaks in at the close of the dark perspective, and opens to view, half seen at first through the tall, narrow opening, columns, statues and cornices, of a light and finished style and looking as if fresh from the chisel, without the tints or weather stains of age, and executed in a stone of a pale rose colour. At the moment we came in sight of them, they were illumined with the full light of the morning sun. The dark green of the shrubs that grow in this perpetual shade, and the sombre appearance of the passage from whence we were just issuing, formed a fine contrast with the glowing colour of the edifice. We know not what to compare this scene with; perhaps there is nothing in the world that resembles it.

So generations of visitors were henceforth to see Petra, the 'rose red city, half as old as time'. When the officers arrived at the Khazna, known as the Nabatean treasury, they were equally impressed: 'the position is one of the most beautiful that could be imagined for the front of a great temple; and the richness and exquisite finish of the decorations offer a most remarkable contrast to the savage scenery which surrounds it'; then, Bankes's obbligato: 'in some respects, the taste is not to be commended.'

Bankes's erudition was much in evidence. On one tomb face, the well-cut letters of an inscription were in a script which baffled the officers. 'None of our party had ever seen these characters before, excepting Mr Bankes, who upon comparing them, found them to be exactly similar to those he had seen scratched on the rocks of the Wadi Maktub and about the foot of Mount Sinai. He subsequently found a passage in Diodorus Siculus, wherein he speaks of a letter written by the Nabathei of Petra, to Antigonus, in the Syriac character, and professed to be able to make out a date.' Bankes was bluffing; many travellers had seen the strange graffiti in Sinai, but these were not to be even partially deciphered until nearly a hundred years later.

When the travellers finally parted, Irby and Mangles for Turkey, and Bankes 'by water to Egypt in the intent of penetrating into Abyssinia by way of the second cataract', it was understood that Bankes was to write a scholarly account of the journey they had undertaken together. But he did not do so; nor did he write the definitive version of the journey east of the Jordan, for which fellow scholars were waiting.

On Bankes's return to England, he enjoyed a brief political career as Member of Parliament for Cambridge University and later for his local constituency of Dorset. Ironically, for the man expected by everyone to make a major contribution to the knowledge of classical remains in Syria, he was best remembered for what the German geographer Ritter called his 'stubborn reticence'. His last, and solitary escapade came to light in 1839 with the publication of the travel memoirs of the French Vicomte de Marcellus.

In 1820, Marcellus had been charged with a secret financial

mission on behalf of a French Catholic order; on his way to the
Holy Land, he purchased the recently discovered Venus de Milo
and sent it back to France. On arrival in Jerusalem, he was taken
up to the governor's residence, like so many other distinguished
visitors, to enjoy the best view of the Noble Sanctuary. The
governor apologized for not being able to take Marcellus into
the Sanctuary itself, but explained that the Moslem dignitary in
charge was still seething over a ruse practised on him by a
European who had penetrated the compound in disguise a few
days earlier. 'Dressed in oriental clothes, this Englishman, who
had left Jaffa the previous evening, arrived at Jerusalem in the
morning; he spent several hours during the afternoon in the
mosque, and left again that very evening for Jaffa, where a boat
was waiting for him. There was no way in which the Mullah
could avenge this profanation.'

Marcellus explained that the secret visitor was Bankes, whom
he had met at Constantinople, and whom he was to meet again in
London, some years later, when they 'laughed together at the
Moslem's discomfiture'. Bankes brought out a portfolio which
contained, according to Marcellus, 'the most unusual drawings'.
If these were drawings of the Sanctuary, they were the first ever
made. But Bankes never published them. By the time Marcellus
published his memoir, other men had stolen Bankes's thunder,
and the Noble Sanctuary was no longer safe from the eyes of the
West.

*   *   *

Palestine now conformed to the painter's ideal of the Picturesque; the site of classical ruins, patrolled by nomadic tribes, and
of a desert refuge which had once sheltered a mysterious
civilization. As the land of the Bible, it was not to fire debate for
another two decades, in a totally changed political climate.
Palestine was to play a different role: as 'evidence' in a trial of a
faith.

CHAPTER III

———◆◆◆———

Palestine and the Authentication
of the Bible

THE MOST SERIOUS CHALLENGE to Turkish rule in the Near East since Napoleon took place at the time when Protestant faith in the literal truth of the Scriptures was being put to the severest of tests. The Egyptian conquest of Syria in 1831, though it was to last barely a decade, enabled the West to gain a foothold in Palestine from which it was not henceforth to be dislodged. From this time forward, Palestine was to be ransacked for 'evidence' of the accuracy of the Bible, not simply revered as the site of the Holy Places.

In 1831 Mohammed Ali, the Albanian ruler of Egypt, nominally the Sultan's vassal, rebelled against his Ottoman master, and his son, Ibrahim Pasha, led Egypt's army into Palestine. One eyewitness to the invasion was Marie-Joseph de Géramb, an Austrian officer turned Trappist monk, evicted from his monastery in Alsace during the anti-Bourbon revolution of 1830. He arrived in Palestine on a pilgrimage to find Jaffa under occupation, and reached Jerusalem just ahead of the Egyptian troops. They were, he observed, dressed in European uniforms, and carried the drums, fifes and bayonets supplied by Mohammed Ali's patrons in the West; and one of Ibrahim's first concerns was to publish decrees instructing local Christians to refuse to pay 'all kinds of punitive tributes and exactions'. Géramb thought this 'merely a cloak for later extortions'. But he was wrong; it was the turning point in the history of the non-Moslems in Palestine.

Since Napoleon's time, France had been the dominant influence in Egypt, while in his quarrel with the Sultan, Mohammed Ali had also sought the help of England as supreme naval power in the region. Both France and England, however, feared the gains Russia might make if the Ottoman empire collapsed under Egyptian pressure, and when Ibrahim swept on north-wards, threatening Constantinople itself, they insisted he confine his gains to Syria. There, he was concerned to show his pro-Western sympathies. Ibrahim Pasha instituted a centralized, pro-Western regime in Syria. The price of agricultural and fiscal reforms, and the greater security of life and property, was the granting of unlimited power to the tax farmers, forced labour, and the conscription of the male population between the ages of fifteen and sixty by the military regime. These measures made the Egyptians deeply hated, and even French travellers deplored their country's support for Ibrahim's despotic rule when they saw children of ten and twelve, scarcely able to hold a rifle, branded and marched off for service in Egypt, and peasant families holding funerals for the sons they never expected to see again.

The Bedouin put up a rearguard resistance, but they were beaten back into the desert. When the peasantry and some of the local sheikhs rebelled in 1834, the revolt was put down with the utmost brutality.

But local Christians – who were not eligible for military service – and foreigners benefited immediately from the new dispen-sations. Edward Hogg, an English traveller who visited Palestine, like Géramb, during the campaign itself, described the 'melanch-oly picture of devastation and ruin' in Acre, where the town reconstructed by Djezzar was once more reduced to rubble. But, he reported, 'the vigorous measures of the new government already have secured the traveller as well from casual plunder as from arbitrary extortion. The notorious Abu Ghosh is no longer allowed to levy contributions, nor indeed did we meet with either interruption or demand in our whole journey from Jaffa to Jerusalem.'

The new spirit of tolerance towards the Christians was particularly noticeable in Jerusalem. Emboldened by this len-iency, and the firm hand exercised by the Egyptian troops, a party of English architects and draughtsmen set out to make detailed plans and sketches of the Noble Sanctuary.

These men came north from Egypt in 1833, where they had been employed by Mohammed Ali restoring ancient Egyptian monuments, and at the same time making the precise and elegant drawings of archaeological sites which were to make the ruins of ancient Egypt famous all over Europe. They included an Italian sculptor, Joseph Bonomi – later to restore St Peter's in Rome – Frederick Catherwood – later to help discover the Maya civilization of South America – and Augustus Pugin, designer, with Charles Barry, of the Houses of Parliament at Westminster. Nothing illustrated the dramatic changes in Palestine more clearly than the fact that Catherwood, with his drawing board and *camera lucida* (a prism arranged so that mirrors projected an image on a sheet of paper, enabling the artist to trace its outlines), was able to sit tranquilly drawing Gerasa where Buckingham and Bankes had hardly dared make notes some fifteen years earlier.

Bonomi was the first to enter the Sanctuary in Egyptian dress. He was fluent in Arabic, having spent nearly a decade in Egypt. He sketched the Dome of the Rock from various angles, while guards and bypassers, believing that he was an Egyptian architect sent to undertake repairs, made no objection. He was followed a few days later by Catherwood, in similar disguise, who managed to sketch the interior of the Dome of the Rock. But the Moslems were now suspicious, and after a hostile crowd gathered, Catherwood was only saved from attack when the governor, who assumed he had a warrant from Ibrahim Pasha, explained his presence and calmed the bystanders. Catherwood spent six weeks surveying and drawing the area, and then, before the governor could discover his mistake – for Ibrahim was on his way to Jerusalem – the visitors left the city.

During his stay in Jerusalem, Catherwood had also made a series of drawings of the city from the terrace of the governor's palace, including scenes from everyday life: the Bedouin coming to market, sheikhs, judges and pipe bearers, the governor holding audience under a canopy, the bastinado of a criminal, and Bonomi and himself at work on the terrace – a documentary of Moslem life in Jerusalem against the background of religious shrines.

Back in London, these drawings attracted the interest of an impresario, Robert Burford, who ran the Leicester Square Pavilion: a huge rotunda where the popular entertainers of the day displayed great murals of foreign scenes and adventures. Burford made gigantic reproductions of the drawings, borrowed costumes from Bonomi to help with the painting of the figures, and in 1836 the 'Panorama of Jerusalem' opened in Leicester Square with Catherwood as live commentator. The display, which covered ten thousand square feet, was visited in its first season by more than 140,000 people, evidence of a revival of popular interest in Palestine which was to continue undiminished throughout the century. In the programme accompanying the exhibit, as much space was devoted to the description of the Dome of the Rock, and its historic and architectural significance, as to the Holy Sepulchre.

The Panorama was eventually destroyed by fire, and Catherwood's drawings of the Noble Sanctuary, lent to an historian of architecture named James Fergusson, disappeared for twenty years. Only one, lent to the master engraver William Finden, for inclusion in a book of illustrations named *The Biblical Keepsake*, was published at this time. Its fate was significant; for before long, Moslem sites and customs were all to be pressed into service as 'biblical illustrations'.

*   *   *

During the 1830s, the controversy over the historical authenticity of the Scriptures, in the light of recent scientific research, reached its peak. The problem went back, in the general sense, for centuries. As Robert Browning wrote in 'Bishop Bloughram's Apology',

> How you'd exult if I could put you back
> Six hundred years, blot out cosmogony,
> Geology, ethnology, what not
> (Greek endings, each the little passing bell
> That signifies some faith's about to die),
> And set you square with Genesis again.

But in the eighteenth century, despite the growth of rationalism, religious belief and scientific progress had managed to coexist comfortably. Successive revelations of the complexity of the physical universe demonstrated the ingenuity of its Maker. In the 1830s, however, the conclusions of geologists, in particular, indicating through the study of fossils that the earth was millions, not thousands, of years old, and had not been created in its final form in a week were dismaying even to many of the scientists themselves. The founder of the science of fossils, Louis Cuvier (to whom French travellers had brought back samples of fish from the Dead Sea), had attempted desperately to reconcile the evidence with faith in divine providence. But between 1831 and 1833, with Sir Charles Lyell's publication of *Principles of Geology*, such exercises became impossible. It was to be many years before scientists gave up thinking in pseudo-biblical terms of the 'single pair' in whom the human race originated, or searching for a 'scientific' equivalent to Noah's flood; but from this point religion and science were to go their separate ways.

Moreover, the new science of philology, which had begun with European penetration of the Near East and the analysis of hitherto unknown languages, produced the analytical study of the Scriptures, particularly in Germany, in their historical and cultural context. During the 1830s, again, the Tuebingen school of bible scholars concluded that the Bible was not one document but a collection of texts from various periods, and pointed out inconsistencies and chronological impossibilities which made it difficult to read the text with faith in its literal truth.

This was not the first attack on the authenticity of the Bible. Freethinkers like Voltaire had done so far more brutally, but while such attacks could be condemned as polemic, the carefully reasoned arguments of the bible scholars were more threatening. While there were those who argued with Coleridge, that religious faith should not be made dependent on a literal belief in every word of the Scriptures, they were in a minority. The more common reaction was that the truths of the Bible had been assaulted and that there were only two ways to defend them: either to reject scientific evidence and linguistic analysis indignantly – a course increasingly difficult to sustain – or to provide equally 'scientific' evidence of the accuracy of the biblical narrative. There was obviously no better place to start assembling such evidence than the Holy Land itself.

The idea of corroborating the Scriptures by reference to the experience of travellers in Palestine appears to have originated with a mid-eighteenth-century Suffolk clergyman named Thomas Harmer. Harmer, though he never visited Palestine himself, compiled an anthology of 'scriptural illustrations' taken from books of travel in the East. He believed that he was thus 'placing [the Scriptures] in a new light . . . not determinable by the methods commonly used by the learned'. Harmer's anthology, which ran into four volumes, was clearly intended as a response to the attack by Voltaire on the veracity of Holy Writ.

Where textual analysis was concerned, a visit to Palestine was irrelevant; but the geologists' work had given an entirely new urgency to explorations of the Dead Sea and Sinai regions, where numbers of clerical and scholarly travellers were now to seek for acceptable explanations of the legends of Genesis and Exodus. The entirely coincidental fact that, under Egyptian rule, Palestine was now open for the first time to Western explorers under reasonably favourable conditions for research led to a break-through in what was called 'scriptural geography' by the American theologian Edward Robinson. Robinson was followed by a long cavalcade of geographers, missionaries and Protestant clergymen, all of whom were concerned primarily with under-writing the truth of the Bible. Every village, tree, plant and stone was scrutinized for its possible relevance to the Scriptures. Parables were found to have living illustrations in local folklore. Puzzling or apparently abstruse biblical passages were explained in terms of Oriental customs, and even the peasantry – who until now had attracted little attention – were closely observed for any insights or parallels their daily lives might provide.

The result of all this activity was an avalanche of books on the Holy Land, most of them illustrated with drawings, water colours and, later, photographs. The landmarks of Palestine soon became as familiar as, forty years earlier, they had been unknown; by 1854, wrote one weary reviewer in the *British Art Journal* of a book by a missionary's wife, 'the subject has been gone over again and again, until the Holy Land is better known in

England than the English Lakes'. Protestant hymns became explicitly geographical; the huge family bibles were illustrated with a combination of Renaissance reproductions, archaeological diagrams from Egyptian excavations, and prints copied from travel memoirs.

It was not only in Protestant countries that bible history was re-examined in the light of modern Oriental life. Any authoritative work on Palestine, such as that of Solomon Munk, a Jewish scholar in the manuscript department of the Bibliothèque Royale in Paris, written from 'a purely rational viewpoint' and quoting from every possible source from the Talmud to the German philologists, ended with a series of engravings from Syrian scenes, and pictures of local artefacts from farming tools to musical instruments. Painters from all over Europe sought not only to correct the distortions of the Renaissance view of Palestine but also to find local, Oriental models for paintings on religious subjects. But the dominant mood was Protestant, and didactic.

The problem with this approach was that Palestine was a Moslem country, Christianity long a Western religion, and the encounter with an Oriental environment as a parallel to that of the Bible was charged with ambiguities.

By the eighteenth century, the religious quarrel with Islam had burnt itself out. The intellectual drive that had produced the new linguistic critics of the Bible was also to encourage the serious study of Islam as an historical religion. Many travellers from the West who were repelled by the rituals of Eastern Christianity compared them unfavourably with the dignified proceedings glimpsed in the mosques.

Nevertheless, the dominant view of Islam as a philosophical system, in the nineteenth century, was that it encouraged fatalism and unreason, resignation to poverty and backwardness, discriminated against women, discouraged the spread of education, and so blocked material progress – nowhere more so than in Palestine. The 'Eastern customs' observed there were thus also deplorable signs of a decadent culture; and to depict Christianity as an Eastern religion was all the more incongruous.

To read the Bible without questioning its literal accuracy was possible in the West, though it went with intellectual stagnation. To attempt to authenticate it in Palestine, however, was to breathe into what Coleridge called bibliolatry an insane dynamic: it was to inspire not only important breakthroughs in scholarship, but peculiar voyages of exploration and wild engineering schemes; to revive the half-moribund turn of the century belief in Prophecy and the Millenium, and partly inspire the ill-fated mission to the Jews in Jerusalem; and to produce some of the most extraordinary, and grotesque, 'biblical' paintings in the history of European art.

*   *   *

Edward Robinson, the scriptural geographer, was a burly, spectacled professor from the Union Theological College of New York, called by his contemporary W. M. Thomson 'the greatest master of measuring tape in the world'. The hundred-foot tape, with which he actually went round the walls of Jerusalem, was his most famous piece of equipment, which also included a telescope (with which he was the first to identify Massada), two pocket compasses, a thermometer, bibles, and the works of Burckhardt and other pioneering explorers. From Seetzen and Burckhardt he accepted the principle that only in the oral tradition of the local peasantry were the original place names of the Bible preserved, and, like them, he ignored the lore of priests and avoided the old pilgrim routes. 'All ecclesiastical tradition respecting ancient places *is of no value* except so far as it is supported by circumstances known to us from the Scriptures, or from other contemporary testimony,' he wrote.

There, however, the resemblance with the early explorers ended. Robinson was a devout Protestant of Puritan New England stock, like the first missionaries. His rigorous training with men like Gesenius, the great German linguist and semitic scholar, whose lexicon of the Bible he was to translate, and Ritter the geographer, some of whose maps of Palestine he carried with him in proof, was undertaken only in order that he might investigate 'the exact sense of Scriptural record'. It was said of Robinson that 'he accepted revealed mysteries without being a mystic, and he used all the lights of reason without being a rationalist'. He was a man so committed to his religion that he could weep at the sight of Sinai and stand on the Mount of Olives, looking down at the Noble Sanctuary, and record nothing whatever on the Temple Mount – presumably because he did not want to register the Moslem presence. For him the desert was a place of 'dreary nakedness', the Bedouin mendacious and venal and all 'Eastern people' unreliable.

The system of enquiry that Robinson evolved depended on reconciling his own accumulated knowledge of the language of the Bible and the evidence provided by early Christian historians with information taken from illiterate men whose language he did not understand. He took with him, therefore, one of the Arabic-speaking American missionaries in Beirut, Eli Smith, who had been a pupil of his in New York. The two men entered Palestine from Sinai, in the spring of 1838, and first tried to identify the exact site where the Law had been handed down. Robinson dismissed the commonly accepted site of Mount Sinai, as it was three miles distant from the plain which he thought a convenient assembly point. The local Bedouin were no help; any name suggested to them they immediately agreed was the very place where the travellers now stood. 'Such is probably the mode in which many ancient names and places have been discovered by travellers, which no one has ever been able to find after them.'

From Sinai, Robinson attempted to trace the path of the Israelites into the Promised Land, but this proved impossible, as the Bedouin idea of a safe route did not coincide with that of the Hebrews. The local Moslems were a nuisance; the Egyptian commander of the garrison at Aqaba kept Robinson up talking when he wanted to make notes: 'The idea of our wishing to be alone was incomprehensible'; and in the coastal plain, local sheikhs pursued them with 'importunate invitations of hospitality', though on one occasion Robinson was pleased to have his feet washed, biblical style, by a female Nubian slave.

Exploring the inland valleys for the New Testament village of Eleutheropolis, he was irritated, in his interrogation of the local people, by 'the indefiniteness and want of precision, [which] seems interwoven in the very genius of the eastern languages and character'. He identified the site by matching distances noted by Eusebius with his own personal walking pace, watch in hand. His speed and persistence were phenomenal; in checking hundreds of sites, about one hundred of them previously unknown, he kept up an average identification rate of eight a day.

In Jerusalem, tape measure and compass in hand, he concluded that virtually every shrine in the city was inauthentic. The Tombs of the Kings probably dated not from biblical but from Byzantine times; the place of Christ's ascension on the Mount of Olives was 'obviously false'; 'Absalom's Tomb' was Greek or Roman, in the style of Petra and the Holy Sepulchre itself, which he visited only once, a 'pious fraud'.

Like later archaeologists, Robinson realized that ancient Jerusalem lay deep below the visible city. Studying the walls of the Temple Mount carefully, he noticed that the lower courses of stones showed traces of antiquity not only for their great size, but because of the style of their bevelling, which was neither 'Saracen' nor Roman. With excitement, he realized that some large stones jutting out from the Western Wall, which at first he had thought displaced by an earthquake, were visible remains of a structure linking the Temple Mount with the old Upper City. What became known as 'Robinson's Arch' was found, over a hundred and thirty years later, to be part of a massive staircase leading down from the Mount, and indeed belonged to biblical Jerusalem.

Robinson was also the first to systematically explore 'Siloa's Brook', the stream that ran between two fountains through an underground passage. Carrying lights and tapes, he and Smith charted the tunnel until the roof became so low that they could go no further. A few days later, having stripped to their 'wide Arab drawers', they crawled nearly a mile on hands, knees and stomachs from the opposite end of the tunnel until they had proved that the two fountains they had entered had been linked, probably by biblical engineers, to protect Jerusalem's precious water supply against a besieging enemy. Forty-two years later, an inscription discovered within the tunnel confirmed Robinson's theory.

What the local people thought of their behaviour is not

recorded. But unlike all their predecessors, Robinson and Smith met with no obstacles to their investigations. 'I am persuaded', Robinson wrote, 'that neither in London nor New York could anything similar be undertaken.' In the countryside, the peasants repeatedly called out to them 'Do not be long', which Robinson took to mean – in liberating the country from Egyptian rule. This was probable; but Robinson further believed that the peasants must be asking for permanent Christian rule: 'Here, as elsewhere, we were supposed to be in search of our hereditary estates . . . this desire for a Frank government or Frank protection we found to be universal in Syria among both Christians and Muhammedans; not excepting even the Bedouin.' In an appendix to his book, he called on England to assert its power, extend its protection to Protestants in Palestine, and extract from the Porte 'the same rights that are granted to other acknowledged Christian sects'.

By the time Robinson published his book, which appeared in 1841 in both English and German, and was acclaimed throughout Europe, Ibrahim Pasha had overstepped the bounds of European tolerance by defeating the Turkish forces sent against him and humiliating the Empire. The English and Austrian armies came to the rescue of the Turks and drove Ibrahim from Syria (Acre was demolished for the third time in forty years) and Mohammed Ali was ordered to confine his rule to Egypt, to the chagrin of his French supporters.

Though once more the Bedouin had free rein, and oppressed villagers fled their fields, the Christian communities and the foreigners maintained the concessions obtained from the Egyptians, the Jews found protectors among the European powers, who established consulates in Jerusalem, and the Protestants were indeed accorded specific rights. The Moslems were forced to accept the privileged presence not only of merchants and travellers, but of the consuls and their protégés. The Catholic missions were upgraded and the Protestant missionaries returned in force.

During this period the impulse to authenticate the Scriptures intensified, as other researchers followed Robinson's advice to clear away 'the mass of tradition foreign in its source and doubtful in its character, grafted upon Jerusalem and the Holy Land'.

Not long afterwards, another American, seeking to reconcile the new science of geology with the narrative of the Bible, undertook the first systematic exploration of the Jordan Valley and the Dead Sea. The events described in Genesis – the destruction of Sodom and Gomorrah and the cataclysm of punishment 'by brimstone and fire' – had long suggested the possibility of a primeval earthquake. The geological examination of the Dead Sea area, it was thought, might illuminate passages of the Bible which were still obscure: where precisely the Cities of the Plain were located, and the 'slime pits' of the 'Vale of Siddim', where the kings of the Cities were consumed; where was that 'valley of salt' where David defeated the Syrians. But there was more to this sudden passion for geological research than the mere identification of sites. One of the central arguments put up by those who defended the Bible as literal truth was that its modern readers simply did not understand the changes that had occurred since biblical times in the Holy Land. These included, it was thought, actual changes in the topography of the country – particularly in the Dead Sea area, where the salt lake diminished periodically because of evaporation or swelled with spring floods from the Jordan. Now Judea and Moab were separated by the Sea; once perhaps they had been connected. The Jordan itself it was thought – though nothing in the Bible suggested this – might have been a great river, flowing south from the Dead Sea to the Gulf of Aqaba.

In 1847, Edward Robinson read a paper to the Royal Geographical Society in London calling on 'all European governments to combine their resources to solve this burning problem' and 'speedily cause the questions raised to be put to rest forever'. Europe did not respond, but an American naval lieutenant, William Francis Lynch, managed to persuade the American navy to send an official team of exploration to Palestine a few months later.

The scientific brief of the expedition was to carry out a thorough geological survey of the Jordan Rift and the Dead Sea, including evidence of volcanic phenomena, to collect specimens of minerals, soils and vegetation, and to observe the wild life in the area. Where the Dead Sea itself was concerned, the expedition established scientific data unrivalled for the next hundred years, and in general was a demonstration of technical ingenuity. But it was nonetheless a prestige venture with no practical outcome, and, where Lynch was concerned, motivated less by scientific curiosity than the desire to take a stand in the biblical debate.

There had been an American naval presence in the Mediterranean from 1815, and American warships patrolled the Barbary Coast in an international policing action against pirates throughout the early century. America had also developed useful commercial ties with the Porte; but the Lynch mission had no political overtones or commercial purpose, and Lynch was warned against any form of political involvement.

He had consulted Robinson before setting out, and his team was heavily armed and hand-picked by Lynch himself – they all had to be teetotallers. They included a trained physician, a 'geological reporter', mechanics and metalsmiths, and took rock-blasting equipment, airtight water bags and all the latest equipment for measuring altitudes and temperatures, including pocket chronometers specially ordered from London. Lynch had ordered the first prefabricated boats, made of specially manufactured copper and galvanized iron, which could be dismantled and reassembled and easily transported. The metal was to stop them being dashed to pieces on the rocks and rapids of the Jordan, or being damaged by the peculiar composition of the water of the Dead Sea.

Lynch himself was an old-fashioned pietist and patriot. He insisted, against local protocol, on carrying his ceremonial sword into an audience with the Sultan, and, on hearing of the death of John Quincy Adams while afloat on the Dead Sea, fired a ten-gun salute from a blunderbuss into the recesses of the deserted valley. He believed that only Christianity could save the Ottoman empire from disintegration, but preferred the religious habits of the Moslems to the 'saturnalia of Rome' or 'the utter debasement of the Parisian worship of the Goddess of Reason'.

So well equipped was Lynch that on arrival in Palestine, in March 1848, he had only one problem: the local people. Despite his firman from the Porte, and the goodwill of British consuls in Beirut and Jerusalem, there was no protection for Lynch against the 'Arab rabble' who, fascinated by the gleaming copper and iron sections laid out on the beach near Haifa, attempted to steal the chains and pins which held them together. The 'miserable galled jades' they provided to pull the wheeled trucks Lynch had brought to carry the boats inland were quite unable to pull the load. To cap everything, the ruling governor of Acre told Lynch that unless he borrowed a hundred-man Turkish guard at the cost of eight hundred dollars – a huge sum of money, and Lynch had been ordered to economize – he would be cut to pieces by hostile Bedouin tribes. Lynch indignantly refused, and the governor advised him to abandon the expedition.

In the event, the support of two remarkable men ensured Lynch's safe passage along the entire route. These were Akil Aga el Hasi, the Bedouin mercenary whose writ ran throughout northern Palestine and who was to become famous throughout Europe;* and the Wahabi chieftain, the old Sharif of Mecca, exiled by the Egyptian Mohammed Ali but respected, with his retinue, throughout the country. Lynch called these men his 'Achilles and Nestor'. Thus escorted, he transported his boats and trucks, pulled by camel power, to the point at which the descent from the plain to the Sea of Galilee began. The boats were arduously lowered to the lakeside, where Lynch acquired a local fishing boat made of wood, the only craft afloat on the lake, which he rechristened the *Uncle Sam*. This was perhaps the same boat observed by various travellers over the previous half century, which subsequently disappears from the literature, since at the first buffeting on the rocks it promptly broke up and sank.

On the Bedouin's advice, the team separated; half rode overland with the Bedouin, carrying stores and keeping watch against sudden attack; and the rest navigated the river. The Jordan was now at full flow, before it could be depleted by the summer heat; but even so the rapids, cascades, false channels and rocks, as the river twisted and turned, showed the Jordan to be

*See Chapter V

less a river than an obstacle course. At times the sailors bypassed the river by portage; at others, they navigated the rapids by securing the boats by ropes to bushes on the banks. Sometimes they had to remove rocks in the boats' way; or walk along in the river up to their waists, easing the boats along beside them; or were forced to excavate a sluice canal. The Jordan was obviously useless, had always been useless, for commerce or for trade. By the time Lynch reached the Dead Sea, he noted that though the direct distance between the two lakes was sixty miles, by following the course of the river he and his sailors had in fact covered two hundred. And as another intrepid sailor on the upper reaches of the Jordan, the Scottish MacGregor, noted, there was nothing Lynch saw from the river that could not have been far more easily documented by a ride along the banks.

The most difficult part of the mission lay ahead. No visitor had ever spent more than a week in the Dead Sea area; Lynch and his team were to remain there three weeks. Again they split up, Lynch mapping the shore, and Lieutenant Dale, his second-in-command, taking depth soundings at 258 different parts of the Sea. They measured its temperature at depth, speculated on the slicks on its surface, noted evidence of organic matter in the water. Eventually, however, Lynch feared that the leaden heat, the sulphurous fumes which rose from the surface of the dense, greasy water were making his sailors ill. On the way through the hills to Jerusalem, they finally established the depth of the Dead Sea as 1316 feet below sea level, or the lowest known place on earth.

Lynch's insistence that the expedition had confirmed the Scriptures obscured its scientific value. His narrative, first published in 1849, described each phase of the journey in its biblical context, and he argued that the same 'general convulsion' which had created the Jordan Rift and the Dead Sea had destroyed the Cities of the Plain. The report submitted three years later by the expedition's geologist, Dr Anderson, included in the Official Report, stated the contrary: that the evidence collected on shore indicated that the depression of the Dead Sea, created either by fissure or volcanic action, had occurred millions of years before the historic era. Many praised these findings as removing the entire question of the fate of the cities from the realm of scientific theory. Twentieth-century archaeological techniques were to establish that the Dead Sea had been the site of Canaanite settlement in about 2000 BC, possibly destroyed by a more modest, and localized, volcanic eruption; but such conclusions would have been too tentative and partial for the mind of Lynch's contemporaries. His journey, far from cautioning other travellers against acting out fantasies, had exactly the opposite effect.

During the mid-century, a number of alternative routes to India were considered to replace the journey round the Cape. The overland route via Suez was established while Egypt ruled Syria, and the British Lieutenant F. R. Chesney carried out heroic but ill-fated journeys to promote the idea of a river route to the Persian Gulf via the Tigris and Euphrates. As the Jordan river, in its present state, could not be navigated, Lynch advocated a route cutting through northern Syria to the Euphrates. But Burckhardt's theory of an ancient watershed which had led south from the Dead Sea to Aqaba survived, and several enthusiasts proposed that modern engineering might encourage the Jordan to flow south to the Red Sea, restoring Palestine's central position – or rather the position it was assumed to have had in biblical times – in the Near East economy and benefiting the commerce of modern, Western, empires.

This ambitious plan was most fully expounded by a British naval officer, W. A. Allen; an engineer who had explored Africa and visited Palestine shortly after Lynch's journey down the Jordan. In 1855 he proposed leading the waters of the Mediterranean through the Kishon – one of northern Palestine's modest streams – to the Sea of Galilee. The consequent rise in the level of that lake, he believed, would then set off a chain reaction in which a vastly swollen Jordan, pounding down the valley to the Dead Sea, would raise its level so dramatically that it would overflow the southern hills and pour down the supposed watershed through the Arava valley south of the lake to the Gulf of Aqaba. All this, he thought, might be achieved by 'blasting operations' to join the Kishon and the Sea of Galilee – a mere twenty-five miles. This, he argued, would be cheaper than the expense involved in digging the 87-mile Suez Canal from the Mediterranean to the Red Sea – an idea already under consideration, and work on which was to begin the following year.

Allen's project would have meant the submergence of about two thousand square miles of the Sultan's territories (including the mainly Jewish city of Tiberias), but he thought that a minor inconvenience compared with the obvious advantages: the revival of ancient Bashan and Gilead, the eastern banks of the Jordan, which would now lie on a thriving trade route; facilities for making the pilgrimage to Mecca by river; encouraging British strategic support for Turkey and repelling potential Russian incursions by moving the British navy into Palestine.

Allen saw his project as introducing a new era which would revive the glories of the ancient world. The Jews, 'who had the ability to keep alive the spirit of commerce', would repeople Palestine, while Britain, 'the new Tarshish', would protect them. He complained that the British treasury refused to back an exploratory survey, unlike the United States, the 'more go-ahead country' which had backed Lynch.

Such a project would have revealed that the steeper slope of the watershed of the Arava valley, from its highest point more than three thousand feet above the Dead Sea, led north – backwards – rather than south to Aqaba. Even when geologists did survey the area a couple of decades later, however, the myth of a full flowing Jordan died hard; the Jordan river controversy persisted well into the 1880s, when the British geologist Hull firmly and finally laid the idea to rest.

*   *   *

'Just as the excavated remains of Nineveh or Shushan or Persepolis enable us to admire the beauty or marvel at the grandeur of those ancient cities, so do the unfading customs of the East lead us to an accurate and satisfying knowledge of the times most influential upon eternity of all the ages that are past,' wrote Robert McEnery, who made detailed studies of the habits of the population of Palestine.

There were still no excavations in Palestine, but the East was scoured for 'illustrations' which would confirm the accuracy of the Bible. The defection of Gideon's followers was compared to the cowardly behaviour of contemporary Oriental fighters against colonizing Western forces; the 'shouting and confused noise' of bible warfare with Zulu battles at the Cape, and the Indian Mutiny. But by far the most popular biblical illustrations were based on the observation of the native population of Palestine.

Biblical scenes on rooftops were explained by reference to Syrian roofs where families gathered, fruit was dried or those under attack by Bedouin took refuge. Marriage processions, even those of the Armenians or the Druse, were compared with biblical scenes, 'eastern salutations' with biblical greetings and partings. Women wailed at funerals and men prostrated themselves before superiors; the language of the Bible only seemed exaggerated now 'to those who are not acquainted with the excitable or emotive temperament of the east'. People in Palestine still washed their hands after meals, anointed their feet, and put off their shoes at doorsteps. The farming methods in Palestine were exactly those described in the Bible, and travellers' reports and sketches showed peasants 'threshing out the corn' with primitive implements or 'grinding at the mill'.

After *Uncle Tom's Cabin*, the most popular book in the United States during the second half of the century was the Reverend W. M. Thomson's *The Land and the Book*. Thomson began his career as a missionary in Beirut during the Egyptian occupation, in 1833. He is believed to have remained in the Levant until 1879, and he became a landmark, known to the Moslems as 'Abu Tangera', the Father of the Cooking Pot, for his broad-brimmed pastor's hat. Thomson buried Lady Hester Stanhope when she died at her mountain retreat in the Lebanon in 1839; he set up a first-aid centre in Safed, in northern Galilee, after the terrible earthquake which devastated parts of Palestine in 1838; he was witness to the anti-Egyptian rebellion of 1834, and the rout of the Egyptian army in 1840; he was escort to Edward Robinson when he made a second visit to Palestine in 1852; and wrote the text for the first exhibition of photographs of Palestine, by Francis Bedford, held in the British Museum, after the Prince of Wales's visit in 1862.

So Thomson did read the country like a book. He knew the

exact technique by which the peasants constructed their earth-roofed cottages; how they hid their grain underground, mingling quicksilver with oil or white of egg and rubbing this into the wheat to protect it from insects; and how a plague of locusts moved, so that the sound of their devouring approach was 'like that of a heavy shower on a distant forest'. Thomson could transpose every biblical metaphor back into its original key: he knew that 'balm in Gilead' was a resinous gum, that local sepulchres were regularly whitened, and he had seen the runners of the Egyptian army literally 'girding up their loins' to take messages. He could illuminate the stranger passages in the Bible by analogy to Palestine farming: what exactly happened when the wild olive was grafted on to the good; what was meant when the seed in Matthew 'fell on stony ground' and why the turtledove was described as 'tabering' on its breast.

One of the first to use Thomson's book as a practical guide was the English cleric and naturalist Henry Baker Tristram, who visited the east bank of the Jordan a dozen years after Lynch and forty years after Buckingham, and reported it a disaster area, formerly cultivated for corn, now ravaged by the Bedouin. Tristram's visit was sponsored by one of the many new organizations set up to increase the scientific understanding of the Bible, the 'Society for Promoting Christian Knowledge', which sent him on a ten-month visit to study Palestine's flora and fauna. Tristram was Canon of Durham, a seasoned traveller and keen ornithologist and zoologist, whose religious faith did not lessen his interest in Darwin's recently published *Origin of Species*. Lynch had consulted Robinson before setting out; Tristram consulted Charles Lyell.

Tristram's Holy Land was that of 'fox-headed bats' seen near Acre, of beehives 'like ovens, or henhouses', of flamingoes shot on the banks of the Kishon, and 'the only crocodile in Asia' trapped in a marsh near Caesaria; of hyenas roaming the deserted valleys, and jays and spotted woodpeckers nesting in the remains of the now decimated forests of the Carmel range. It was only in the perennially well-defended countryside around Nablus that he found a flourishing economy – due mainly to the fact that because of the American Civil War, the local cotton industry prospered once more. 'The hum of the cottonbow murmured on every side, and the walls were dripping with the juices of cochineal and indigo, as the webs of silk and cotton were hung out to dry.'

In Jerusalem, a city where Tristram felt 'as if . . . visiting a father's grave, or the house of one's youth', he discovered swallows nesting in the eastern wall of the Temple Mount, where olive and palm, lemon and cypress grew, and where he caught specimens of the turtledove, the titmouse, the thrush and the wagtail. He noted the unusual call note of the raven, the most common bird of Jerusalem, and as specimens could only be captured at nightfall, he and his companions ambushed the birds just before sunset, outside the city walls.

The local peasants and Bedouin who helped and guided them were bewildered by travellers who hunted animals they had no intention of eating, and who sought no treasures in ancient tombs. Near the Dead Sea they shot a wild boar, only to find that the local Bedouin would not transport it, lest the mule be defiled. Another helper, not realizing that Tristram wanted his specimens whole, retained only the edible parts of an ibex and threw away the head and horns. When one of the party started playing Mozart, the Bedouin tried to accompany this strange music with a 'fantasia' of gunshots.

At the Dead Sea, Tristram's conclusions regarding the rival claims of the Bible and geology typified the position now reached by those who could not reject the evidence of science but were not prepared to relinquish their faith. He accepted that the cataclysmic events which had formed the Jordan Rift had taken place 'in a geologic epock [sic] far remote from the appearance of man on earth'. On the other hand, he wrote, 'if every occurrence in Sacred History is to be thus tested and accounted for, the whole question of miraculous intervention has been surrendered to the enemy, and modern scientific knowledge, not legitimate criticism, is made the test of Scriptural authenticity'.

*   *   *

Geology could be accommodated, and flora and fauna were not controversial models, while local customs were illuminating of the biblical narrative. But the more closely the local inhabitants were scrutinized, the more problematic the biblical parallels became.

The view that the Bedouin, as an ancient nomadic people, must be the nearest approximation to the biblical patriarchs had long been current, though not acceptable to the Church. 'Abraham was a Bedawin,' Richardson had written in 1818, and most travellers in Sinai jumped to the same conclusion. But when the Dean of St Pauls, Henry Hunt Milman, published his lively *History of the Jews* in 1829, describing Abraham as an 'Eastern Sheikh or Emir', there was such an uproar that the book was withdrawn.

The closer examination of the Bedouin which took place in the mid-century disqualified them on more literal grounds. Thomson, for instance, pointed out that the Bedouin did not keep large herds, till the ground, or 'accommodate themselves' to life in the towns.

The Jewish inhabitants of Palestine posed an even greater problem. The Ashkenazi Jews dressed like Polish noblemen of centuries earlier, and kept to their European habits, while even the Sefardi Jews, who looked suitably Oriental, had nothing in common with their warlike and agrarian ancestors. The Christian missionaries who had some intercourse with the Jews – those not converts themselves – were ignorant about many of their practices and their origins. Thomson, for instance, did not know the biblical injunction relevant to the Jews' earlocks (he called them 'dandyism'), nor the origin of the custom of binding plylacteries on arms and foreheads, which he compared with the local Moslem habit of tattooing the face and arms with a blend of gunpowder and paint. The difficult question of the Jewishness of Jesus he begged by arguing that he was 'perfectly and divinely original'.

If both Bedouin and Jews were eliminated as contemporary 'illustrations', only the domesticated Moslem peasantry remained as heirs to the people of the Bible. This did not mean, however, that the Moslem presence in the Holy Land was really accepted or that the peasantry was seen as other than misguided and semi-barbaric, and – since most of those involved in 'authenticating' the Bible were clergymen – even the most

affectionate account of their customs was tempered by ex-
pressions of regret at their unregenerate state. Little hope was
held out for improvement. Virtually every European traveller
or resident described an absence of 'patriotism' whether of
Moslem, Jew, or other ethnic group. The country's hetero-
geneous composition was an obstacle to its moral redemption,
as 'they could neither be united for religious nor for political
purposes'.

Moreover, despite the apparent confirmation, in the customs
of the country, of the truths of Scripture, there was less
confidence as to whether it also confirmed the current belief in
Prophecy. The revival of interest in Palestine among the clergy
became a bone of contention between the Evangelicals, many of
whom were ardent believers in the Return of the Jews, and the
Tractarians who, seeking a closer relationship with the Catholic
Church, strongly disapproved of prophetic 'enthusiasm' and the
obsession with the Old Testament which went with it; a clash
which reached its climax with the establishment of the Anglican
bishopric in Jerusalem in 1841.

One of the major controversies related to Palestine during the
mid-century was the disagreement between A. P. Stanley,
professor of religions at Oxford and later Dean of Westminster,
and Alexander Keith, a leading member of the Scottish church
and an ardent believer in the Return of the Jews, both of whom
spent several months in Palestine at this time.

Stanley was the very model of the Broad Church moderate
whose views on Palestine, as on other subjects, reflected the kind
of cautious pragmatism which was to outlive both the Evangelical and the Tractarian fevers. He went through Palestine with
Robinson's book in his pocket, though Robinson was strong
meat for the average clergyman: the popular Reverend Gadsby,
whose own book of Palestine travels included many 'biblical
illustrations', thought him a 'semi-infidel'. Stanley carefully
examined Palestine for its connections with the biblical record,
but delicately sidestepped more controversial issues such as
miracles and their possible scientific explanations. He approved
selectively of illustrations of the Bible by Oriental customs
'which it is an unworthy superstition either to despise or fear'.

But he warned against using modern Palestine as a forcing ground for prophecy. Though it had demonstrably been the most fertile country of the Near East, he wrote, it was useless 'to seek for the fulfilment of the ancient prediction' in literal terms, 'staking the truth of Christianity and the authority of the Sacred Records on the chances of local and political revolution'.

Wandering Arab shepherds might be reminders of the primitive infancy of the faith, Stanley conceded, but Christians would do better to study the coastal towns like Caesaria, where the apostles had gathered, 'in order to trace back to its origin the first contact of the religion of the East with the power of the West. It is as if Christianity already felt its European destiny strong within it, and, by a sort of prophetic anticipation, gathered its early energies round those regions of the Holy Land which were most European and least Asiatic.'

This very prudent view of the passion for authenticity was vigorously attacked by Alexander Keith, who, a few years earlier, had toured Jewish communities throughout Europe and the Near East in order to calculate the chances of an early Return. Stanley's view of Palestine, Keith argued, was altogether 'too vague and poetical'. Every visitor to Palestine over the past half century, he insisted, including the Oriental scholars and even the freethinkers, had 'involuntarily and unconsciously' confirmed Prophecy in their reports; even the British consuls, in their commercial despatches, did so by using the word 'tenfold' when describing the depopulation of the country. Keith was particularly outraged by Stanley's ingenuous comparisons of practically all the ancient Israelites to the 'lawless Bedouin'. The Jews, Keith argued, had certainly not been 'wild Ishmaelites' or troops of plunderers, but city dwellers with a developed civilization. It was not part of the Evangelical vision to confuse Jews and Moslems, when the Jews' destiny was to become Christians in the foreseeable future.

The lessons to be drawn from Oriental Palestine in theological argument were also highly ambivalent. The most famous heretic of the Anglican church during the mid-century was Bishop Colenso, of Natal, who was expelled from the Church for arguing that in discussions with his African charges he had been unable to defend a literal interpretation of the book of Joshua. Josiah Porter, a clergyman who had spent years in the Levant, attacked Colenso, on the grounds that before questioning the Bible's veracity he should have studied the lives of the desert Arabs; Stanley — always the peacemaker — *defended* Colenso by reference to Palestine, arguing that the exaggerations regarding numbers in the Bible were only what was to be expected, given the Oriental passion for hyperbole.

Not only clergymen, but lay Christians found that a visit to Palestine threw new light on the problem of faith. Harriet Martineau, the popular philosopher, travelling through Egypt and Palestine in 1846, came to the conclusion that faith could be preserved not by fighting 'what can be proved to be scientifically true, in geology and some other directions', but by analysing the part ancient Egyptian beliefs and rituals had played in Judaism, how they were slowly discarded, and how far the Christian superstitions so viable in Jerusalem had been superimposed on the 'pure and reasonable' message of the Gospels. Like Coleridge, she condemned 'the awful error of mistaking the Records of the origin of Judaism and Christianity for the messages themselves'; and her dog-eared old bible, she wrote, had never seemed so relevant to her as in the wastes of Sinai, where she believed the Hebrews had waged a long struggle to put aside Egyptian superstitions for 'a pure moral law'.

Wearing black wire goggles and a broad-brimmed hat against the glare of the desert sun, sleeping in a linen bag of her own design to keep out vermin, and walking between ten and fifteen miles a day because she disliked the motion of the camel, Martineau cast a conscientiously liberal eye over the Palestine countryside. In Hebron, visiting the supposed tomb of the Patriarchs, now covered with a mosque, she inadvertently recalled the Crusaders and immediately corrected herself, 'was ashamed of the absurd, illiberal emotion; and as I looked upon the minaret, felt that the Mohammedans had as much right to build over sacred places as the Empress Helena; though one must heartily wish they had all let it alone'. In Jerusalem, she deplored Protestant efforts to convert the Jews, since in industrial England the working class lived without religion: 'While we have millions of savages in our own island – heathens without heathen gods – I cannot see why we should spend on a handful of strangers who already have a noble faith of their own, the resources which would support Home Missions to a much greater extent.' This was a remarkable volte-face by a writer who had begun her literary career by writing prize-winning conversionist essays, intended to proselytize, for Catholics, Jews and Moslems.

Martineau's manuscript, which had been commissioned by John Murray under the mistaken impression that she was to commend in it a proposal for the Anglo-Egyptian railway, was instantly returned 'as a conspiracy against Moses'. When finally published, it aroused great interest; Martineau's view of early Eastern religions and Judaism as stages on the way to Christianity prefigured her enthusiasm for Comte, whose work she translated into English and helped to popularize. Martineau eventually became a freethinker.

Most controversial of all contemporary attempts to place the Bible in its historical and geographical context were two biographies of Jesus which eschewed all reference to supernatural events. David Strauss's *Leben Jesu* appeared simultaneously with Lyell's geological studies in 1835, and was translated into English by George Eliot in 1848. Strauss, a German biblical scholar, treated the Gospels purely as literary texts, but concluded that while they were historically unreliable, 'the dogmatic significance of the life of Jesus remained inviolate'. The French Orientalist scholar Ernest Renan was to make a different defence on behalf of his *Vie de Jésus*, which appeared in 1863, and which, unlike Strauss's work, was set against the background of contemporary Palestine. Renan's book was excoriated both by the Catholic and the Anglican churches; it enjoyed an enormous success in France, where it became the second most widely read book after the Bible.

Renan claimed that he had written the book 'with the absolute detachment of an historian'. The *Vie de Jésus* was, however, a highly romantic critique of the Gospels, clearly influenced by Renan's two-month visit to Palestine in the spring of 1861 – an offshoot of his work at the head of a French archaeological mission to northern Syria. Asserting that Jesus was born not in

Bethlehem but in Nazareth, 'perhaps the only place in Palestine where there is relief from the general oppression and neglect [of Ottoman rule]', Renan portrayed Jesus as a simple village preacher in an idyllic Galilee, among a farming community 'lacking in aesthetic sense, indifferent to comfort', but 'exclusively idealistic'. Against this natural birthplace of pure faith (which Renan suggested had later been corrupted by the Catholic Church) he pictured a physically and spiritually barren Jerusalem 'like today, a city of pedantry, . . . dispute, hatred and narrowness of spirit', a city which, Renan insisted, 'had always been hostile to Christianity'.

The Protestant clergymen who had tried to authenticate scriptural miracles in terms of Palestine's flora and fauna had more than a little in common with Renan, a rational Christian who saw Jesus as a social revolutionary and moralist; both shared a profound ambivalence towards the Levant as the physical source of Christianity. On the one hand, Renan shared the Protestants' discovery of the local origins of Christian parables; on the other, he echoed their belief that Jesus was 'divinely unique' and that what Renan termed his 'exquisite theology of love' had emerged largely in defiance of first-century Judaism and the culture of the Levant.

'The races here have changed immensely,' wrote Renan to the historian Taine during his stay in Syria: 'there is, however, such a thing as a Syrian mentality . . . whose dominant characteristic is duplicity.' The precise cause of Renan's irritation was the fact that Syrian merchants were continually badgering him with reports of archaeological 'treasure'. Renan's portrayal of the Galilee was, however, less the result of his actual observation than the need to find some Palestinian correlative to the purity of Jesus' faith; he was only able to explain Jesus' emergence in Levantine society by placing him in an idealized community of unspoiled peasant disciples.

*   *   *

Well into the second half of the nineteenth century, painters of biblical subjects faced a dilemma both religious and aesthetic. The huge family bibles carry illustrations of the Hebrew patriarchs as Bedouin chieftains; this is no longer a shocking image. But as the Scriptures narrate the advent of monotheism (or Moses) the Hebrews undergo a strange metamorphosis, assuming classical draperies and European features. In some cases this is because the editors of the bibles simply reproduce a Renaissance classic as illustration. But when contemporary works are used, the disciples, and the Holy Family, tend to wear clothing somewhere between the burnous and the toga, and their features are not semitic. The only recognizably semitic features of the figures in the famous 'Biblical Gallery' of scriptural illustrations printed by the engravers Dalziel belong to models chosen by Simeon Solomon, a Jewish colleague of the Pre-Raphaelites. Gustav Doré, the arch romantic of biblical illustration, hovers between the Orient and the stormy Alps, while English bibles are decorated with instructive archaeological sketches of Near East antiquities. Only at the very end of the century, as the rage to authenticate the Scriptures loses its original impetus – for evolution is now assimilated and an historical approach to Christianity no longer revolutionary – does James Tissot's illustrated bible appear. Tissot, a fashionable society painter, turned devout Christian, visited Palestine in 1886 and his bible represents all the scriptural figures in Arab costume, with the Magi as sheikhs riding out of the desert and a Bedouin Jesus in an Arab Jerusalem.

The search for authentic versions of biblical scenes was not initially a Protestant preoccupation but merely the natural consequence of rediscovering the East. Travellers as early as Firmin Didot, in 1816, had expressed regret that 'most painters had not been able to see for themselves the sites, the customs and the countries they are obliged to depict'. He added the reassurance that authenticity 'would not have detracted from the nobility of their style'.

At the beginning of the century no such thought, however, disturbed the romantic painters whose Palestine landscapes were neither particularly accurate nor overshadowed by didactic considerations. Travellers regularly appealed to a contemporary Poussin to paint the more fertile areas of the Galilee, or a new Salvator Rosa for the bandit-ridden Judean hills; the placid landscapes of a Cassas or Marilhat, and the lowering crags and fortress monasteries of an Adrien Dauzats, satisfied the romantic eye. But Palestine scarcely attracted the painters famous for their Oriental scenes; save for a handful of paintings – Carl Friedrich Werner's splendid interior of the Dome of the Rock, painted in 1863, and Carl Gustav Bauernfeind's street scenes of Jaffa and Jerusalem, painted towards the end of the century, are notable exceptions – the lustrous colour, exotic detail and of course the erotic subjects, are totally missing.

Palestine was too poor, and too respectable, to merit the treatment given to other parts of the Near East by what are now called 'Orientalist' painters.

The English painters Bartlett and Roberts, both of whom visited Palestine in the late 1830s, were intent on topographical accuracy, and Roberts was praised by Robinson as the first painter to show Palestinian landscape as it actually was. Roberts himself complained that he was unable to render the extraordinary rock formations of Judea, and his famous views of the Holy Land are essentially reproductions of the Picturesque ideal in an Oriental setting: in the foreground, native figures in statuesque poses, or fragments of ruined monuments; in the middle distance, a town, and panoramic hills beyond – Palestine in the eye of a talented scene painter. Horace Vernet, a military painter, came up through Sinai with his nephew, Goupil-Fesquet, in 1840, Fesquet taking the first daguerreotype photographs of Palestine as aids to Vernet's paintings. Fesquet insisted that neither took a particular interest in the history of local architecture or archaeology 'which we absolutely lack . . . we are painters'. And Vernet, who painted several biblical scenes, took the view that as all the characters of the Bible had looked like Arabs, it was legitimate to paint Judah as a Bedouin sheikh, Tamar as a rather forthcoming and leggy houri.

The idea of authenticity in biblical paintings grew not from the encounter with Palestine but in Europe, as part of the rejection of academic painting and the desire to return to early Renaissance models. Lord Lindsay (who had visited Palestine in 1838) advised painters, in his *Sketches of the History of Christian Art* published in 1849, to 'seek out the neglected relics of an earlier, a simpler and more believing age, talk to the spirit that dwells within them . . . and listen reverently for a reply'. This was the spirit behind the German Nazarenes, who worked in Rome on their biblical paintings, and the Pre-Raphaelites in England. Neither group – with one notable exception – saw any point in seeking inspiration in Palestine itself.

It was the English painter David Wilkie who was the first to be seriously concerned by the problem of 'accuracy' in painting biblical scenes and to suggest that it could be solved in Palestine. Wilkie went to the Holy Land in 1841 with the idea of painting an authentic Christ in a correctly designed setting; he was drowned on the return voyage to England, but his unfinished painting of Christ before Pilate, and his reflections on the subject, survived him. It was significant that Wilkie was disturbed by the possibility that 'authenticity' might prove unacceptable if taken to its logical conclusion. It was impossible, he thought, to portray Christ and the disciples eating the Last Supper cross-legged on the ground, and although he knew Christ should look Jewish he chose a Persian prince who looked European as his model. Wilkie believed that biblical painters should first acquire as much knowledge as they could about their subject, then discard whatever was incongruous to the Western eye – more or less Stanley's view on the lesson of Palestine, where its stones and brooks were concerned.

Wilkie's ideas were influential, and English painters began to read widely around the subject of biblical scenes. Catholic writers argued that so literal an approach deprived the subject of a wider, spiritual dimension; critics from Gautier to Burne-Jones, Eugène Fromentin in particular, thought that Arabizing the figures of Christian narrative meant depriving the subject of dignity. But the trend persisted, finding its way into the family bibles and the work of the Pre-Raphaelites. It remained as controversial as the problem of authentication was in other respects. Only one important painter of the period – the exception among the Pre-Raphaelites – adopted it whole-heartedly.

William Holman-Hunt paid four extended visits to Palestine between 1854 and 1892, spending months at a time in Jerusalem and taking infinite pains to study the background of his biblical subjects. He set off in 1854 against the advice of all his patrons and friends. His colleagues Rossetti and Millais had also been influenced by the idea of realism in biblical paintings: Millais' 'Christ in the House', exhibited at the Royal Academy in 1850, had shown a carpenter's shop in authentic detail and was duly criticized for 'irreverence'. Going to Palestine was another matter. Ruskin 'refused to admit that any additional vitality could be gained by designing and painting in Syria' and wanted Hunt to train a new school of art in England. Coventry Patmore, the poet, told Hunt that he would find no new flora to illustrate his scenes but only 'overgrown weeds', and that if it was beauty he was after, he would do far better at home. Wilkie's death was still fresh in all minds and Palestine still fever-ridden.

Hunt's initial impressions were all the more favourable because he had been warned so often that the country was barren and the climate dangerous. From Jaffa he wrote back to his friend Combes at Oxford: 'The luxuriance of the vegetation is I believe double that of any part of England I ever saw'; and from Jerusalem, 'you can never conceive the extreme beauty of the place without seeing it . . . there were thousands of effects of light to choose from' and he was unable to understand the country's reputation for unhealthiness: 'The air is the most delicious I ever breathed . . . I believe when the absurd notion about the danger of this climate is corrected that many English people will immigrate here, instead of going to bleak uninteresting places as Australia or America. When I turn farmer, I shall certainly bring my father, mother and sisters here, keep a flock of camels and grow artichokes and palm trees.'

Within a few months, however, Palestine had soured on him completely. By August he was writing 'the country is cursed, and everyone who comes here shares in the evil'. He denied rumours that he was turning Moslem and marrying a local girl; he would allow 'no dirty greasy Eastern woman to come near enough to me to hide the clear pink and white of clever beautiful English girls'. 'Arabs, Turks, Egyptians and Jews [Hunt originally added Greeks, then crossed the word out — it went against the grain for an artist to condemn the Greeks wholesale] are the kind of people who give the key to the commandment to destroy the Canaanite which I once regarded as unintelligible.' 'The only vice the Arabs avoid is the eating of pork, no! they will have to die out and be driven out as the wolf and the wild boar were in England.'

Authenticity with a vengeance. Hunt's near paranoia was caused by the difficulties of finding models, both human and animal, in the real Jerusalem of the Crimean War period.

His first project was 'The Finding of Our Lord in the Temple by his Mother and Joseph', a painting of the boy Jesus among the rabbis. Hunt consulted the Talmud and Josephus as well as checking every detail in the Scriptures; and he had decided that the figures of the Jews should not be idealized. The Polish Jews were obviously unsuitable, but even the Sefardi Jews, introduced to him through members of the Protestant Mission, were at first reluctant to sit for him. Hunt had arrived in Jerusalem at the same time as an emissary of the Rothschilds, sent to open a hospital for the local Jews, who until now had patronized that of the mission. Hunt, as one of the Protestant community in Jerusalem, was immediately suspect as a potential stealer of souls. He eventually did find sitters among a group of Sefardi 'enquirers' or would-be converts, and had an even more grotesque problem to deal with. One man, modelling a rabbi, suspected that the image might take his place at the Day of Judgment not as a Christian but as an 'unregenerate' Jew, and thus the likeness in the painting was formally baptized (as Jack Robinson).

His encounter with the Moslems was more disastrous. When Hunt tried to sketch a threshing floor at the village of Siloam, the villagers continually increased the price for 'sitting', and then, when Hunt would not agree, pelted him with stones. There is an echo of this experience in the strange 'The Plain of Refaim from Zion', and Hunt wrote bitterly and constantly about 'Moslem venality'.

Despite the Jews' belief that Hunt belonged to the Mission, he found the Protestant community tiresome and philistine. It was hard to get canvas, and he complained that both the consul and the Bishop took in the *Athenaeum* and the *Examiner* – both journals notably hostile to Hunt's painting; and he became involved, with the photographer James Graham who was the Mission's lay treasurer, in a bitter local feud against Bishop Gobat.

All these, however, were minor ordeals compared with Hunt's experience while painting 'The Scapegoat'. The idea itself was bizarre: an attempt to portray the biblical penitential goat in Leviticus, sent into the wilderness to its death. From the Talmud, Hunt learned that a scarlet strip of cloth tied round the goat's head to signify sin turned white when the sacrifice was accepted, but he decided that the goat itself must be entirely white to symbolize innocence, and in order to be fully authentic had to be painted on the shores of the Dead Sea itself. In the winter of 1855, therefore, attended by a party of Bedouin to whom he was unable to speak as he knew not a word of Arabic, Hunt spent seventeen days at the Dead Sea, rifle in one hand and paintbrush in the other. He suffered intermittently from fever, and on the way back to Hebron was caught between two battling Bedouin tribes. The goat had meanwhile died of exposure to the heat. A second goat, purchased for a very high price, turned out to be black-faced, and also died the following day; and the third goat sitter was painted standing in a not entirely authentic pan full of salt, in Hunt's Jerusalem studio. When Hunt left Jerusalem he was still without a model for the boy Jesus. His search ended at a Jewish school in Red Lion Square in London, to which the Jewish philanthropist Frederick Mocatta, who had interceded for Hunt in Jerusalem, had ensured his admission.

Neither painting was popular with the critics. *The Times* thought 'The Scapegoat' 'an excellent likeness of Sir Stratford de Redcliffe', the British ambassador at Constantinople.

Perhaps the only observer to perceive the mental torment behind 'The Scapegoat' was Henry James, who was deeply affected by it, describing it as 'so charged with the awful . . . I should have feared to face it all alone in a room'. In 'The Golden Bowl', Hunt's painting became the image of Maggie's despair; far more potent, for James, than the work of the French painters, who, he wrote, 'have ransacked and rifled the Oriental world of the uttermost vestige of its mystery'.

The paintings did not earn Hunt commissions from the church, and according to Dean Farrar, the popular theologian who was one of his admirers, it was the working men from Lancashire and Yorkshire who came in their thousands to see his paintings and purchase engravings. The 'Finding of Our Lord in the Temple' was bought by a brewer for £5 500 – the highest price paid at that time for a work of art by a living artist.

When Hunt next returned to Palestine he chose a Greek Orthodox Arab as his model for Christ; the Turkish governor of Jerusalem and the Greek patriarch were more interested than the English clerics had been in his work. They came to his studio to finger the fresh paint and see how the figures appeared on the reverse side of the canvas. The Armenian patriarch even asked Hunt to contribute a portrait of Mary and Jesus to his church (as Fesquet had noted, none of the visiting painters to Jerusalem ever thought of donating their work to the local churches – though all deplored the poor quality of the icons and paintings which hung there). But the Latins disapproved strongly of 'The Shadow of Death', in which Mary turns to see the shadow of the Crucifixion appear behind the young carpenter's raised arms, as 'the representation of the Holy Virgin with the face hidden was denounced as a Protestant indignity to the Madonna'.

No artist, professional or amateur, who visited Palestine ever attempted to show the poverty, dirt and commercial exploitation of the Holy Places described by every visitor, though Hunt planned – but never executed – a 'series of etchings to prove that in our day there is as much idolatry in the world as in Isaiah's time'. But on his last visit to Palestine, in 1892, he prepared sketches for his last major painting, on a subject no painter had attempted before him: the Miracle of the Holy Fire.

Hunt's idea was to 'perpetuate for future generations the astounding scene which many writers have so vividly described', believing that now, as European costumes and habits were everywhere, there was little time left to witness that ceremony which 'echoes in many respects the mad excitement of the Asiatic mob in the temple at Ephesus'. Hunt, who was going blind, laboured for seven years on this painting, only to find that it was totally incomprehensible to the viewing public in England. He found his 'Oriental' sitters with the help of the manager of the paupers' Asiatic Home in Limehouse. It was perhaps the epitaph to the whole subject of biblical authenticity.

CHAPTER IV

———◆●◆———

'King Consul'

'IN JERUSALEM', wrote an English visitor, Ridley Herschell, in 1844, 'which is in a commercial point of view but a paltry inland Eastern town without trade or importance of any kind, sit the consuls of the five great European powers, looking at one another, and it is difficult to say why and wherefore.'

The consuls were in Jerusalem, however, not to report on the sale of olive-wood souvenirs or to nursemaid European travellers, but for quite another reason.

After the European powers had debated whether to restore Turkish rule to Syria at a conference in 1840, France and Prussia both proposed plans for an international regime in Jerusalem. The French wanted international Christian supervision, the Prussians an European protectorate which would ensure autonomy to all the local sects and protect the Jews; Metternich alone argued that Jerusalem was a Moslem city. But mutual suspicion prevented the creation of extraterritorial status for the Holy City.

Nevertheless, only in Jerusalem could the West claim an historical dimension for its political interests, and the wellbeing of the local Christians and Jews was entrusted to the consuls who now, following the British example of 1839, took up postings in the Holy City. Their task was essentially that of watchdogs, monitors of the new Turkish reforms which were supposed – *inter alia* – to end discrimination against non-Moslems throughout the empire.

The powers claimed that they were acting not only in the interests of Christians, but of Moslems and even the Porte itself. This meant an involvement in local affairs which went far beyond normal consular duties. In Jerusalem, with its multireligious groups, each consul gathered round him a little protectorate of his own. Officially, the consuls could claim jurisdiction only over foreigners; but in practice, their influence spread much further.

*   *   *

The Western consuls in the Levant had for years been the flagbearers of the little trader communities living in the coastal towns. The old system of extraterritorial privileges, the Capitulations, renewed by France in the late eighteenth century, had been intended originally as an assurance of safe passage and free commerce for foreigners, mutually beneficial to Europe and the Porte. It soon became a protective network stretched around not only the traders but an entire section of the local population which depended on them.

Edouard Blondel, a French merchant who spent two years in Syria between 1838 and 1840, observed that 'European merchants pay neither taxes nor duties; the local people whom they employ as agents or as servants enjoy the same privileges. What is even more surprising, is that they then cease to depend on their own government and rely only on the consulate of their masters, which owes them help and protection as it does to its own nationals.'

By the 1840s the French consul in Beirut, Eugène Poujade, observed that the English political and commercial influence in Syria had overtaken the French 'thanks to their excellent travellers, their missionaries, and principally the immense development of their industrial goods'. But though mid-century Palestine, like the rest of the Levant, was flooded with cheap Manchester cottons, Palestine did not become an important market for European goods, and its varied agricultural exports exceeded its imports for most of the century. Curiously enough, the one commodity for which Syria was dependent on imports – first from America and later from Russia – was kerosene oil.

Far more significant than the imports from abroad was the growing circle of Western influence spreading from the consulates. When the poet Gérard de Nerval visited the governor of Acre in 1851, the Turk complained bitterly of 'Consular trickery': 'Imagine, he said, a great city where a hundred thousand individuals are outside the framework of local laws; there isn't a thief, a murderer or a delinquent who does not succeed in putting himself under the protection of some consulate or other. There are twenty police forces which cancel one another out; yet it is the pasha who is supposed to be responsible.'

In this manner, what developed was two parallel systems of law: one for the local Moslems, and the *rayah* – the non-Moslem subjects of the empire – and the other for the Europeans and their protégés. Even the *rayah* were eventually drawn into the European sphere by the activities of the missionaries and the priests.

* * *

The consuls walked about Jerusalem preceded by their 'kavasses', Turkish janissaries in gold and blue uniforms delegated for their protection, carrying the silver-topped maces which were the consular symbols of office. When all the consular corps and their families appeared together on public holidays, as Lynch commented in 1848, the kavasses looked like 'so many drum majors of a marching regiment'. The consuls' presence was obligatory at all ceremonies in the Holy Sepulchre, where each had his chair and prie-dieu and his correct place according to protocol, the merest infringement of which meant a diplomatic incident.

The little foreign community adapted Moslem houses to European or American use, putting in glass panes (hitherto little used in Jerusalem) and taking down the wooden shutters, which, it was complained, shut out the view and let in the dust. Views from private houses were a Western innovation; the Moslems preferred their walled privacy.

The consuls' contacts with the local 'notables' were generally restricted to formal occasions, though consular wives might be invited to the women's quarters of Moslem neighbours; the Prussian consul Rosen's wife visited the harem of 'Musa Effendi'. Between June and September the entire foreign colony moved out of the dirty, overcrowded city, where the water in the depleted cisterns bred disease, and lived in tents on the surrounding hills.

In winter, they flocked to the Jerusalem Literary Society meetings organized by the British and Prussians, and the consular hostesses organized recitals of Handel and Rossini.

The consuls' handymen were the Jewish artisans, who baked the only European bread and provided mechanics and glaziers; Christian Arab women cleaned their houses; and Egyptians groomed their horses.

The consuls were an odd collection. The British, as befitted the most politically stable of European nations, enjoyed the longest terms of office – the second British consul, Finn, took no holiday during seventeen years of duty. The French tried desperately to assert hereditary rights as supreme Catholic power, handicapped by the seesaw of regimes at home and the absence of French priests and colonists in any significant number; the Austrians were the most professional of diplomats; the Prussians tended to be Orientalist scholars who wrote learned tracts on the archaeology of the city.

The Finns were the most famous consular couple, and also the most controversial, for their involvement with the Mission to the Jews.

Their French contemporary was Emile Botta, a French archaeologist who had combined consular duties in Persia with his researches at Khorsabad, and whom Maxim du Camp, on a visit to Jerusalem in 1850, described as 'a man of ruins, in the city of ruins, [who] believes in nothing, and appears to hate everything save the dead'. Of a series of American eccentrics, the first consul, Warder Cresson, was the oddest. His initial accreditation was withdrawn while he was still on the high seas (America did not formally establish a consulate until 1857) but this did not prevent Cresson from acting as self-styled consul for years. Thackeray, who met him *en route*, wrote: 'He has no other knowledge of Syria but what he derives from Prophecy . . . as soon as he arrived, he sent and demanded an interview with the Pasha; explained to him his interpretation of the apocalypse, in which he discovered that the five powers and America are about to intervene in Syrian affairs and in the infallible return of the Jews to Palestine.' Cresson subsequently became a Jew, and married a Jewish woman with whom, according to Holman-

Hunt (whom he assisted in the search for Jewish models), he had not one word of any language in common.

Elizabeth Finn, in one of her lightly fictionalized portraits of Jerusalem life, describes a social evening in the British consulate: the Prussian consul explains 'antiquarian difficulties' in fluent English to visiting clergymen; officers discuss European politics and the 'late revolutions' with the Austrian consul (Pizzamano), a titled Venetian; a visiting banker's wife is astonished that the Copts 'should pay to be close to the Holy Fire, as we pay in Europe for a good box at the opera', and English and German aristocrats exchange anti-semitic reflections on the 'hardened, reprobate Jews', and the truth of blood libels as witnessed in Wallachia.

Botta had another way of relieving the tedium of the 'paltry eastern town', to judge from the account of the French antiquarian Félicien de Saulcy, who spent a wet Christmas with the French consul in 1850. 'Same weather as yesterday. Impossible to set foot outside . . . I help the abbé to arrange his collection of herbs. Mohammed goes to the Haram and brings me back mosaic cubes' (presumably filched from the Dome of the Rock). 'Dinner with Botta, hashish binge, delicious effects of music. At ten thirty we all go home drunk as lords, night full of agreeable dreams.' The next night the hashish was swallowed before dinner. 'Very lively dinner; during dessert, with my first mouthful of tobacco, feel I'm going mad. From that moment, terrible crisis which lasted all night. Horrible, never try it again.'

*   *   *

The consuls had their own courts of justice, which were the authority for foreign residents, protégés, and visiting tourists; Turkish police and soldiers were forbidden to enter their residences. Their protégés enjoyed freedom from military service and from most Ottoman taxes, as well as trading privileges; most of the import trade was in the hands of Europeans, Armenians or Jews.

The consular employees, some of whom – like the kavasses – were Moslems, were not very well paid, and sometimes not paid at all. Isaac Zachariah, a veteran Jewish dragoman, or interpreter, whose patent of 1802 had been signed by Lord Elgin, served British consuls in the coastal towns for thirty-eight years without pay, was hounded out of Jaffa during the transition from Egyptian to Turkish rule and died in poverty in Jerusalem.

But the privileges acquired by consular staff generally made up for the poor pay. A Jewish convert in the employ of the Americans commented: 'The Kavasses attached to the consulate engage themselves not only out of consideration for the pay they get, but for the protection the place affords them to carry on their own business more successfully, for the perquisites they get, and for various other privileges.' One wonders what Mussa, the kavass of the Austrian consul Count Pizzamano, did out of consular hours; he had been official executioner to Ibrahim Pasha.

Consular service offered rich opportunities for intrigue; employees tended to pass on their jobs from father to son, plotted against rivals, threatened their employers with defection to other consulates if their demands had not been met, and often used their authority for private purposes. From 1830, many of the consular agents had been Ottoman subjects – merchants, landowners, and even tax farmers – and profited from the very system which the consuls, in their reports, so consistently deplored.

Relations between the consuls and the governors of the city were often strained; some of the consuls could claim to know the country better than its official administrators. In the first years of Turkish rule after the restoration of Palestine to the Sultan, the governors were replaced almost annually. For some years they were not salaried, but paid the Porte for the right to hold office. Thus they could only recover their costs by taking bribes or imposing extra taxes. 'The only check on the government's arbitrary tax laws and cupidity, is the fear of rebellion,' wrote the French consul in 1844, 'since the governor's only duty is to keep peace in his district' – and the actual policing was done by another official, the local *serasker*.

As Judea was controlled by rival, heavily armed clans in the hill towns, this was easier said than done. Hence the consuls' frequent complaints about the insecurity of life and property often fell on deaf ears. The governors of Acre and Jerusalem, moreover, had no authority in criminal cases, which were referred to Beirut or Damascus, the regional Turkish centres of administration. The most effective Turkish weapon against the consuls was procrastination: if sufficient time passed after a complaint was heard, it was likely that the governor himself would be serving elsewhere before action was taken. The consuls' weapon was a direct appeal to their ambassador at the Porte, but it was one that could not be used too often.

The Jerusalem consuls saw themselves as in the vanguard of progress. In practice, given the conditions of the country, they were drawn into the very system they criticized. The notion of 'protection', as the American consul Beardsley noted, being part and parcel of Eastern practice, it became vulnerable to every kind of abuse. The consuls, in protecting the non-Moslems and their hangers-on, reinforced the privileges of one section of the community at the expense of another. Unable otherwise to ensure the safety of Western travellers, they bribed the Bedouin and sought favours from highwaymen for their own nationals. They suffered from what was known in the chancelleries of Europe as *la fièvre Hierosalymitaine*, and the painter Edward Lear called 'Jerusalem squabblepoison' – the hysteria which periodically gripped the isolated, inbred Christian sects. They became involved in the most trivial local disputes and solemnly informed the Foreign Ministers of Europe of such matters as the theft of chickens and the escapades of adulterous wives; and they battled ferociously over potential protégés.

*   *   *

This rivalry began in the early 1840s. Until then, Britain had run the only consulate in Jerusalem. Its origins were curious. During a British consular reshuffle in 1838, one of the Syrian consuls pointed out that while Russia's interest in the Greek Orthodox community was growing, and France was traditionally the protector of the Latin Catholics, Britain had no standing in the Holy City. Palmerston, the British Foreign Secretary, having decided in principle on the establishment of a consulate, then warmed to the idea of a Jewish protected community there proposed to him by his Evangelical son-in-law, Lord Ashley, later Lord Shaftesbury. Hence his famous injunction to the first consul 'to afford protection to the Jews generally' – the Jewish population of Jerusalem then consisting of about five thousand souls.

Russia, which despatched mass pilgrimages to Palestine annually, claimed a paternal interest, in the name of their Greek Orthodox Church, in the local population of twenty thousand Arab Christians, and had no need at this stage to despatch a consul to Jerusalem. For Louis Philippe and his successor, the revival of French historical claims over the three-thousand-strong Latin community was one way of restoring French prestige as an imperial power. In 1843 France opened a consulate. The other European powers followed, and later, America.

There was, however, one drawback to the gathering of the eagles in Jerusalem, and that was the pecking order of the local birds. Once European prestige was harnessed to the petty quarrels of the Christian clergy, the merest hiss from an angry priest was audible in the chancelleries of Europe. The theft, in 1847, of the silver star which hung, symbolizing Latin rights, in the Grotto of the Nativity in Bethlehem – a shrine dominated by the Greek Orthodox – triggered a struggle for prestige between France and Russia. When Russia finally demanded sovereign rights over the Greek Orthodox population throughout the Ottoman empire, a diplomatic battle was set in motion which ended in the Crimean War. No one paid much attention to the fact that the affair of the silver star – a small incident, as holy battles went, in Palestine – was resolved in December 1852, a few weeks before the outbreak of war; by that time, it was of no importance.

*　　*　　*

The consuls were far from welcome in Jerusalem. The Porte only grudgingly produced the firman for the first British vice-consul (Britain later upgraded the post), Edward Young; and when he entered the Pasha's Divan to present his credentials, he was discourteously made to stand in the presence of the seated city notables. His first consular action brought him up against local usage: he posted a sign warning all British protected persons that it was against British law now to employ slaves. One of his first practical duties was more mundane: to obtain ground for a Protestant graveyard, as the local Christian sects refused Protestants burial. A traveller from Switzerland had lately been buried by the roadside, where his remains were promptly dug up by dogs and jackals.

Young's first attempt 'to afford protection to the Jews generally' resulted in Young's dragoman, who had tried to rescue a Jew attacked in the street, being set upon by an angry crowd. But Young soon discovered that the most passionate persecutors of the Jews were not the Moslems, but the Greek Christians.

The first French consul, Lantivy, ignorant of local protocol and, as a servant of the *ancien régime*, obsessed with the idea of restoring France's lost glory, flew the French flag over his consular office; it was immediately torn down, dragged through the streets, and the flagstaff crowned with an old Turkish slipper. Lantivy's demand for formal redress in the form of a twenty-one-gun salute to the humiliated *tricolor* was ignored, and consular gossip had it that the Pasha himself was behind the riot.

The relations of the first French and English consuls with the governors consisted mainly of registering complaints about attacks on Jews or thefts of property from the few visiting Europeans. The second French consul, Helois-Jorelle, reported in 1847 that the task of keeping order in the region had been entrusted by the governor to 'a notorious sheikh' (Mrs Finn identified him as Khaleel Aga er Ressas) who circulated freely in the city and only acted efficiently against criminals 'when he was refused his share of the loot'.

As for the protégés, their attitude to their would-be protectors was at first anything but promising. For the warring groups of Christian Jerusalem, the arrival of the consuls was a signal for an intensification of hostilities. A short time after Young's arrival, he was asked by a visiting Irish priest to intervene in a clash between Latins and Greeks. Young declined, remarking accurately enough that 'these disputes may at some future period become a question for political consideration'. The establishment of the joint Anglo-Prussian bishopric in 1841 in Jerusalem, where there was no real diocese but for the missionaries and their handful of Jewish converts, added to Young's troubles; he objected to having to protect Germans and had no specific instructions to that end – but they expected his protection.

Moreover, Dr Edward MacGowan, the Exeter physician to the Mission who was its natural leader, continually provoked the Moslems and was the cause of friction between the consul and the governor. Despite the local custom by which Moslems guarded their houses and wives jealously from foreign eyes, MacGowan opened sealed windows looking into a neighbour's courtyard and ignored repeated requests by Young to reseal them. There was an Ottoman law against foreigners acquiring land; MacGowan purchased property in a village near Jerusalem through intermediaries, planted vineyards, and announced his intention of making wine – another infringement of Moslem law. The villagers who had sold him land were imprisoned by the governor, and the rest of the village protested so violently that he had to leave. It was scarcely surprising that the doctor, whom Young described as 'of a litigious disposition and too ready to repel what he sees as the insolence of the Arabs', was constantly attacked in the streets.

The French claim to represent the interests of the Latins in the Holy Land was met with unequivocal suspicion by their potential protégés, who were Spaniards, Italians and Sardinians. The first consuls strained in vain to hear a word of French spoken in the churches, and were unable to locate a single French priest in the Latin convents. The Franciscans were under the jurisdiction of Rome, and did not appreciate French intervention, especially as the French financial contribution to the churches fell far behind those of the other Catholic states. Lantivy complained to Paris that 'only a minority of Franciscans accept the protection of France frankly and loyally'.

The Sardinian priests, backed by their consul, delighted in baiting the Frenchman, arguing that 'their order had only God as their protector', and when the Pope re-established the Latin Patriarchate in Jerusalem in 1847 – followed by a challenge to the Greek Patriarchate – the French consul was disturbed to learn that the Patriarch, Father Valerga, was also 'a Sardinian patriot'.

The superior of the Latin convent in Jerusalem went so far as to enquire of Young whether the convent could be placed under British protection to avoid the unwelcome attentions of the French. Again, Young prudently demurred.

The Turks, old hands at this game, played off one church and consulate against another. When the silver star disappeared from the Grotto in Bethlehem, tension between the French and Sardinians meant that it was some time before Jorelle took up the Latin cause, only to be told that the governor 'did not recognise France as protector of the Holy Land'. The infuriated consul advised Paris: 'What we need is a crusade, with battleships to back up every discussion; for every day there are fresh quarrels over a carpet, a lamp or a nail.'

Battleships did patrol the shores of Palestine throughout the middle decades of the century; but they were not only French, but British, Russian, and ultimately Prussian battleships, effectively neutralizing one another. Parties of European sailors regularly trooped up to the Holy Sepulchre, watched with intense suspicion by the rival consuls. French battleships traditionally sounded a twenty-one-gun salute as they sailed by Mount Carmel, on which the old Carmelite monastery, razed by Djezzar's successor, had been rebuilt with French money. But there was no crusade.

*   *   *

If Britain had embarrassments with resident Protestants, France with her Catholic protégés, both were mild compared with the complications all the foreign powers experienced in the task of protecting and aiding the Jews.

Between 1838 and 1882, the Jewish population of Palestine grew from about 8000 to about 27,000 souls. By 1870 Jews outstripped both Moslem and Christian communities combined in Jerusalem to become the largest single religious community in the city. There were many possible reasons for this increase: the disastrous earthquake of 1837 in Safed and Tiberias, followed by a Druse rebellion, drove thousands from the Galilee holy cities to Jerusalem. From the 1830s onwards Jews left Eastern Europe both to escape the tyranny of the Czar's poverty, and growing secularism spreading from central Europe. Turkish reforms had improved the lot of the local Sefardi Jews most of whom were Ottoman citizens; but for the Ashkenazi population, most of whom were foreigners, the greatest advantage of living in Jerusalem was to be under the protection of one or other of the foreign consulates.

Only about a quarter of those Jews eligible for British protection, however, took advantage of Palmerston's instructions; they were too apprehensive of the proselytizing Protestant community. In 1847, when Russia cancelled the passports of Jews who had not returned to Russia after a six-month absence, about seven hundred Jews were left stateless. Finn did all he could to ensure their adoption by England and an agreement was reached with Russia on this score. But according to the Austrian records, the vast majority of these, some six hundred, sought Austrian protection and were ultimately granted it. As many Jews had also immigrated from regions under Austrian rule, the largest number of Ashkenazi Jews was thus protected by the Austrian emperor.

Young, the first British consul, believed Britain should abstain from all religious activities 'thus strengthening our ability to protest over French and Russian interference with the Christian subjects of the Porte', and helping missionary activity meant 'to cast plain and obvious duties, with sound reason, overboard'. This advice was ignored by Finn, Young's successor, whose excessive involvement with the Jews ruined him; and towards the end of the century the number of Jews formally under British protection diminished. After 1890 Britain limited the number of its Jewish protégés to those with prior claims to citizenship or protection, ending what one British consul in Syria termed 'a fruitful source of dispute and contention'.

For where the Jews were concerned, the European consuls were dealing with a tightly organized community with its own laws and sanctions, which would take any help offered in the struggle for survival but did not welcome interference in its communal life.

The consular courts, though empowered to deal with their protégés' personal status – including marriage and inheritance laws – were not recognized as an authority by the rabbis. The

Ottoman authorities, however discriminatory their treatment of Jews and Christians, had nevertheless respected the autonomy of their communities on all personal matters. Such autonomy was basic to the 'millet' system by which each religious group controlled the personal affairs of its members – a system foreign to Europeans.

While Finn continually fell foul of the Jews on this point, other consuls were more tactful. Emile Botta tried to reconcile Jewish and French laws when dealing with the affairs of immigrants from French Algeria. When Jewish law insisted that the property of Jews who had been supported by charitable funds should revert to the community on their death, Botta thought this just, and found a compromise with French law, which favoured individual inheritance.

Where Finn was concerned, he allowed renegade members of the community, converts in particular, to appeal to foreigners over the heads of their own community leaders. So while on the one hand the British consul frequently took the part of persecuted Jews, the rabbis often sought the help of the Turkish governor against the English missionaries and the consul's arbitration.

In 1842, a Russian rabbi, Bordaki, who was also the Russian and Austrian consular agent in Jerusalem before the first consul's arrival, protested to the governor that Jewish converts had taken refuge with a German missionary working with the bishopric from the just wrath of their own community. Other rabbis sought Turkish help against those who had buried a Jewess who died in the Mission hospital. On another occasion, the governor imprisoned a would-be convert, at the Jews' request, for three months, in an unsuccessful bid to prevent his conversion. In such cases, several consuls thought themselves bound to uphold the idea of freedom of conscience and worship. If this meant a change of faith, however, it went against Moslem and Jewish belief, and was resented by the heads of the rival churches.

In Jerusalem, whenever a foreigner, or a protégé, changed his or her religion, it became a highly public matter. Converts fled the fury of their families and took refuge in consulates or missions; diplomatic incidents duly followed. By far the greater number of such incidents concerned Jews; one of the more complex was the case of Mendel Diness, an Austrian Jew who was to become Jerusalem's first professional photographer. When Diness sought to convert to Protestantism, both the Russian consul-general in Jaffa, who employed Diness as a translator, and the Austrian consul, under whose protection Diness came, joined in the protests of the family to the British consulate and took every means to prevent the conversion. They were unsuccessful.

But the conversion of Christians by other Christians also exacerbated rivalries between churches. The second Anglican bishop, the Prussian nominee Samuel Gobat, chose to proselytize among the Greek Christians rather than the problematic Jews. This in itself was enough to cause hostility between the bishop and Consul Finn, and reached a pitch of hysteria when Gobat accused Finn's dragoman, a Jewish convert named Simeon Rosenthal, of dishonesty in his business practices. In the uproar which followed (pamphlets flew back and forth in London like brickbats), Finn exercised his full authority against Gobat forbidding him to leave the city; the Prussian consul, Rosen, lodged a formal protest, and Finn was brought to heel by the Foreign Office.

The French and Prussian consuls battled over the daughter of the head of the Church Missionary Society, Charles Sandretzki (himself a convert from Catholicism), when she disappeared from her home and joined the Catholic French Sisters of Zion. According to French law, Miss Sandretzki, aged twenty-three, was legally independent; according to the Prussian consul, she was still subject to parental authority. While the Latin Patriarch tried to mediate between the family and their cloistered daughter, and the French consul appealed to Paris for instructions, Miss Sandretzki fled the city and sailed for Rome on a French warship.

There was trouble, too, over the education of the children of converts; British and French consulates clashed when children were transferred from a Protestant to a Catholic mission school.

This was nothing, however, to the trouble the consuls involved themselves in by helping Jewish philanthropists in the West to open schools teaching secular subjects to the strictly orthodox

Jewish community. In the 1850s the Austrian consul Count Pizzamano facilitated the opening of the famous Laemel school, only to have it anathematized and banned by the heads of the Ashkenazi community. In 1865, another Austrian consul, Count de Caboga, tried to help the school's patrons introduce the teaching of languages, mathematics and science; again they were defeated. The French consul de Barrères had the same experience with schools set up by the French-based Alliance Israelite Universelle in the late 1860s.

All the consuls dreaded Holy Week, when any incident could arouse the suspicions of the Moslems (tradition had it that the Christians would rebel against Moslem rule at Easter) and when Greek Christians were most likely to attack the Jews. The French consul de Barrères complained 'of the need to keep watch constantly over public order in the Church [of the Holy Sepulchre] which means that the Consul has to remain there permanently, for many hours, by day and night, especially when the celebration of the ceremonies by the various Christian cults coincides'. It was not the easiest consular posting in the East.

*　　*　　*

If the establishment of the foreign consulates in Jerusalem marked the beginning of extensive Western influence in Palestine, the Crimean War of 1853–6 was its watershed. When Britain and France, fighting beside Turkey, defeated Russia at Sebastopol in 1855, flags flew boldly from all the foreign consulates in Jerusalem for the first time. The French consul, de Barrères, demanded – and got – the twenty-one-gun salute which the governor had refused Lantivy twelve years earlier. While the war still went on in the north, the governor read out the terms of the Hatti Humayun, a new programme of reforms which promised equal rights to Christians and other non-Moslems, protection of their persons and property, freedom of worship, and other privileges, including permission to hold land in their own names – though this was not actually implemented until more than a decade later.

In Jerusalem, the Sanctuary was opened in daylight to Europeans equipped with firmans, three European noblemen toured the Moslem ·as well as the Christian Holy Places, and Palestine was thrown open to the middle-class parties of tourists who were soon to outnumber the travelling elite in the Levant.

During the years which followed, Moslems who insulted Jews publicly were often forced to make public redress; the stinking tannery near the Holy Sepulchre, and the slaughterhouse at the entrance to the Jewish quarter were relocated, and the stone barrier which held up the entrance of pilgrims to the doorway of the Holy Sepulchre – 'the annoying reminder of past humiliations', as a French consul put it – was demolished. Public order, at least within the city, was improved. The police now routinely disarmed peasants entering the city, who previously, as an American consul reported, had been 'walking magazines'.

In 1856, when the war ended, Consul Finn, who had observed that the local population saw the Crimean War as a battle between Moslem and Christian forces, now reported 'a steady diminution of fanaticism and disturbance'. Whereas twelve years earlier, green paint (the colour allowed to Moslems only) had been scraped off the door of the Anglican bishop, Finn now reported seeing a Jew at the main gate of the city, wearing 'a complete dress of a most peculiarly Moslem shade of green'. Sentinels presented arms to the consuls going in and out of the city, and the governor of Jerusalem had attended an English church service at Christ Church, the Protestant church, on the previous day. 'In a doctrinal point of view, it was looked upon as a remarkable coincidence for Epiphany day that in a church with the commandments and creed inscribed in Hebrew, there should be a Turkish pasha standing at the Te Deum with our prayer book in Turkish in his hand, in Jerusalem.'

Finn's optimism was somewhat premature. In 1856 there were anti-Christian riots in Nablus and foreign flags were torn down. The Hatti Humayun had proclaimed that the Old and New Testaments were the precursors of the teachings of Mohammed; but the distribution of bibles by the missionaries, as the British ambassador to the Porte, Henry Bulwer, acknowledged in 1864, continued to be a provocation in Moslem towns. In Jerusalem the life of Christians might be more secure, but foreign colonists who took seriously the relaxation of previous prohibitions on land purchases found that they still needed firmans for settlement. They could only set up colonies, moreover, in the teeth of local hostility which sometimes led to violence.

When a group of colonists, the Dickson and Steinbeck families who farmed outside Jaffa, were victims of murder and multiple rape in 1857, the American and Prussian consuls in Jerusalem, acting on behalf of the two families involved, had to literally pursue the governor of Jerusalem around the country to get him to hear their complaint. The American consul reported, 'The Pasha of Jerusalem is an enemy to the Christians and will not move on this matter until he is forced to.' The case was eventually heard in Beirut, where the large American Protestant colony formed a strong pressure group. When the first American tourists arrived in Palestine in 1868, packhorses intended for and paid for by the Americans were removed at the last moment by muleteers, at the governor of Jerusalem's orders, and served him for a pleasure outing in the Judean hills. Foreign visitors without royal pedigrees were still denied entry to those Christian shrines sacred also to Moslems; and in 1862, when the Prince of Wales visited Palestine, even his progress was halted by a Bedouin force which allowed him to pass only when they had ascertained that a certain Turkish officer, with whom they had a blood feud, was not among his escorts.

Consular relations with the governors were not much easier, partly because the growing Western presence in Palestine, the Turks feared, was only the prelude to a military intervention aimed at turning Palestine into a Christian state. Frequent changes in the administrative status of Jerusalem indicated that the Porte was well aware of the new importance of Jerusalem in Western eyes.

Two of the three governors who served long terms of office in Jerusalem between the Crimean War and the 1880s – Sureya Pasha and Rauf Pasha – were hostile to the West. While Sureya's behaviour was more subtle, Rauf Pasha, disturbed by the chanting processions of Christians through the streets of Jerusalem at Easter, encouraged the old Moslem pilgrimage to Nebi Musa to become a competitive event, in which Moslems beating on drums and cymbals, preceded by whirling dervishes, were for the first time recorded by Western visitors.

Proposals for technological improvements by Western representatives were received coolly. Consular complaints about bad road communications evoked a response only in 1868, when a road of sorts, built with forced labour from the villages *en route*, was patched together between Jaffa and Jerusalem, only to fall apart with the first winter rains. Fuad Pasha, the Turkish Grand Vizier, was reported to have said during this period: 'I shall never concede to these crazy Christians any road improvement in Palestine, as they would then transform Jerusalem into a Christian madhouse.'

Nevertheless, communications with the outside world were improved during the 1860s, including an efficient Austrian-run postal service and, in 1865, a telegraph service which linked Jerusalem to Jaffa and thence to Beirut and Constantinople. These changes increased Turkish control over the province and were thus fully in the Ottoman interest. And the Turkish reaction to the Western proposals for improving the water supply in Jerusalem shows a certain ambivalence. In 1870, the water question provoked a major diplomatic incident involving Jerusalem, Constantinople, Damascus and Paris.

The filthy state of the city's cisterns, and the absence of a direct water supply from outside Jerusalem, had long been a cause of Western complaints. In 1865, a British army engineer, Charles Wilson, carried out an ordnance survey of the city, financed by an English philanthropist, Angela Burdett-Coutts. A few months after Wilson left Jerusalem, a cholera epidemic broke out which claimed 621 lives, or one in every twenty of the population. The governor, Izzet Pasha, under the pretext of accompanying an Ottoman dignitary to his ship, left the city for Jaffa – both men thus breaking the quarantine rules – and remained there. The French, Austrian, Prussian and English consuls, having evacuated their families to the hills, remained to distribute food and water, and the Latin Patriarch, Valerga, and a handful of priests tended the sick.

Five years later, Lady Burdett-Coutts tried again, proposing the construction of an aqueduct to bring water from the suburbs into the city, at her own expense; her one condition was that the newly founded council should contribute to its maintenance. But the council argued that it had no funds for this purpose.

The new governor, Kiamil Pasha, however, was more receptive to ideas for improvement than his predecessors, particularly since in 1870 Jerusalem was suffering from a persistent drought. Affected no doubt also by the newly undertaken explorations of Western engineers in the city – the Palestine Exploration Fund was now digging away for dear life in search of biblical Jerusalem* – he now decided to send soldiers to reconnoitre for ancient cisterns and conduits beneath the sanctuary which, though no longer in use, might again be reconnected.

One such source was the Twin Pools, cisterns once fed by a Roman aqueduct and which had been rediscovered during excavations for the construction of the French Catholic convent, the Sisters of Zion, two years earlier. Kiamil Pasha suggested that here was an ample source of water which might be tapped; a Prussian doctor resident in the city had pronounced drinkable the water oozing into the cellar of the convent, and a Prussian architect suggested ways in which Kiamil might reconnect the source.

But the convent was French property. The French consul – Joseph Adam Sienkewitz – was moreover extremely sensitive on the question of French prestige on the eve of the Franco-Prussian War. He saw Kiamil's proposal as a Turkish plot to assail France's rights as protector of the Holy Places, aided and abetted by the cunning Prussian residents. Sienkewitz insisted that the water was no more than a brackish trickle, and refused the Turks access to the convent cellar. Kiamil was not to be deterred.

On a hot Sunday morning in June Turkish soldiers clearing their way through an underground channel leading from the Sanctuary area to the Via Dolorosa, where the convent stood, burst through the door which led to the cellar. Sienkewitz rushed from the consulate and ordered the soldiers out; from then on he spent sleepless nights watching all the entrances to the cellar. But on 13 July he learned that the mayor of Jerusalem, a Turkish officer and several soldiers had once more forced their way into

*See Chapter VII

the cellar from an underground passage. Donning his full consular regalia and waving a sword, Sienkewitz rushed into the breach. He was outnumbered, however, and forced to retreat. When he attempted to contact his superiors at the Porte via the newly installed telegraph services, he discovered that despite the fine weather the telegraph poles were down. While Sienkewitz fumed, the governor sent a special messenger to Jaffa with his version of the incident, which was that the French consul had physically attacked Turkish soldiers who were only trying to improve the city's water facilities. This message preceded that of the consul to Constantinople. It was not until several weeks later, after exhaustive diplomatic enquiries involving Rashid Pasha, the pro-Western governor of Damascus, that the cellar was returned to the French nuns, and not till the fifteenth of September that the breach was closed and French honour satisfied. By then, of course, Sedan had fallen.

*   *   *

The arrival of hundreds of Christians as residents in Palestine – missionaries, priests and colonists – had raised the standard of living in the towns if not by improving facilities then by increasing investment in the country, particularly in building. Huge ecclesiastical compounds rose in Jerusalem: churches with belltowers which challenged the minarets (bellringing was permitted since the reforms); pilgrim hospices, of which the largest was the Russian Compound which changed the skyline of Jerusalem from the West; and synagogues financed by Jewish philanthropists in Vienna, Paris and London.

The consuls reported a fourfold rise in land prices over the six years following the Crimean War. The reforms in the land laws opened the market to foreign purchasers, as well as encouraging the local notables to buy up land cultivated by tenant farmers. The change in registration laws, introduced with the aim of centralizing administration and improving the tax yield without increasing investment on Turkey's part, forced the peasants who occupied most government land to either register it in their own names or to see it taken over by wealthy townspeople, merchants and foreign colonists, who paid off the backlog of taxes and

'The Finding of the Saviour in the Temple' by Holman-Hunt (1854–60).

Hunt's models for the rabbis were Sefardi Jews in Jerusalem, most of them 'enquirers' or potential converts from the Anglican Mission. The figure of the boy Jesus was modelled on a pupil of a Jewish school in Red Lion Square, London.

Below left: Horace Vernet was a military painter who – unlike Hunt – was not interested in making detailed research for the purposes of 'authenticity'. He accepted, like many French Orientalist painters, the idea that the biblical figures looked like contemporary Arab sheikhs. The 'Tamar', however, looks more like a model from the Folies Bergères. 'Judah and Tamar' (1840).

Below right: Akil Aga by Carl Haag. Akil was the *de facto* ruler of the Galilee and protector of Christians and Jews for some thirty years, and his system of alliances with England and France (which he used in his relations with his Turkish overlords) would not have shamed a European politician.

Khan el Tujjar, the great weekly market in Galilee during the mid-century, was at the centre of Akil's territory.

Haag's sketch of the reception of the Prince of Wales by Akil Aga records a visit to Mount Tabor in the spring of 1862. The two mares on the left were presented by Akil to Prince Edward, as described by A.P. Stanley, later Dean of Westminster, who was also present.

European tourists in the mid-century were often poor riders and no longer wore disguise. Their pack animals were overloaded with the complex paraphernalia of 'Tent Life'.

employed the peasants to farm the land for them. Most of the peasantry took the second course.

From the beginning of the century, Western visitors had assumed that more efficient administration would ensure better conditions for the peasants. Now, despite increased prosperity in the towns, however, there was little change, according to the consuls' reports, in the condition of peasant life during the thirty years following the Crimean War.

In 1849, just before the war, Consul Finn, on a visit to the south of the country, found 'valleys of wheat reaching to our horses' backs and scarcely any population visible; the district was wastefully sown, grain covering the beaten roads, and there trodden down and rolled upon while growing by soldiers, horses and camels'. The farmers, he said, had diminished by three-quarters, having fled to avoid taxation, as the villages were always a year in debt.

In 1872, well after the land reforms had taken effect, the American consul Beardsley described a similar picture of neglect. And in 1880, the Austrian consul, the Count de Caboga, explained that while the area of land under cultivation had actually doubled over the previous decade, because of greater success in keeping the Bedouin at bay, there was no change in the state of the peasants and most arable land was hopelessly neglected. Caboga's report, one of the most detailed despatched by any foreign consul, made it clear that progress in Palestine was essentially progress for a handful of rich local landowners, or the few foreign settlers whose farming experiments had by now dramatically raised the productivity of their little estates, just as Western money had created a building boom in the towns. The missions now educated thousands of Christian Arabs in the English, French or German traditions, Caboga reported, and this 'to the disadvantage of students who are separated from their natural environment . . . nowhere are uneducated Arabs made into educated Arabs'. Jerusalem, Caboga observed, had become a European city.

Charles Warren, the British army engineer who mapped the biblical topography of Jerusalem despite determined opposition from the Turkish authorities, summed up the accepted view of

˙the changes in the city: 'King Consul rules supreme, not over the natives of the city, but over strangers; but yet these strangers for the most part are the rightful owners; the natives, for the most part, are usurpers.'

*   *   *

During the 1860s, a new problem was added to the consuls' already complex relationship with their protégés: the presence of the first Western colonists.

James Finn paid dearly for his attempts to change the status of the Jews in Palestine, but the actual cause of his downfall was an ambitious convert colonist; Victor Beauboucher, fifth American consul, became hopelessly involved in the disastrous affairs of the Adams colony at Jaffa; and the German consuls von Alten and von Munchausen were drawn into the struggle of the Templar community both with the Turkish authorities and the local population.

The only known portrait of James Finn shows him in full consular dress, sheathed sword at his side; the uniform looks uncomfortably tight, and Finn, chosen to succeed the pragmatic Young in 1845, was not in fact 'an old Levant hand'. He had no experience either in commerce or in consular service, and his only (rather remote) qualification for the post was that he had written a treatise on the Jews of China. It seems likely that his appointment was rather the result of his connections; he had been tutor to the family of Lord Aberdeen, the former Secretary of War, and was about to marry Elizabeth, daughter of Alexander MacCaul, the most famous authority on, and missionary to, the Jews in Europe and friend of Lord Ashley.

Whether or not it was the influence of Finn's father-in-law that kept the difficult consul in Jerusalem for seventeen years, Finn consistently exceeded his brief. There can scarcely have been another British consul who was reprimanded, consecutively, by four separate Foreign Secretaries, yet continued to function in his post.

No other consul did so much for the Jews and yet incurred so much opposition from them. It was Finn who first brought the plight of the Russian Jews, left stateless in 1848, to Palmerston's attention; Finn who instructed Jews as to how they could best obtain British protection; Finn who investigated every case of harassment or violence towards Jews and took it on himself frequently to punish their tormentors; Finn who intervened personally to help Jews deprived of charitable support from Eastern Europe, when the Crimean War cut them off from their main source of income. Perhaps his most extraordinary efforts were his plans, and those of his wife, to provide employment for destitute Jews in 'agricultural labour' – actually little more than clearing stones from the hillsides – on plots of land near Jerusalem. Finn even tried to convince the Foreign Office 'to persuade the Jews in a large body to settle here as agriculturalists on the soil', in partnership with the Arab peasantry, an idea passed on to the Porte but which elicited no response; the Turks had no desire to encourage more Western protégés to flock to Palestine.

The Jews, however, not only saw in Finn a useful protector but suspected that his ultimate aim was their own conversion; the leaders of the community ostracized those who accepted Finn's help, confronted him frequently for asserting his consular authority where would-be converts were concerned, and on one important occasion appealed against him to Sir Moses Montefiore, the Jewish philanthropist periodically involved in Jewish affairs in Palestine over a period of some sixty years. By the end of the 1850s Finn's position was precarious. His various welfare projects for the Jews had been financed mainly from his own pocket, and he was borrowing heavily from Jewish moneylenders at high rates of interest. He had crossed swords too many times with the Anglican bishop and Edward MacGowan of the Mission to the Jews, and the file of complaints against him in the Foreign Office was extensive. But it was his association with a convert colonist family, the Meshullams, which proved fatal.

For someone who believed, as Finn did, in the conversion of the Jews and their rehabilitation as farmers in Palestine, the Meshullam family were a continual encouragement. John Meshullam, an English-born Sefardi Jew, ran the first 'Hebrew Christian' farm in Palestine at Artas, near Bethlehem. Converted by the legendary (convert) missionary Joseph Wolff, John

Meshullam was a Crusoe-like figure who had made and lost a series of fortunes when he was cast up on the shores of Palestine in the early 1840s. After a brief spell as market gardener for the Mission, and, as hotelier, he acquired land near the Pools of Solomon for the price of settling a blood feud, and grew fruit, vegetables, corn and grapes. With Finn's help, he employed Jewish poor in seasonal labour and distributed surplus crops among them during famine.

John Meshullam's elder son, Peter, was an ambitious young man educated in England and America, who had served in the signal corps of the British army during the Crimean War. On his return to Palestine Finn employed him at the consulate as his deputy and, in 1860, sent him on a mission to the Galilee and Mount Lebanon to check on the conditions of local Christians and Jews during the period of the Moslem and Druse massacres of Christians in Damascus and elsewhere. But Finn had not troubled to advise the Foreign Office in advance, and when he began sending back Meshullam's reports, he was sharply rebuked for exceeding his brief, operating outside his allotted area, and wasting consular funds.

To make matters worse, Peter Meshullam now began to use his consular authority to lay down the law in the Bethlehem area. The Meshullams' relations with their Moslem neighbours had always been difficult and Peter Meshullam now chose to settle the families' scores as well as trying to crack down on petty thieves and extortioners – in particular, waging a private war against a local Moslem who was alleged to have seduced Meshullam's sister. Moslem Bethlehem turned against the family, despite John Meshullam's efforts to disown his son's tactics, and scandals multiplied around Peter Meshullam, spread by his enemies. Finn was inevitably implicated, and his enemies in the Mission were jubilant.

At this moment the Prince of Wales arrived for a visit in the spring of 1862. He was bombarded with petitions of every kind against Meshullam. The moneylenders, sensing Finn's downfall, stopped his credit.

Now only the Ashkenazi Jews, alarmed, came to his defence. They appealed directly to Queen Victoria, begging her not to recall the consul; were Finn to leave, they wrote, 'and until the coming consul shall subdue the men of this land, we fear for our lives, lest the inhabitants should swallow us up with wrong-doing'. But they were too late. Finn had been accused of handling consular finances 'in an offhand, irregular and neglectful man-ner', and in January 1863 he was reposted to the Dardanelles, a posting he never took up as he was by now a sick man.

In May, the Foreign Secretary sent Sir Edmund Hornby, judge at the consular court in Constantinople, to Jerusalem to investi-gate the affair, which was complicated by the fact that in March Peter Meshullam had been murdered by his enemies. Hornby's conclusion was that while 'there was nothing fraudulent or criminally improper in Finn's conduct', there had been 'much to blame', notably his unfortunate choice of consular employees. Hornby induced most of Finn's creditors to come to an arrangement, sold off his assets and castigated the Mission, the Jews and the Evangelical Protestants as all having contributed to his ruin. Hornby warned the Foreign Office that any official who arrived in Jerusalem was forced to take sides on the question of the future of the Jews and other religious controversies, and concluded his comments: 'In all times, toleration in such matters has been rare. In Jerusalem, it would seem to be impossible.'

*   *   *

Victor Beauboucher was a Belgian journalist who had gone to America during the Civil War to fight with the Massachusetts volunteers because of his hatred of slavery. He lost part of one leg in the battle of Cold Harbor and was subsequently recommended officially for the post of American consul in Jerusalem. The language in which his first consular despatches were written was very odd: describing a plague of locusts, the consul predicted that 'the misery of the inhabitants will increase by the augmentation of all things nearly inaccessible'. The State Department enquired worriedly as to their new consul's nationality, and Beauboucher replied: 'Is not my naturalization evident by the fact of my services rendered to my adopted country?'

The State Department appears to have conceded the point, for Beauboucher continued to serve his adopted country for another three years, having prudently acquired a bright young multilingual vice-consul, from an Austrian-Jewish family of converts, named Benjamin Finkelstein, to write his despatches. Beauboucher's gammy leg gave him trouble throughout his term of service, and he repeatedly asked to be reassigned to some more civilized posting, such as Italy. Instead, he was called upon to handle a particularly tricky case involving American colonists in Jaffa, and simultaneously to discipline his indispensable, but rebellious, consular staff.

The American consulate had to all intents and purposes been run by its protégé staff for some years. No fewer than five consuls had been sworn in between 1857 and 1865, the year of Beauboucher's appointment, and during the long periods between the departure of one consul and the arrival of the next, the local staff had the run of the premises. This meant one family in particular, the Armenian Murad family, who were officially under Prussian protection.

The first Murad in American service had left Jaffa as the result of the investigation of the Dickson murders, hounded out by the suspects' relatives. A second Murad, Simeon, took over as vice-consul after the first Murad's death and was alone in the office during the tense six months of the anti-Christian uprising of 1860. During the American Civil War, one consul failed to arrive, and the next sent no despatches save to request a new set of consular silver-topped maces (the first set had disappeared). Lazarus Murad, the third of the dynasty, sat out the terrible cholera epidemic of 1865 alone and made no secret of the fact that he expected to be made consul himself. Instead, Beauboucher got the job.

One of his first official acts was to sack Lazarus, who had not only failed to register receipt of Warder Cresson's personal effects (the first 'consul' had died in 1860) but had 'extorted of travellers considerable sums imploring their commiseration, under the pretence of an insufficient salary'. Murad had also pocketed half the fees the consuls now paid, on behalf of travellers, for permission to visit the Dome of the Rock; and after he left, it was discovered that he had taken with him a brand-new American flag and most of the consular stationery.

A short time later, Beauboucher was warned by the American legation in Constantinople that a large group of American colonists was on its way to Palestine without a firman from the Sultan, adding that their sponsors 'should not have encouraged families to embark from America until the result of their application to the Porte was known'. Beauboucher replied asserting his willingness to protect the newcomers, firman or no firman. They proved very difficult to protect.

The colonists were a group of families, mainly artisans and farmers, from Maine, and they were henceforth to be known as the Adams colony after their leader, George Washington Joshua Adams, an American lay preacher and believer in the Millenium. Adams had composed an extra book of the Bible (Enoch), compared the settlement of Palestine to that of the United States, and assured the men and women who followed him that Jaffa was an important port, a dollar worth ten in their homeland (the cost of living was in fact double that in America) and Jerusalem a thriving modern city. Adams, like other cult leaders, exercised an extraordinary power over his followers; but this quickly wore off when they found themselves homeless on the wintry Jaffa beaches.

Thirteen of the colony died during the first two months alone, most of them children, although Adams managed to get hold of land previously mortgaged to Americans and to put up the clapboard houses the settlers had brought with them, a strange transplant from the eastern American sea coast. But with no experience of the climate, or of semitropical farming, with tools many of which proved unsuitable, and faced with the hostility of the local people, most of the colonists were soon clamouring to be sent home.

Beauboucher's sympathies were all with the colonists whom he described as 'honest artisans and labouring men', but he was torn between this sympathy and his duty as an accredited representative to the Porte. Adams tried to persuade the colonists that the consul was their worst enemy. Meanwhile Finkelstein, in composing the consul's despatches, lost no opportunity to request American citizenship for himself, while pointing out that no real American citizen would work for so shamefully low a salary.

The governor of Jerusalem, Izzet Pasha, complained immediately to the consul about the illegality of the settlement. Adams, spotting a way out, applied for Turkish citizenship, and Beauboucher 'detained' him for twenty-four hours to argue him out of the idea. Having involved himself with the settlers, Beauboucher now began advancing them money. By the spring of the following year, he had given them some four hundred dollars – about half his annual salary – with no guarantee of repayment, while Adams had managed to get through several cases of brandy and arak and was piling up debts as fast as hangovers. Despite the consul's help, most of the settlers were soon destitute.

The State Department enlisted the help of an elderly American clergyman Mr Bidwell, on a Levant tour, to investigate the situation. But Bidwell was taken in by the plausible Adams, who insisted that all was well, assisted by a fourth Murad, Serapion, nephew to Lazarus, who now found a way to revenge the family's wrongs on the unfortunate consul. Serapion Murad testified both to Bidwell and in the visitors' book of the Carmelite convent on Mount Carmel, where he stayed, that 'never had any colony been so defamed by its consul or had any colony been more prosperous'.

By this time, however, the plight of the colonists had reached the American press. Consuls now descended on Jaffa from Beirut and Alexandria, and with their help the first group of immigrants re-embarked for America in the summer. Serapion Murad was found guilty of defamation and sentenced by the Prussian consul to a week's imprisonment.

In September, the first American tourist ship, the *Quaker City*, steamed into Jaffa's waters, carrying, among others, two American journalists – Samuel Clemens (Mark Twain) and Moses S. Beach of the New York *Sun*. Beach advanced fifteen hundred dollars in gold to ensure that the remaining Americans who so wished could be repatriated via Egypt, back to Maine, since, as Twain wrote: 'It was evident that practical New England was not sorry to be rid of such visionaries and was not in the least inclined to hire anybody to bring them back to her.'

But this was not the end of Beauboucher's troubles. The nucleus of the colony remained in Jaffa, many of them still loyal to Adams. The new governor of Jerusalem, Nazif Pasha, complained that the colonists who, despite the lack of formal permission, had begun to cultivate the land, paid no Ottoman taxes; the colonists, for their part, demanded that Beauboucher cease dealing with their affairs and promised to settle their debts with the government by themselves.

They kept this bargain for fully six months, after which they were once more quarrelling among themselves and appealing to the consul for arbitration. During a brief absence of Beauboucher from office, his replacement, Lorenzo Johnson, wrote to Washington: 'Their affairs are bringing great disrepute upon the American character; should it be necessary for me to interfere again, I shall not fail to apply the law to their cases so fully as to place beyond doubt the fact that our government does not tolerate such dishonest and disgraceful proceedings.'

Adams and his wife finally left for England in the summer of 1868, nearly two years after their arrival, without paying their creditors. Three months later Adams surfaced in Liverpool, still lecturing about 'four crops a year' to would-be settlers, and, a year later, a solitary candidate for redemption turned up in Jaffa from Liverpool with a crate-load of pots and pans he hoped to barter for local produce.

Beauboucher had still not been reimbursed. In the autumn of 1868, unable to pay Finkelstein his salary, he dismissed him. He himself finally left Jerusalem a year later, without appointing a replacement. In January 1870, his last appearance in the consular records, he turned up in Washington, with another request for the money he had advanced to be repaid, this time to a Jaffa moneylender to whom he had transferred his debts. Finkelstein battled obstinately for reinstatement for three years; eventually another consul took his part and re-employed him. Having earned his passage, he emigrated to America.

Serapion Murad went on to bigger and better consular intrigues in the German consulate.* Two of the surviving Jaffa colonists, Rolla Floyd and Herbert Clark, made good as tourist guide and travel agent respectively. Clark even became an American consul himself, some years later.

The houses and lands of the Adams' colony did not stand

*See Chapter VII

empty long. In 1869 they were purchased by new arrivals in Palestine, the sober, strictly disciplined German Templars, a Pietist sect which was in trouble both with government and established church for its visionary, sectarian views.

*   *   *

The Templars believed that Palestine should be under Christian rule, and that German armies would be the instrument of creating a Christian state in Lebanon and Syria, with Jerusalem at its centre. Some such idea had been put forward during the period of Egyptian rule by Helmuth von Moltke, Prussian military adviser to the Sultan and later the architect of Prussia's European victories; but at this period of German history Bismarck had no interest in challenging British and French supremacy in the area, and the Templar colonies, though they came to be the largest and most solidly established of all the foreign settlements in Palestine before 1882, were not used by Germany as a pretext for claiming political rights.

Nevertheless, the Templars believed themselves in the vanguard of enlightened Christianity, warriors in the 'peaceful crusade'. Their work was universally admired by Western visitors to Palestine. Paul Lortet, a French professor of medicine who visited Palestine in the 1870s, believed that their colonies 'would become a centre of regeneration for the soft and infantile peoples of the Orient', regretting only that their presence clashed with French interests. Laurence Oliphant, the British writer who lived near them in Haifa for several years, wrote that 'the Templars' well-cultivated fields, trim gardens and substantial white stone mansions form a most agreeable and unexpected picture of civilisation upon this semi-barbarous coast'. The Templars set up model communities of artisans, and professionals; they experimented with European farming methods and indicated, especially to the more independent-minded Jews, that European colonies could succeed even in a hostile environment.

The Turks saw the Templars rather differently. Turkish policy was only to encourage newcomers prepared to adopt Turkish nationality and their attitude to Western investment fluctuated. The Templars were definitely German, and their colonies self-contained; they believed that they were the true heirs to the Holy Land, where they were to create a 'spiritual temple' as an example to 'degenerate mankind'. They had no interest in proselytizing among the local Christians or Jews, but their view of the Moslems was that 'the oriental is impudent and arrogant, his characteristics those of thievishness and beggary, and he only respects power and money'. This dislike was returned, with interest. The Templars' Moslem neighbours stole one-third of the crops from the fields of their one agricultural settlement in the plains; and in Haifa and Jaffa there were numerous violent incidents, particularly when the Templars took it upon themselves to physically chastise signs of 'immorality'.

Their relationship with the German consuls in Jerusalem was thus ambivalent. The German Lutherans and Catholics in the Holy City, proselytizers concerned with orphanages and schools, were hostile to the Templars and for some time the consuls kept their distance from the new settlers along the coast, leaving the day-to-day affairs to be settled by the local consular agents. The Templars complained of lack of support by the consuls in their battles with the authorities, notably in Haifa.

The lands they had purchased in Haifa, through an intermediary, could not be registered in their own names, as they had no firman for settlement. The Turkish officials refused to recognize one of the Templars, Friedrich Keller, as the local German consular agent; and in the plain of Esdraelon, where they had also acquired land, officials ordered them off the land, leaving behind fields already sown.

Their first notable victory was when they established themselves as carters plying the route between Jerusalem and Jaffa port. The town council had objected to the Templars driving their carts through the narrow, congested streets of the town to the quayside. The Templar leader, Christoph Hoffman, complained to von Alten, the consul in Jerusalem, that this was 'simply the resistance of barbarism to the advance of culture', and that he 'had therefore to take refuge in the might of the German empire'. In November 1874, by von Alten's mediation, the Templars were allowed to pass through Jaffa for three hours each day while a road bypassing the town was constructed.

Their contribution to the road services in Palestine was held up as evidence of their claim to having brought culture to the Holy Land. They invested their own money in building a road from Haifa to Nazareth, and from 1875, again with von Alten's help, worked a carriage service from Jaffa to Jerusalem, which proved more successful than previous transport services organized first by Jerusalem Moslems, and then by one of the American colony's survivors, Rolla Floyd.

The Templars were still however without legal rights, existing on Turkish sufferance, and there was no evidence that Germany was behind them. The turning point came with the Russo-Turkish war of 1877/8.

For years the Templar leaders had been clamouring for German warships to patrol the coast, in order to demonstrate support for their colonies and deter attacks from the local Moslem peasantry. Berlin had steadily ignored these requests; and the consuls, mindful of correct relations with the Porte and Berlin's policy of non-intervention, did little to help them. But in the spring of 1877, on the eve of the war, two things happened: the consul in Jerusalem, von Munchausen, became increasingly nervous of what would happen to the German community in Palestine if war broke out; and a German naval officer commanding a frigate visiting the Syrian coast toured the Templar colonies and was impressed by what they had achieved.

Von Munchausen had special reason to be alarmed. The Russians, on evacuating Jerusalem, had entrusted their affairs to the German consulate, which was now obliged to fly the Russian flag as well as its own. Moreover, as invariably happened in time of war, the Turks prepared to withdraw most of their garrisons from Palestine for the front line – leaving the minority population undefended.

On Easter Monday, the corvette *Gazelle*, commanded by Count von Hacke, visited Jaffa. The count was received by Hoffman and conducted round the colony, where he saw the workshops, schools and fruit orchards; the two men co-authored Hacke's subsequent report to the German Admiralty. This spoke of the Templars having left Germany 'to bring progress to their country and humanity' (in fact many had left to avoid military service as well), reported that German exports to Palestine now ranked third after England and France, praised the Templar schools, and played down the frequent disagreements and even violence between the Germans and the local Moslems. Von Hacke suggested that the presence of a warship in the region, on an annual basis, would be beneficial to German interests. This report was passed on to the German Foreign Ministry, to join von Munchausen's despatch warning of danger to the Christian communities in general, and the Germans in particular (of whom the Templars were the most exposed), when the Turkish soldiers were withdrawn.

Russia declared war against Turkey at the end of April, and the Turkish troops were duly ordered north. Bismarck was still very cautious before committing a German naval force to the defence of the settlers. He first consulted France and England, assuring both that all he intended to do was to help protect the Christians of Palestine, as he had no political aims in the region; and only when sure of their consent, despatched a squadron of five German battleships to the Palestine coast. Throughout July the squadron, commanded by Rear Admiral Batsch, staged an awesome display of Krupp firepower in manoeuvres offshore while, as the Templar journal *Die Wärte* described it: 'The Arabs opened their eyes and mouths wide' as the *Gazelle* saluted the German colony at Haifa, all its cannon blasting away . . . 'which could so easily have turned the Moslems' town to ruins in a few seconds.'

Von Munchausen, though gratified at the appearance of the squadron, was apprehensive at the thought of using the German navy to settle the Templars' scores with the local Turkish authorities, as they wished him to do – particularly since his instructions were that the navy was not to participate in any diplomatic negotiations. Nevertheless, on 19 July, both Admiral Batsch and von Munchausen appeared at the headquarters of the governor of Acre, where they were received with unprecedented honours.

Von Munchausen raised the question of the transfer of land documents to the Templars and the recognition of Keller as German consul in Haifa – both of which were granted immediately. The Germans went to extraordinary lengths to indicate to the unfortunate governor that there was no connection at all between the battleships lying offshore and the diplomatic visit. Admiral Batsch remained silent during the interview, save for an aside to von Munchausen to end the exchange of courtesies and get to the point. Von Munchausen explained that he had merely taken advantage of the squadron's little trip up the coast – hitching a ride, as it were – to visit the governor of Acre on this occasion.

Thus the Templar tail had successfully wagged the German dog and, as they thought, advanced the cause of the 'peaceful crusade'. They expected that, at the peace treaty of 1878, Palestine would be awarded to Germany.

However, while the Templars henceforth enjoyed a measure of official support, and even some financial help, from the German government, the later rapprochement between Germany and Turkey effectively ended their hopes of a German regime in Palestine. The lesson of the affair, as in that of Finn and Beauboucher, however, was that while King Consul might rule supreme in Jerusalem, he was very much the subject of his protégés.

CHAPTER V

---•◦•---

Feudal Palestine: Akil Aga

MONDAY WAS MARKET DAY in Galilee during the mid-century. Within the half-ruined walls of the fifteenth-century Khan el Tujjar, a few miles from the foot of Mount Tabor, peasants, merchants and craftsmen gathered from both sides of the Jordan. Caravans of pack animals carrying sacks of barley, wheat, sesame and Indian corn made their way from the upland district of the Hauran, from the swampy Huleh valley, and from the nearby plain of Esdraelon. Cattle, goats and sheep were driven across the Jordan from fertile Bashan and Gilead. Bales of cotton were brought down the winding mountain tracks from Nablus. Local pedlars, tailors, farriers and saddlers set out their stock, and cobblers offered everything from rough hairy sandals to yellow and red moroccan boots.

Well before dark, however, the market was dismantled; merchants and craftsmen took shelter in Nazareth, up in the hills nearby, and the peasants returned to the villages behind their stockades of prickly pear. For every trodden path converging on the Khan was dangerous.

In the east, across the Jordan, lived the three great Bedouin federations which terrorized Palestine: the Aneze in the north, the Bene Sakhr southeast of the Sea of Galilee, and the Adwan to the south. Beyond Tiberias, the banks of the lake, surrounded by treeless hills, were almost unpopulated. The Jordan valley, with its rich volcanic soil, was deserted save for a few poor villages and a handful of semi-nomadic tribes, beekeepers whose clay hovels were scarcely higher than the heaps of manure deposited by their animals. Wild boars roamed the wadis linking east and west and scavenger dogs policed the villages. From the Jordan, south of the lake, to the foothills of the Carmel range to the west – beyond which lay Acre and the sea – stretched the plain of Esdraelon, eight hours' ride on horseback, where the crops grew high but without a single village in sight. The peasants travelled miles to sow and to harvest, muskets on their shoulders, but when hostile tribes or bandits were rumoured to be near, especially in the summer when the Bedouin were short of fodder for their horses and camels, they let the crops rot unreaped, to be pillaged or trodden beneath the feet of the Bedouin's horses.

Nazareth, in the hills, was somewhat more secure, with clusters of villages, both Moslem and Christian, in the country around it – a town of mosques, and fortified churches. On the ridge of hills between Nazareth and the Sea of Galilee lay a saddle of land with twin pommels, remnant of an extinct volcano, known as the Horns of Hittin: at its base the site of Nebi Shueb, or Jethro's Tomb, sacred to the Druse.

All this territory was the stamping ground of an extraordinary Bedouin chief, Akil el Hasi, who first came to the attention of the West as Lynch's escort on his journey down the Jordan. Akil's black tents might be pitched between Shfar'am and Nazareth, on Mount Tabor, or in the Jordan valley south of the lake. When he was further off, the entire region was at risk from the tribes across the Jordan or from local bandits. His women took precedence at village wells; townspeople sought his friendship, and villagers paid for his protection; his name alone was allegedly enough to deter marauders. From the mid-century, for twenty years, the story of his exploits was told in consular despatches, travellers' memoirs and missionary chronicles, for he was chief protector of the Christians and the Jews of northern Palestine, whose plains and valleys he regarded as his own territory, in the manner of a feudal chieftain, for a period of nearly thirty years. In his youth the head of a band of horsemen from his own tribe, he was said in his prime to be able to call on up to three thousand horsemen from among allies he made among the Bedouin east of the Jordan.

But his power was neither absolute nor constant. He was alternately a mercenary in Turkish service, and a rebel against

Above left: The Moabite Stone. This inscription, discovered in Bedouin territory east of the Jordan in 1867, was the only corroboration in writing of the history of the Holy Land as related in the Old Testament. The stone was reconstructed from many fragments, as the Bedouin, convinced by Western interest that it contained treasure, had smashed it to pieces.

Above right: One of the 'Moabite potteries', forgeries which deceived Prussian scholars and the amateur archaeologists of the Palestine Exploration Fund. They were recognized as fakes by the great French epigrapher Clermont-Ganneau, who perceived that their lettering was 'palaeographic nonsense and philologically untranslatable'.

Below: The sarcophagus of Queen Saddam (Helena of Adiabene), a first-century convert to Judaism. The antiquarian Félicien de Saulcy, who discovered the sarcophagus, assumed it to be that of King David's sister, Seruya, but pretended to the Jerusalem Jews that it was a Roman relic.

Above left: 'Sir Moses Montefiore' by Salomon Alexander Hunt (1846). Montefiore visited Palestine seven times between 1827 and 1875. He was a major link between the poor and orthodox Jews of Palestine and the emancipated Jews of the West.

Above right: Ashkenazi Jews, by the Palestine Exploration Fund photographer Sergeant H. Philipps. This photograph is probably inauthentic for several reasons. It exists in two versions, in which the models have exchanged hats and kaftans. The striped kaftans here indicate that the men were married students of Kabbala; in the other version, they wear different clothes. The models may have been 'enquirers' or prospective converts from the Anglican Mission.

Below: Jews at the Western (Wailing) Wall by Adrien Bonfils. This photograph – unlike many others – appears to have been taken behind the Jews' backs, and unposed, so it is probably authentic.

Turkish authority. His survival depended on his ability to exploit Turkish weakness, foreign ambitions, and Bedouin greed, with equal facility.

*   *   *

Before the Crimean War, some sources estimate that of just under a thousand Turkish troops stationed in Palestine, only about a hundred and sixty were at the disposal of the governors to police the countryside. The Jordan valley and the Galilee were wide open to the tribes, who pillaged the peasants both from necessity and for sport, robbed caravans and stripped travellers, and were even called in as reinforcements to fight in the private wars of the clan leaders in the hill towns of Mount Nablus. The minorities in the Galilee, Christians and Jews, many of whom were protégés of foreign powers, lived in Nazareth, Safed and Tiberias, and in villages near them. They were equally remote from Jerusalem and from Beirut, strongholds of the foreign consuls. The governor of Acre, nearest in time of trouble and nominally responsible for their welfare, did little to protect them.

The system the Turks adopted in order to control both the sheikhs in the mountain towns and the Bedouin was to incite one clan against the other, or to use 'irregular cavalry', mercenaries drawn from the Kurdish or Druse communities in the north, or the Egyptian Bedouin in the south. In theory the foreign consuls deplored this system; but in the south of the country they went along with it, and dealt regularly with the predators themselves. James Finn employed Bedouin sheikhs from 1845 to protect European travellers on the dangerous route to the Dead Sea. He was frank about these negotiations in his reports; even more revealing is the account provided by Holman-Hunt in a private letter, describing Finn's reaction to Hunt's harassment by Bedouin in the Dead Sea area in August 1854. Finn told Hunt that he himself would not have gone to the Pasha for redress, but to the tribe of Arabs (Bedouin) with whom he made 'treaties' for the Dead Sea and Edom travels (to Petra). These, at his bidding, 'would have fired the village and murdered right and left'.

French envoys and consuls consistently bribed the sheikhs of Abu Ghosh, who had terrorized and blackmailed all other travellers throughout the first half of the century. Both Chateau-briand and Lamartine – who held confidential talks with their chieftain during his visit in 1836 – openly boasted of the special relationship between the bandit sheikh and France, and in 1844 the first French consul, Lantivy, reporting that Jerusalem was protected only by 'twenty men with fixed cannons', said that only French influence and 'some gifts made at the right time' prevented the powerful Abu Ghosh chief from taking the city as his own. So certain was this clan of French support that in 1846, when the incumbent sheikh was accused of the murder of Turkish officials in Jaffa and Ramle, he assumed – wrongly this time – that he could count on French protection to avoid arrest and punishment by the authorities.

In the Galilee, however, there was no local sheikh upon whom the Europeans could depend to protect their interests. It was this vacuum that Akil el Hasi exploited so effectively.

* * *

Akil el Hasi was the second son of a Bedouin chieftain from the Nile delta, Musa el Hasi of the Henadi tribe, who had ridden north in the early years of the century to serve the governor of Acre as head of a band of irregular cavalry. The connection between the governors of Acre and the Henadi went back to the end of the preceding century, when Djezzar, 'the butcher of Acre', had served in Egypt with the Mameluke Beys. After Djezzar's death in 1808, the Henadi continued to serve his successors, Suleiman and Abdulla. In 1814, Musa el Hasi was put in charge of the southernmost area under Acre's control, Gaza, where he and a force of fifty horsemen patrolled the desert approaches of Palestine against the incursion of other Bedouin from Sinai.

Musa el Hasi had married a woman from a Turkoman tribe and had three sons: Ali – of whom nothing is known – Akil and Salih. Musa died in 1826, leaving his horsemen and his large flocks of goats and sheep in charge of Akil. Five years later, when Ibrahim Pasha invaded Palestine, numbers of Egyptian Bedouin rode with him, including the main body of the Henadi tribe from which Akil was descended. Henri Cornille, a French traveller in

Palestine at the time of Ibrahim's siege of Acre, and temporarily a captive of the besiegers, saw how Bedouin troops – perhaps the Henadi – formed the spearhead of the Egyptian assault force in the first, reckless and unsuccessful attack on the city. The Bedouin gave warning of their attack with resounding war cries, alerting the city's defenders, and were cut down by the Turks' cannon. Cornille watched them brought back, mutilated and dying, crying out that they had been defeated not by men, but by evil female spirits flying through the air.

It was during this siege that Akil quarrelled with his patron, Abdulla of Acre, and went over to Ibrahim's side. In November 1831 a force of irregular troops was sent to protect the roads and villages between Nazareth and Tiberias from Ibrahim's enemies; the Henadi appeared to have first entered the Galilee at this time, but Akil and his followers remained in Gaza, and for several years it seemed that he had thrown in his lot with the Egyptians.

The Bedouin of Palestine, however, were among those who resisted Ibrahim most strongly. In 1834 the peasants rose against Egyptian rule; Akil, whose Bedouin instincts were clearly stronger than his links with Egypt, joined the rebellion. When it failed, the Egyptians dispersed the Henadi and exiled their leaders.

When, in 1841, British and Austrian forces drove Ibrahim from Palestine, Akil was recalled to Ottoman service and appointed head of a fifty-man troop of horsemen patrolling the area around Nazareth and Mount Tabor. From this time forward, he was to regard Galilee, including Esdraelon, the Sea of Galilee and the Jordan valley, as his personal fief; and it was during this period that his links with the local Jews and Christians were established.

The notables of Nazareth, unlike the sheikhs of Mount Nablus, were not a warrior breed; they were merchants and clergy and they realized quite soon how useful the Bedouin chief could be to them. In 1845, a dispute arose among members of the Latin Church, which grew to such dimensions that the Turkish governor of Acre, Muhammed Kubrusli Pasha, decided to dismiss the community's head, Yusif Elias, and put in a candidate of his own. Elias asked Akil to intercede for him with the governor – which he did, unsuccessfully. But the community, emboldened by Akil's support, decided to challenge Kubrusli, and refused to accept Elias's dismissal. Kubrusli, infuriated by a mere Bedouin's attempt to play politics, summoned Akil and his cavalry to Acre for a formal review. When the Bedouin were lined up before him, Kubrusli told Akil that he and his men were forthwith dismissed.

Akil now proceeded to demonstrate to the Turkish authorities, on what was to be the first of many occasions, the cost of offending him or dismissing him from Ottoman service. He crossed the Jordan with his horsemen and joined the notorious Bene Sakhr Bedouin. For two years, Bene Sakhr and Henadi forces terrorized the Jordan valley, pillaging and killing wherever they went. The challenge to Ottoman authority was so flagrant that Kubrusli, one of the ablest of Turkish administrators, was forced to take notice. In 1847, he summoned Akil to Acre under pledge of safe conduct and asked him to explain the behaviour of his men.

Akil replied that the Henadi were neither merchants nor farmers. Their only skill was fighting, and if they were not employed by the Pasha they had no choice but to revert to the Bedouin way of life as raiders in order to survive.

Kubrusli accepted – or pretended to accept – Akil's argument; it was far safer to have the man in his service than at large. He appointed him Aga, or Turkish chieftain, at the head of a force of seventy-five horsemen. Henceforth, Akil patrolled the countryside he had so recently savaged, keeping other Bedouin at bay. But this did not mean that his alliance with the Bene Sakhr ended; he did all he could, in fact, to reinforce it, marrying the daughter of one of their sheikhs. Later events show that he was able to use the threat of Turkish retribution as skilfully against the Bene Sakhr as he used the Bene Sakhr – and thousands of their armed horsemen – against the Turks.

By this time, Akil Aga was a local legend. It was Lynch's expedition to the Jordan, and his account of the man himself, which was to make Akil famous in the West.

Lynch met Akil under the roof of Kubrusli's successor, Sa'id Bey, shortly after the Americans landed in Haifa.

Around the room were many officers, and there were a number of attendants passing to and fro bearing pipes and coffee to every newcomer. But what especially attracted my attention was a magnificent savage enveloped in a scarlet cloth pelisse richly embroidered with gold. He was the handsomest, and I soon thought also the most graceful, being I had ever seen. His complexion was of a rich mellow indescribably olive tint, and his hair a glossy black; his teeth were regular and of the whitest ivory, and the glance of his eye was keen at times, but generally soft and lustrous. With the tarboosh upon his head which he seemed to wear uneasily, he reclined, rather than sat upon the opposite side of the divan, while his hand played in unconscious familiarity with the hilt of his yataghan. He looked like one who would be 'steel amid the din of arms/And wax when with the fair'.

*   *   *

It was not long before Lynch learned that his handsome escort had been until recently little better than an outlaw. But the moral categories the lieutenant applied to Europe and Turkey (he deplored European decadence and Nelson's 'dalliance' with Lady Hamilton) obviously did not apply to the Bedouin.

> Looking at his fine face, almost effeminate in its regularity of feature, who would imagine that he had ever been the stern leader of revolt, and that his laughing careless eye had ever glanced from his stronghold in the hill upon the Pasha's troops in the plain, meditating slaughter in their ranks and booty from the routed Turk; or searched the ravines and the hillsides . . . for the lurking fellahin and their herds?

Akil, Lynch concluded, belonged to a different age; he was a medieval robber baron. Akil described to him the division of the spoils among the tribes, and Lynch witnessed a *sulha* or peace ceremony between Akil and a rival sheikh whose herds and horses he had carried off during the raids of 1847. Lynch also saw Akil as a 'cattle rustler', making off with a young camel which had strayed from a nearby tribe; and at one village, 'an Arab woman screamed out and wept bitterly at the sight of Akil. In him she recognized the murderer of her husband, in a foray the previous year.' Like all Bedouin, Lynch noted, Akil despised the fellahin, and when Lynch told him 'that many of our most

147

eminent men were tillers of the ground, his smile was more of a contemptuous one than we had ever seen upon his handsome features'.

Near the Dead Sea, Akil was wounded keeping an Adwan force away from Lynch's party; 'a genuine barbarian, he never sleeps beneath the frail covering of a tent . . . ever found at night slumbering, not sleeping, near the watch fire, his yataghan by his side, his heavy-mounted, wide-mouthed pistols beneath his head'.

Lynch did not specify in his narrative how much he actually paid Akil for his services, but he indicated that Akil had more in mind, when offering them, than money. Towards the end of their journey together, Akil dropped a number of hints in order to discover whether the Americans 'would aid an association of the tribes in an avowed object'. Lynch concluded that Akil contemplated a Bedouin uprising 'for the purpose of throwing off the thraldom, here almost nominal, of the Turkish yoke . . . and establishing a sovereignty for himself . . . he might hope that if we were involved our country would sustain us'. But Lynch was sceptical as to whether Akil could in fact unite the Bedouin, but even more aware that he would be sharply criticized 'if we became voluntarily embroiled either with the tribes or the Turkish government'. Nevertheless, Lynch concluded, 'Their God is gold, and fifty well-armed, resolute Franks, with a large sum of money, could revolutionise the whole country.' Later travellers were to assume the same was true of the Arabs of the Hejaz.

Lynch's book was published in 1848, and it could only have reinforced suspicions at the Porte that their hired troops in the Galilee could easily get out of hand. During the next few years, at all events, the Turkish governors in Syria made repeated efforts to put an end to Akil.

During a Druse rebellion in 1852, Kubrusli became military commander, or Serasker, of Syria; he first sent Akil north to the Hauran to put down the rebels and later ordered him to keep open a road along which a Turkish ammunition convoy was to pass, and which the Aneze Bedouin had under ambush. But Akil returned from both these missions triumphant and unharmed.

He knew Kubrusli was still hostile to him, and was careful to keep within his own territory and on no account to enter the Turkish stronghold at Acre unless he was provided with a safe conduct. In 1853, however, he was tricked into coming to Acre by the offer of a fake firman supposedly sent by the Sultan himself. No sooner had he entered the town when he was seized by Turkish soldiers, put in chains, and sent by ship from there to Constantinople. The Turkish authorities accused him of complicity with the Druse and decided to exile him to the fortress of Widdin in Bulgaria, where they no doubt believed him sufficiently remote from Palestine and his followers.

Meanwhile, the Crimean War had broken out, and all available troops were withdrawn from Syria. Kubrusli Pasha, too, was recalled to Turkey. Akil succeeded in escaping from Widdin after no more than six months' imprisonment.

According to Arab historians, he had travelled on the same ship to Constantinople as the Latin Patriarch of Jerusalem, Valerga, who, knowing of his friendship with the Christians of Galilee, lent him money which enabled him to buy false papers in Bulgaria. According to the British consul in Beirut, he escaped from the fortress disguised as a Greek monk. At all events, by the beginning of 1854 he had returned to Palestine – on foot, some said.

At this stage of Akil's career his name began to appear in the consular records of both England and France.

During the Crimean War, Consul Finn was disturbed by the threat of local hostility to the Jews both in Judea and in Galilee, as well as by Bedouin encroachments everywhere. Among the Bedouin tribes who began once more filtering through into Palestine from the south was Salameh el Tawahi, a Bedouin who while serving as a tax farmer to the Khedive of Egypt had allegedly stolen large sums of money. The governor of Jerusalem maintained that he had no knowledge of Tawahi's presence in Palestine, but on one of Finn's tours of inspection near Gaza – where he hoped to recover property stolen from British travellers by Bedouin – his kavass recognized Tawahi, with a large force of followers.

Tawahi came from a tribe related to the Henadi, and moving

north, he joined up with Akil. Together, they now constituted a formidable threat to the governor of Acre. Finn reported from Jerusalem that 'the most serious aspect of recent disturbances in the north ... in which the very name of Government was laughed to scorn, was that a rebel force of considerable amount is assembled in or near Nazareth, headed by Akil Aga, a chief of some notoriety who escaped lately from exile to which he had been sent for suspected assistance to the Druses'. Akil and Tawahi, Finn went on, 'have recently sent repeated messages of defiance and threats to the Pasha of Acre. So serious a state of the country has not occurred since the restoration of the Sultan's authority in 1840.'

Finn sent his 'most faithful Kavass' through the hills (where the sheikhs were once more at one another's throats) to the rebel leaders' encampment in the Galilee, warning them that he knew of their conduct, and reminding them that the Turks 'had most powerful nations as allies'. To the Foreign Office, Finn explained that 'in these days I conceive myself warranted in taking steps which at other times would be useless'. There was no Pasha nearer than Beirut who could take effective action, he added, the 'feeble personnage' in Acre being unable to deal with the situation.

Finn clearly thought that he was dealing with one more Bedouin sheikh to whom he could read the riot act. But Akil, for the second time, had glimpsed the chance of finding a Western patron, and he responded quickly. Finn's kavass, who had found Akil and Tawahi camped near the Horns of Hittin, returned 'bearing a long letter from each sheikh, signed with the impress of their signet rings', explaining and justifying their conduct. Akil argued that he was no rebel, but that all his property had been seized during his imprisonment, and his arms sold to the Abd'El Hady family of Nablus, whom he accused of responsibility for his exile to Widdin. Tawahi argued that he had left Egypt because of persecution by the Khedive, who had imprisoned his sons.

Finn believed neither of them, but was gratified by the conciliatory tone of the chieftain's letters. Akil did more to convince Finn of his good intentions. He promised to guard all the district now once more under his influence, including the towns of Safed and Tiberias, 'on account of the English-protected people living in them'. According to the information Finn received subsequently from his agents in the north, Akil also countermanded a 'marauding expedition' he had planned, and sent letters everywhere informing the local sheikhs of his promises to the English consul. He even tried to placate the Turks, by sending his brother Salih to fight in the Crimean War. Salih was later to divert many European travellers by describing how he had commanded five hundred Bedouin fighting on the banks of the Danube.

Akil now set up a system of alliances which would not have shamed a European politician. As soon as he had concluded his arrangement with Finn, he presented himself to the nearest British vice-consul, Rogers, in Haifa, and promised obedience to the Ottoman government if he could be restored to favour by English mediation; he then went to the clergyman of the Church Missionary Society in Nazareth, Pastor Zeller, and asked for a certificate declaring him to be a Protestant. How Zeller managed to deal with this request is not recorded; but henceforth Zeller was to be one of Akil's most assiduous chroniclers, as well as providing liaison between the Bedouin and Western travellers concerned with safe passage through northern Palestine.

Soon afterwards, Akil sent word to the French consul in Acre that he was actually of North African origin (France had recently consolidated its conquest of Algeria), and thus owed allegiance to the French. In the French diplomatic despatches he was henceforth referred to as 'a Bedouin of the Barbary States'. The French consul promised Akil his help, and personally escorted him to Beirut. There he met the French consul-general de Lesseps, whom he impressed with his determination to protect the Christian population of Galilee. De Lesseps forthwith interceded on Akil's behalf with the Turkish governor of Beirut, and pledged his word for the Bedouin's future good behaviour.

Akil was promptly reinstated in Ottoman service for the fourth time, given command of two hundred horsemen, and returned to his encampment. He was now in favour with both the British and the French and responsible for the safety of the entire non-Moslem population of the Galilee; moreover, he had once more forced the Turks to recognize his supremacy in northern Palestine.

He had not, however, forgotten his alliance with the Bedouin across the Jordan. Immediately on his return to the Galilee, Akil rode off to join the Bene Sakhr at Samakh, at the southern end of the Sea of Galilee, and personally guided the tribesmen across the plain of Esdraelon to attack a village in the hills not far from Nablus — the Bene Sakhr having contracted, as frequently happened, to intervene on behalf of one of Nablus' warring clans. In this case, it was that of Abd'El Hady, of whom Akil had so recently complained to Finn.

Finn had word of this fresh outrage, but this time decided to turn a blind eye to Akil's escapade as long as his personal agreement with Akil still held. 'Meanwhile, having the whole of Uppcr Galilee absolutely at his disposal,' Finn wrote to the Foreign Secretary, 'he abstains from doing the least injury on the Jews or the other inhabitants of Safed and Tiberias because in February last he promised me to be their guardian; he seems to regard the district north of Tabor as his home, and that south of Tabor as a foreign land.'

This was true enough. Two years later, the head of the Abd'El Hady clan rather rashly decided to extend his operations to Akil's territory, and led his men into the Esdraelon plain, where Akil and Salih were collecting taxes for the governor of Acre. This time, Akil warned the Nablus sheikh that he was out of his own territory; when Abd'El Hady refused to retreat, he was beaten back into the hills.

While the consuls were content with their arrangement, the Turks, not unreasonably, still regarded Akil as a menace. It was only under pressure from the French that Wameck Pasha, the Turkish governor in Beirut who had exiled Akil to Widdin in 1853, had reluctantly accorded him a formal pardon. Wameck could not break his agreement with France; but on his return from a term of service in Damascus, he evolved a plan to rid the Turks of Akil for good. This time, he used the stratagem of calling in another, and formidable, militia — that of the Kurdish chieftain Sa'id Aga Chamdin, who had served Wameck in Damascus.

Chamdin was appointed military governor of Tiberias, in the heart of Akil's territory. One spring morning, Akil discovered Kurdish soldiers feeding their horses on the pastureland leading down to the Sea of Galilee. Akil accused the Kurdish chief of trespassing on his territory. Chamdin produced the official papers he had received from Constantinople.

What happened next became a legend in the north of Palestine, the story of a great battle passed down from father to son in the villages and also, as it happened, reported in detail by the consuls. On 30 March 1857, a rainy, misty evening, Bedouin and Kurdish troops faced one another on the plateau between the Horns of Hittin, high above Tiberias and the Sea of Galilee. Akil's horsemen were outnumbered by at least two to one, though he had called in his allies from among the Bene Sakhr; the Kurdish force numbered about seven hundred. The Kurdish troops were armed with matchlocks, the rifles ignited by striking a spark on the charge of gunpowder in their chambers; the Bene Sakhr had only swords and spears.

But the Kurdish soldiers had only recently marched hundreds of miles from the north, and were in strange territory, while Akil was on his home ground. In the damp air the gunpowder in the matchlocks failed to ignite; yet at first the Kurds' superior numbers told and Akil's force began to fall back. But Akil had held Salih and his followers in reserve, and as the Kurds pressed forward, confident of victory, Salih attacked them, killing Sa'id Chamdin's brother, and the son of the governor of Jenin, a town with which the Kurds had friendly relations. With two of their leaders killed, the Kurds panicked and fled. Some retreated to the Druse sanctuary of Nebi Shueb; local legend had it that those who actually took refuge in the sanctuary were spared at Akil's shouted order. But the fact that the Kurdish dead were reported as strewn over a wide area 'from Tabor to Tiberias' suggests that Akil's men pursued every fugitive and killed every man they found.

Finn's account described thirty killed on Akil's side, and between 100 and 180 among the Kurds; and travellers reaching Jerusalem shortly afterwards spoke of seeing vultures feeding on the Kurdish corpses for two days before the local peasants dared to bury them.

Both the French and British consuls deplored Wameck's provocation of Akil. De Lesseps saw the hand of Britain in the affair; he thought Wameck 'in order to please the English' had tried to get rid of Akil, 'the only person to assure the safety of our traders, our pilgrims and our religious establishments in Mount Carmel, Nazareth and Tiberias, this vast region where the Sultan's authority is but nominal'. Moore, de Lesseps's opposite number in Beirut, commented: 'Wameck Pasha's chief ability seems to have consisted in setting one party against the other and thereby introducing a state of general insecurity and lowering the dignity of the government.'

Despite Finn's fears that the defeat of the Kurds would be a signal for widespread fighting between their allies in the north and the Bedouin, the battle of Hittin confirmed Akil's power. The Turks made no further effort, for the next seven years, to remove him by force.

*   *   *

Akil now boasted that he had both the English and the French in his pocket. When Finn visited him, on a tour of inspection in the Jordan valley, he told the consul that 'he was now styled a Frenchman in Turkish service'; he ostentatiously broke the fast of Ramadan by eating and drinking, 'while he laughed at those fools of Mohammedans around him'.

He was now in the position to set whatever price he liked on his services. Finn reported that 'the English-protected people of Tiberias, all Jews, are wellwishers to the cause of Akil Aga from fear – he having of late years protected them in their farming of taxes on receipt of a share in their gains' – and from now on he became as celebrated a businessman as he was a soldier, taking protection money from all the villages in his territory. In this task he had an unusual ally: a Hassidic Jew from Tiberias.

From the 1830s onwards, a strange figure on horseback could be seen galloping back and forth between Tiberias and Jis'r, a Moslem village about ten miles south of the Sea of Galilee. Tall and thin, with spiralling earlocks peeping from beneath his fur-trimmed Jewish *streimel*, dressed in a long black Polish kaftan and slippers, he rode a thoroughbred Arab mare and was armed with a Turkish sabre, a brace of pistols and a Bedouin dagger. In the panniers slung across his horse's back he carried the goods he peddled to the peasants and Bedouin of the region: bolts of Damascus cloth, tobacco, and sugar cane for the children.

Reb Leibkes Toister (nicknamed Konstantinover from his home town in Russia) was a member of the distinguished Karlin Hassidic sect. His family had arrived in Tiberias in the early years of the century, part of the migration of orthodox Ashkenazi Jews from Eastern Europe. While most Jews were suspicious of their Moslem neighbours and terrified of the 'wild Ishmaelites', Reb Leibkes had played in the streets of Tiberias with Moslem children and spoke fluent Arabic; his imposing height, and his fearlessness, enabled him to travel freely through the Arab villages, at a time when most Jews saw the Bedouin as a local version of the Cossacks who had terrorized the Jewish villages of Russia.

According to Jewish oral tradition, Toister, known as Abu Zalmania (father of Zalman, his eldest son) to the Moslems, served Akil as tax farmer for a number of years; he also helped the Bedouin defend those villages under Akil's protection from marauders. Among the Jews he was known as Akil Aga's 'finance minister'; by the time of Tristram's visit to Palestine in 1863, he had been replaced by a Christian 'secretary'.

Akil also extended his territory westwards to the Carmel range when, as Tristram noted, members of 'a notorious village in the plain of Esdraelon, plundered and drove out the people of seventeen villages in Carmel till but three, and those Druse and Christian, have been left in the whole district. These, fearing the same fate, sent a deputation not to their own governor, the Pasha of Acre, but to the Agha, and offered to pay him tribute for his protection, since which time they have remained unmolested.'

Akil was now prosperous. In 1848, Lynch had portrayed the tribe feeding on 'a primitive mixture of flour, river water and rancid butter' cooked in a huge kettle stirred with driftwood, which the Bedouin scooped out in the hollow of their hands. The missionary Thomson, who visited Akil frequently, described a visit to Akil's encampment in Esdraelon a few years later very differently: 'A sheep or calf will be brought and killed before you, thrust instanter into the great cauldron which stands ready on the fire to receive it, and, ere you are aware, it will reappear on a great copper tray, with a bushel of burghul or a hill of boiled rice and leben.' And for a mascot, Akil had acquired a tame predator: a panther trained to hunt gazelles, prowling, half invisible, in the grass and stubble.

*   *   *

Towards the end of the 1850s the Henadi were at the height of their fame. Eliza Rogers, sister of the British consul in Haifa, called Akil and Salih 'the most powerful and formidable people in the Pashalik of Acre, with between three and four thousand armed horsemen under their command', a 'tolerated tribe of marauders' thanks to whose energy highway robbery and murders were rare. In local Arab tradition, Salih was a ferocious womanizer, who thought nothing of taking village women as his tribute unless called to order by Akil, but Miss Rogers heard nothing of this. When she visited Salih's tents near Haifa, he entertained her with a show of wresting, gazelle hunts, with his small son mounted on a horse 'whose pedigree went back to Solomon'. Salih expressed amazement at Miss Rogers's tiny handwriting, and he allowed himself to be sketched: 'his eyelids were kohl tinged, and he looked rather fierce, on the whole.'

In 1859, the Orientalist painter Carl Haag travelled up to Palestine from Cairo. The main purpose of his journey was to paint the famous Bedouin chieftain and his tribe, but he encountered many obstacles. Akil was not easy to locate; because of his poor relations with the Turkish authorities, he had left the tribe's encampment and stayed at a different town or village every night. It was only due to the help of Tanuus Qiwaar, a friend of Akil in Nazareth, that Haag was able to trace Akil to Salih's home at Iblin, a village between Nazareth and Haifa. There Akil sat to Haag for a portrait; but when Haag wished to continue painting on the following day, Akil became impatient and refused to pose in the same attitude as before. Haag was able only to paint Akil's head; the figure and dress were completed only later, from a model.

In 1860, Akil faced his greatest challenge. In that year, the suppressed hatred of the Christians among the Moslems of northern Syria was released in an outbreak of violence which shook the Levant and threatened to endanger the agreement by which the European powers had undertaken not to overturn Turkish rule. For over fifteen years, the French and English had been intriguing against one another in Syria: France on behalf of the Maronite Christians of Mount Lebanon, Britain with the mountain Druse. In 1859 Druse and Maronite rivalries led to armed clashes, and by May 1860 the situation in northern Syria was one of civil war.

The reforms which had given the Christian subjects of the Porte equal rights with the Moslems had never been willingly accepted, and the fact that so many of the Christians in the cities were merchants who profited from the Capitulations, or were privileged protégés of the consulates, exacerbated the resentment. Moslems killed Christians all over northern Syria and in the provincial capital of Damascus. British estimates were of a hundred and fifty Christian villages burned, five hundred killed in the fighting, and between five and six thousand massacred by the Druse. Even before the notorious slaughter of Christians in Damascus, which took place on 9 July 1860, there were indications that the Shiite or Metawali Moslems were joining the Druse and that the conflict might spread south into Palestine.

On 12 June, the vice-consul of France in Haifa reported that near Safed and the plain of Acre, Metawali Moslems and Druse had razed three villages to the ground, and that Haifa itself was threatened, left without a single soldier to defend it. Though the governor of Acre was rounding up a small force, the vice-consul feared that it would be unable to halt the 'homicidal masses'.

There was bad news from Nazareth, the French report went on: 'Akil Aga has announced to the townspeople that they cannot count on him, as he will be busy elsewhere. Whether or not this counts as a defection, the situation is critical.' A few days later, on 19 June, consul Finn reported that 'native Christians all through the country experience some degree of apprehension from the Moslems', though, in his view, the worst thing for them to do was to show their fears.

It was Finn who indicated the nature of Akil's business elsewhere. The real threat in Palestine was not from the native Moslems, but from a huge, locust-like invasion of Bedouin. According to Finn, six thousand Bene Sakhr had crossed into Tiberias, where they were 'levying a heavy tribute . . . and consuming the wheat and barley of the neighbourhood'. The mills which served Tiberias, powered by springs on the north shore of the lake a few miles outside the town, were unprotected, and Finn wrote that the Jews of Tiberias were threatened with famine, since 'these Arabs have stopped all communication between the town and the mills, and threaten, when they have finished with Tiberias, to advance further into the country.'

No Turkish troops were at hand. But, Finn added, 'to meet these Arabs, Akil Aga has received reinforcements from Gaza, and with these he promises to attack them.' The most dangerous enemy the country faced was a huge force with ties to some of Akil's allies.

This was one reason why Akil apparently did not risk open conflict and was at first unprepared to commit himself; another was that he was heavily outnumbered. The French estimated that at this time he could summon, at the most, two thousand horsemen. According to a local Arab historian, he warned the Nazarenes, through the Nazareth Christian, Tanuus Qiwaar, that the Bene Sakhr were advancing, and the Christian and the Moslem notables of the town prepared to defend the town together. Meanwhile, Akil parleyed, as it later emerged, with his fellow Bedouin.

The European powers began slowly to move into action. On 6 July, the French government proposed to send an international commission to Syria, but widespread suspicion of French motives held up the expedition. While the West hesitated, the worst massacres took place in Syria, and it was not until August that the first detachment of a twelve-thousand-strong international force, half of which was French, was sent to the Lebanon on the understanding that the occupation would last no more than six months and that its sole purpose was to restore order.

The danger to the Christians of Palestine lasted, therefore, from the middle of June through most of July, during which time the only sign of European interest was the presence of French and

Russian battleships cruising offshore. During those weeks, according to Count Bentivoglio, the French consul-general in Beirut, only Akil Aga protected the Christians of Galilee. 'The plot was ready, and only awaited the cooperation of Akil Aga to be put into effect. This brave Bedouin not only refused formally to associate himself with all action against the Christians, but told the more fanatical Moslems of Acre, of Chafamer [the town of Shfar'am] and the Bene Sakhr Arabs that whoever moved against the Christians would have Akil Aga to reckon with.' What appears to have happened was that the 'fanatical Moslems' were not numerous enough to act on their own; with the Bene Sakhr, pillaging the villages, behind them, they might have constituted a serious threat. Akil prevented this from happening, and according to the French report did so entirely by argument. He may have demonstrated his relations with the foreign powers and the terrible vengeance they would take if any harm came to the Christians. For during this period Akil was in constant contact with the French and English consular representatives in Haifa, Acre and Beirut.

He was also doing very well out of his new position as the only defender standing between the minorities and their enemies. On 2 August, Finn reported that 'in Northern Palestine, the country is kept quiet by . . . Akili Aga, who is making considerable gain by affording protection to Christians and Jews'. Later in the month, Finn's envoy, Peter Meshullam, visited Akil and urged him to keep up the good work; the message he carried from Finn was that 'in a short while he will be very glad that he had protected the Christians and the Jews, as he will soon hear how those who had injured the aforesaid will be punished'. On 16 August, the French expeditionary force landed in Beirut, and with thousands of foreign soldiers only a short march away, the threat was lifted. On 27 August, the captain of the British frigate HMS *Firefly*, which stood off Haifa for eleven days, made an official visit, with Rogers, to Akil's encampment.

The Turks punished the offenders in northern Syria savagely. Fuad Pasha, the Turkish Grand Vizier, was sent to Damascus by the Sultan to restore order and handle relations with the French. But he was in no mood to reward Akil, despite French

representations to the Porte and a personal appeal by Bentivoglio.

The French ambassador to Turkey obtained an assurance from
the Porte that Akil would be rewarded 'as he deserved', but Fuad
Pasha 'turned a deaf ear' to Bentivoglio's embassy. Later,
however, the French consul heard that Fuad Pasha had sent Akil
a letter, and a pair of cheap pistols. This was not considered
adequate recompense by the French, and Bentivoglio renewed his
requests to the French foreign minister, Thouvenel, for a sign of
recognition of the Bedouin's outstanding services; in due course a
jewelled sword arrived from Paris, with instructions that it be
formally presented to Akil as a sign of the Emperor's recognition
of his 'honourable conduct'. When the Turkish governor of
Beirut heard the news, he asked to be allowed to present the gift.
But Bentivoglio refused, insisting that the entire populace,
Christian and Moslem alike, should witness the public honour
conferred by France on a defender of Christians.

Accompanied by several army and navy officers, and preceded
by the flag from a French warship, Bentivoglio took the sword,
and a pair of pistols (superior no doubt to those of the Turks) to
Akil's encampment at the foot of Mount Tabor. Akil rode out to
meet the consul, dismounted, and led him into the encampment
grasping the consul's horse by the bridle. A great crowd gathered.
'From every side of the plain we were crossing, more Bedouin
appeared, running to see the gift of the Great Sultan of the
French,' Bentivoglio reported. The presentation ceremony was
witnessed by a huge crowd, in total silence, and 'the news spread
rapidly throughout Syria, and to all the Bedouin of the Desert,
from Nejd to Baghdad'. 'We must hope', wrote Bentivoglio, 'that
this example will serve to encourage other chieftains to imitate
Akil Aga's example, to the great advantage of the Christian
population of this part of Syria.' Akil dictated an elaborate and
rather incoherent letter to the Emperor, which ended:

> As to myself, I, most humble slave, with all that belongs to me,
> my men and my goods, my tribe and my friends, and
> possessions of the right and left hand, offer our blood and
> unlimited devotion to the Government of His Happiness and
> are ready and willing to serve him in these territories. To this

end I take the liberty of presenting this humble petition to the Palace of his Lordship, to express to him all my thanks and profound gratitude and obedience, continually addressing to God fervent prayers for the continuation of his government in triumphs and victories and for the long life of his Imperial Happiness, crowned with glory and happiness by the Creator of men.

This document would not have pleased the Ottoman authorities.

Meanwhile, the prolonged French occupation of Syria was beginning to try the patience of the other European powers. The six-month period had officially ended in February 1861, but the French stayed on, Paris refusing to recall the soldiers until the position had stabilized. An international conference held in Paris debated a new constitution for the province of Syria, in which Mount Lebanon was to become autonomous, with a Christian governor appointed by the Porte; Turkish control was restored at the price of a new area of French influence. While the terms of the constitution were being drawn up, Thouvenel informed Bentivoglio that Akil Aga had been awarded the Légion d'honneur. A week later, he announced that France would evacuate its expeditionary force on 9 June. The presentation of the honour to Akil Aga was thus designed and carried out to make it appear that despite the French withdrawal, France was still the most important foreign influence in the Holy Land.

Fuad Pasha could not have been pleased that yet another French honour was to be conferred on the rebellious chieftain. But the French diplomats and officers again buckled on their arms and decorations and prepared for a new ceremony, this time on board a French battleship, the *Eylau*, anchored off Haifa. Invitations were sent to all the notables of the coastal towns and the agents of other powers.

On 22 June, Bentivoglio arrived from Beirut and Akil from Tabor, with an escort of five hundred horsemen. On the morning of the 23rd, the crew of the *Eylau* stood to attention on deck, as Akil was welcomed on board by the captain. Bentivoglio presented Akil with the warrant of the Légion d'honneur, a translation was read to him, and the captain of the warship handed him the cross and made him swear to continue to protect the Christians against their enemies. The crew then filed past Akil, a formal inspection in reverse. The native population, Bentivoglio reported, was impressed, and Akil and his men toured the ship 'exclaiming with surprise and admiration' at the guns and fittings. In the afternoon, the Bedouin disembarked and escorted the French officers to the convent on Mount Carmel.

Strange honours to be conferred on a Bedouin; let alone one who had so consistently challenged the authority of the legal government of Syria.

＊   ＊   ＊

The ceremony on board the *Eylau* in 1861 marked the climax of Akil's career; it also presaged his decline. Henceforth, as the next French consul in Beirut noted, 'his services to a foreign government could only increase [the Turks'] justified suspicion'. At Constantinople it was rumoured that Akil was planning a general uprising in Palestine against the Porte with French connivance. For their part, the French realized that Akil was becoming an embarrassment. At the beginning of the following year, three sheikhs appealed to the Beirut consulate asking to travel to France 'to present their respects to the Emperor'. One was Akil Aga. The French consul, Outrey, conveying the request to Paris, recommended that it be turned down, as 'his journey would have as many disadvantages for him as for us'. There is no record of what happened to Akil's panther which, as Thomson described, was sent off to France, very seasick, as the chieftain's personal present to the Emperor.

Akil was now poised uneasily between his French patrons and his Turkish masters. The French could not disown him completely; the Turks could not get rid of him without antagonizing the French. It was in both their interests that Akil should be tamed, and made to serve the Porte as part of the regular forces in Syria. But this was precisely what Akil had always avoided.

By this time, the Turks had begun to tackle the problem of discipline among the mercenary troops. Fuad Pasha was particularly concerned to bring all the Bedouin sheikhs to heel, and he sent word to Akil to visit him in Beirut as a demonstration of fealty to the Sultan. Akil refused; ever since his arrest in 1853 he had steadfastly avoided visiting the coastal towns unless in the company of Europeans. As the French noted, he trusted no Turkish promise of safe conduct. But his refusal to wait on Fuad, as the French consul Outrey commented, 'on the part of such an influential man, was not conducive to the efficient administration of the territory to the south'.

Eventually the Turks swallowed their pride and asked Outrey to persuade Akil to come to Beirut. The French consul's condition was that the Turks must formally guarantee safe conduct to and from Beirut not to Akil himself, but to the French consulate. This was agreed, and 'to the great astonishment of the entire countryside through which he passed, and of the town of Beirut', Akil duly appeared, was respectfully received, and 'regularised his position'.

The reconciliation did not last. A year later, all the mercenary troops in Syria were integrated with the Turkish army. Akil discovered that his men would be expected to wear Turkish uniform, and immediately resigned his commission. The Turks appointed a replacement. But no other Bedouin dared risk Akil's displeasure, and they were forced to reinstate him.

Akil was still as famous in Europe and America as in Palestine, and every important traveller was taken to meet him. In 1859 he had told the painter Carl Haag that he wished to visit the Queen of England and declare himself her loyal servant. In the spring of 1862, he had his only meeting with European royalty. The young Prince of Wales, Edward, sent off to Palestine by Queen Victoria after his father's death, in what was intended to be an improving experience, was accompanied by A. P. Stanley, now the leading British authority on Palestine, who stopped for a sermon in every wadi.

When the royal caravan reached Tabor, Stanley recounted Akil's life of adventures 'somewhat similar to those of David at the court of Achish', and the Prince's reception of Easter Sunday, in Akil's tent, was in Stanley's eyes one more biblical illustration. During a three-course meal, for whose inadequacies Akil repeatedly apologized 'in true Oriental style', Stanley noted the similarities between Akil's demeanour and the biblical account of patriarchal life.

It is almost needless to point out in this the familiar reminiscences of the tent of Abraham and the tent of Yael, those
two Biblical pictures of Patriarchal life. There were the en-
treaties to stay, and partake of the hospitality . . . there is the
meat from the flocks or herds 'tender and good', there is the
'cream in the lordly dish', 'the host standing by whilst the
guests did eat'. There is the wife's tent close at hand, but free
from the intrusion of strangers. There is the divan on which
the sleeper might recline, and, concluded Stanley enthusiastically, 'there is the strong peg or stake of the tent, and the
huge wooden mallet to drive it into the ground, or into the
sleeper's temples.'

The visit concluded with an exchange of gifts. The Prince of
Wales gave Akil a jewelled revolver, and Akil who 'kissed the
Prince's foot in the stirrup', offered him two mares – which the
Prince declined to accept; a curious insult to Bedouin hospitality,
perhaps regarded as prudent by his escorts, who were officially
guests of the Porte.

The royal visit was later the subject of a watercolour sketch
by Carl Haag. The visit of British royalty did not improve Akil's
relations with the Porte. For the following year, when Canon
Tristram arrived in Palestine on his zoological mission, he
learned that, on the Sultan's orders, Akil had been dismissed
from his post earlier in the year and, in order to save his life, had
taken refuge in Gaza. Once more, however, Akil's departure
was the signal for an orgy of banditry on the roads of Galilee,
and, once more, the man known throughout Palestine now as
'the ruler of Tabor' was recalled – one week before Tristram's
arrival. 'This was very good news', wrote Tristram, 'as we had
placed all our hopes for a visit to the east side of the Jordan on
him.'

By this time, visiting Akil was a little like visiting royalty.
Tristram had to await Akil's waking from sleep, and noticed that
during their conversation, Akil handed his Christian 'secretary'
his pipe in order to keep the tobacco burning; and he offered
Tristram gracious compliments on the birth of the Prince of
Wales's son. When Tristram explained his mission, Akil promised him that the presence of five of his men alone would ensure

his safety across the Jordan, though, he explained, he had no actual fighting force there. His men's ammunition was too precious to be wasted hunting animals for Tristram, but should they capture tigers, or other animals, they would naturally present them to him.

Akil's promise of safety held good, and though Tristram witnessed scenes of horror on his journey in the Dead Sea region – entire villages sacked and their inhabitants slaughtered by Bedouin raiders – he and his companions passed everywhere unharmed.

On his return journey through the Galilee, Tristram revisited Akil's tents in order to enjoy the offers of hospitality he had previously postponed. On this occasion, Akil seemed to Tristram like a landed gentleman collecting his rents: 'We were invited to dinner, but no business conversation ensued, though business was being carefully transacted, as the Aga vouchsafed one half of his face with a pleasant smile to us, and the other half with a keen glance to his secretary on the other side, who was receiving rents and counting dollars on a handkerchief at his elbow.' Though no 'business' took place between Tristram and Akil, the Englishman presented Akil with a gold watch and chain; 'this he received with a bow, and handed it to his secretary without even casting a glance at it.' Perhaps more important, to Akil, was Zeller's promise that, should Akil's men faithfully protect Tristram on his journey northwards, the 'Western powers' would intervene on his behalf at the Porte.

Even had it been in Tristram's power to ensure such intervention, it probably would have helped Akil very little. His last years proved as lawless as his first. They were recorded not in the consular records but in the pages of the earliest Hebrew newspapers to be published in the Holy Land.

*   *   *

The education of the reporters in these papers was in the bible class and Talmudic seminary, and their accounts were written in a vividly archaic style which Stanley might have admired. For the Jews, Akil was less a biblical hero or protector, however, than a tyrannical marauder from whom they bought protection, and from fear of whom they begged the help of more powerful Jews outside Palestine.

According to these sources, in 1864, the year after Tristram's first visit, Akil was captured by the soldiers of the governor of Beirut, manacled, and thrown into prison. There is no record of intervention by the French. Hearing of the arrest of their 'protector', the Jews of Tiberias sent an urgent plea for his release to the most powerful Jew in Syria at that time – Shemayahu Angel, a Turkish banker and merchant settled in Damascus since 1832. Angel, whose generosity to his own people was only matched by the financial aid he had provided to the Sultan, had been decorated personally by him for his assistance during the troubles of 1860. Angel now intervened with the Sultan on Akil's behalf, and Akil allegedly promised obedience to his officials thereupon.

Shortly after his release, however, the governor of Acre, Kabouli Pasha, demanded a share in the protection money Akil was collecting for himself in Galilee. Akil refused; and henceforth, according to the Jewish sources, he reverted to his old habits as an outlaw. In January 1865, the Hebrew paper *HaLevanon* reported that despite his promises to Angel, Akil was at the head of Bedouin robbing travellers on the roads between Nablus and Tiberias. The governor sent troops against him, who failed to track him down. In June, David Ze'ev Sofer, the paper's correspondent in Safed, reported that Akil's brother Salih, at the head of twelve hundred horsemen, was terrorizing the Mount Nablus area, confiscating the local peasants' firearms and stealing their flocks. This, together with a new plague of locusts, had caused a sudden rise in the price of food, and 'the people's countenance is darkened like unto the edges of a cauldron on the fire'.

In July 1865, *HaMevaser*, a Hebrew paper published in Lemberg, an Austrian frontier town and important Jewish centre, published a report from Sofer which they claimed was a journalistic scoop 'not to be found in any other newspaper'. It ran like this:

> If ye know not, surely have ye heard, that great contention prevails throughout our land. At the head of the wild dwellers in tents, bands of robbers, rides the prince of murderers, Akil Aga, and his tribe, the Indian [sic]; their aspect is like fire, their war cry

like that of the wolves of Arabia. Cruel and merciless are they, and all are destroyers. The Arabs gather round them, numerous as the fish of the sea, riding their steeds like tigers and bearing spears and daggers. Their horses fly like eagles, they neigh like the sound of trumpets, and the war cry of their riders shakes the land.

Though the Sultan had appointed these robbers to protect the Holy Land, Sofer went on, and set thieves to catch thieves, Akil had not kept the peace after his release by the intervention of the Jews. Thus

the Sultan's order went forth to apprehend Akil Aga and all his host. And there was found a man of greater valour than Akil, Rash'el Aga, chief of the Kurdish tribes, and with him five hundred men, all valiant warriors, and with them the soldiers of the government with rifles and even with great cannon [Kanonen]. And they came unto Akil Aga to give battle with him, shouting 'Rash'el Aga and the king's army are upon thee'. And Akil took his host, the sons of Henadi, and the wild Arabs his allies and departed, and Rash'el Aga fell upon them and smote whosoever did not flee them, their tents and their flocks, their donkeys and their camels did they sack and plunder. And Akil Aga fled into the wilderness to a place called Balagah and pitched his tent there. And the Kurdish host invaded all the Jordan valley and the place of the Holy City of Tiberias and set a guard where the camp of Akil had stood.

The Kurdish force then pursued Akil across the river, and for a time it seemed that Akil's old enemies had turned the tables on him. But, Sofer reported, Akil had many allies across the Jordan, among the Bene Hassan, and together they routed the Kurds. 'On the night of the twenty-seventh of Nissan [April 1865] the Henadi fell upon the Kurds, and killed their guard, and smote all their soldiers and the dwellers in their tents, and now they boast that Rash'el Aga will fall into their hands. And may the Lord have mercy on our land, and cast out this evil from its borders.'

* * *

In the West, Akil's reputation was fading. With the replacement of romantic adventurers by steamship travellers, and renewed speculation, after 1860, as to the political future of Syria, there was less enthusiasm for the excitement of protection by a man who, biblical illustration or not, was a brigand. In the second edition of Tristram's book in 1866, many passages relating to Akil were deleted, and more details put in about Pastor Zeller and his mission centre in Nazareth. Finally the admiring portrait of Akil by Lynch was replaced by a chapter devoted to Akil Aga in a book published in 1866 by W. Hepworth Dixon, writer and traveller, editor of the *Athenaeum* and amateur criminologist.

Akil, Dixon concluded, was 'clever, daring and unprincipled'. His power was not only the result of his native cunning and 'serpentine manners' but of local anarchy and ethnic strife. Dixon accused Akil of having deliberately fomented trouble in Palestine in order to make himself indispensable. 'The charities and affinities which in Europe soften men's hearts are here unknown. Love of country and pride of race are phrases which convey no meaning to a Syrian ear. In Syria there are now no Syrians; nothing but hostile races and rival sects . . . in such a community, power lies in the strong man, not in the just law . . . when he is daring, like Akeel and Abu Ghosh, he may enlarge his power.' It was still inevitable that Dixon should compare Akil to a biblical character – but this time it was not to David. 'Such is Akil Aga; a man racy of the soil; one who has had his counterpart in every age of the history of Galilee. What Akeel is today, Judas of Gamala was in the days of Christ, and Joshua ben Sapphias [an Edomite mercenary] was in the days of Paul.'

Akil died in his tent at the Tabor encampment a year or two after this portrait appeared; the exact date of his death is unknown. He refused to the last to obey Turkish rules and regulations.

Many Bedouin sheikhs whose tribes had become semi-nomadic – as for long periods the Henadi were, despite Akil's contempt for the fellahin – laid claim to the government lands on which their flocks pastured and agreed to pay the necessary taxes. As the new land laws first passed in 1858 were slowly implemented, several sheikhs registered the lands in their own names. Akil was wealthy enough to do the same. But according to local Arab tradition, he did not. 'Wherever my horse treads, is my territory,' he was alleged to have said, and it seems unlikely that a man who refused to the end to wear Turkish livery would have allowed an Ottoman clerk to define the limits of that space.

By the time of Akil's death, the Turks enjoyed a measure of control over northern Palestine; but the territory across the Jordan and around the Dead Sea, as well as the southern deserts, remained in Bedouin hands. When Tristram paid his second visit to Palestine in 1872, with no Henadi escort, he was taken prisoner by the Sheikh of Kerak and only freed after the payment of ransom. In 1877, when war broke out between Russia and Turkey, the Tarabin Bedouin from the southern desert took advantage of the absence of Turkish troops for the last time and plundered villages as far north as Jaffa, Ramleh and Jerusalem. Akil Aga had no successors, and the Bedouin menace to the borders of Palestine ended only with the fall of the Ottoman empire.

CHAPTER VI

Popular Palestine

THE IDEA OF TAKING ordinary middle-class travellers through the Holy Land in organized groups began when two remarkable men met at a Temperance League meeting in Leicester in 1844. The meeting was addressed by James Buckingham, now in his late fifties, and chaired by the young Thomas Cook, a printer and Baptist lay preacher. Cook had recently begun to arrange excursion trips to Liverpool and London for the labourers of the Midlands, not only to Temperance meetings but to holidays at the seaside and the big cities; he was one of the first to see that the invention of railway travel meant the end of the confinement of the working class to the area around their homes. In much the same way, the newly prosperous middle classes were beginning to travel abroad; but at this stage, travel to the Levant was far beyond their pockets or their imagination.

Buckingham used his experience as a traveller to publicize temperance, contrasting the drunkenness of Christian nations with the sobriety of the Moslem countries, where 'on nothing stronger than milk and sherbert, the athletes of Persia and wrestlers of upper Hindoostan excelled'. He and Cook had more in common than a passion for temperance. Buckingham was by now famous as a campaigner throughout England and America, for such causes as freedom of the press, colonial self-government, anti-slavery and the improvement of city life for the labouring masses. Cook's interest in travel for the people was dedicated to the idea that to introduce people to foreigners was to lessen the fears and hatred that led to war, as well as to make such journeys accessible to other than the privileged few.

Both Buckingham and Cook were active pacifists; Cook

opposed the celebrations of the anniversary of Waterloo and invited his 'brethren of France' to cross the Channel and inaugurate a new era of peace. Buckingham was a delegate to the first world peace congress in Brussels in 1848. By 1850, Cook was arranging trips for the middle class to Paris, Italy and the Alps, and in that year he sought Buckingham's advice as to how to organize a round trip to Egypt and Palestine.

But for years, the idea Cook had so much at heart remained impracticable. The 'Eastern Tours' project was postponed until Cook had built up a solid American, as well as an English, clientele, and was only firmly established when railway links across Europe, through the newly built Mont Cenis tunnel, had cut travelling time drastically between London, Paris and the Mediterranean or Adriatic ports. Only then could Cook's tourists take advantage of the steamship routes which had already made Palestine more accessible to Catholic pilgrims from France and Italy.

The first tourists who were neither wealthy nor antiquarians began arriving in Palestine at the end of the period of Egyptian rule. Perhaps one of the earliest was David Holthaus, a German journeyman tailor who stitched his way round the world for seventeen years, finding work in every port, arriving in the Holy Land in 1838. Holthaus never thought of posing as an Oriental, and added only a straw hat and uncomfortable Turkish shoes – when his own wore out – to his European clothes. He was aware of, but not interested in, the scholarly debate on the authenticity of the Holy Places; he would not, he wrote, 'presume to pass judgment on Robinson . . . yet, in my simplicity, I could not help fancying that the sacred spots must have been much more accurately and readily determined in the third and fourth century than now in the nineteenth'. He was cheerfully ignorant of Islam; at the Noble Sanctuary, when chased out by the Nubian guards, Holthaus concluded that 'a harem may probably be connected with the mosque'; and he returned loaded with souvenirs – rosaries, mother-of-pearl tablets, crucifixes, petrified olives and peas, and a certificate of his visit to the Holy Sepulchre.

Italian priests also travelled light: 'most wretched is the man who carries a trunk', wrote Tommaso Christ, a Friulano who organized his own little international caravan, advising such travellers not to set out before the age of thirty-five, when their ecclesiastical studies would be over, or after fifty, when they would be too old for the rigours of the journey. Tourists like this little group were undeterred by theological dispute or by the barren aspect of the country: as Tommaso Christ wrote, the disputes changed almost daily, but for the Holy City 'Eternity, like a meridian, passes through Jerusalem.' Padre Francesco Cassini da Perinaldo, who dedicated his huge travel memoir to Ferdinand of the Sicilies, was dismissive of well-educated sceptics, preferring to travel with 'men rich in piety and poor in letters'. He agreed with Holthaus that since centuries of the faithful had respected certain sites, he was not going to question them, though his horror at the 'schismatic Greeks' rituals was no less than that of Protestant and French Catholic visitors. Like all Italian Catholics, however, his real contempt was reserved for the Protestants, newly ensconced in Jerusalem: 'the Presbyterians without a priest; the Episcopalians without bishops; the Evangelicals who do not practise the Gospels . . . and a host of others, too numerous to even remember'.

Priests and clergymen were in the vanguard of the new travellers who boarded the new steamships in the 1850s. The trip to Palestine was still an ordeal. The new Turkish quarantine laws introduced in the last years of Egyptian rule ensured that all travellers coming from danger spots in the East (and few travelled to Palestine alone) were shut up in lazarettos for up to a fortnight at the port of entry, provided only with (often mouldy) bread and water, kept behind wire fences and fumigated with 'brimstone vapours'; trumpets were sounded to warn away the local people. Middle-class travellers could not afford a separate escort to visit the Dead Sea, and when they tagged on to the pilgrims from the East, who were driven down to the Jordan like cattle by the Turkish soldiers, they were treated roughly. The British consul reported that the English Reverend Higgins, and his friend, a Cambridge student named Dalton, accidentally strayed out of a protective line of soldiers at the pilgrim encampment near the Jordan in 1848. Higgins was 'assaulted by a soldier in undress with a large stick when he went out of a "nominal gate"; he having in his hand a fine net for catching butterflies, let it fall to save it from being broken and tried to take the stick from a soldier.' Dalton, an athletic youth, collared the soldier and found himself surrounded by another thirty; he was so badly beaten that both his eyes were closed.

The rules of Western travel, elaborated by the elite, were now changed. The Reverend Josiah Porter, writing a new guide to Palestine in 1854, warned that : 'to adopt the native custom when one is not only ignorant of the language but unable to conform to the mode of salutation, sitting, walking and riding of the people, is just an effectual way of rendering oneself ridiculous . . . Firmans are of little or no use. They can neither secure respect nor command attention to wants . . . English gold is the best passport in Syria.'

So the Western travellers became instantly identifiable by their long overcoats (the English wore tweed), the veils which floated from beneath their sun helmets, their sunglasses, and their green lined umbrellas. The gold they carried went straight into the pockets of the dragomen (interpreter guides) who, until the advent of the organized tour, charged what they wished and had the travellers at their mercy. The classic mid-century dragoman was Yussuf Badra, made famous in the American John Ross Browne's account of 1852, *Yussuf, or the Journey of the Frangi*: mendacious, a shameless blackmailer, but entertaining (in retrospect) and indispensable. Yussuf boasted of slaughtering Bedouin but turned tail at the first real danger; led his charges to foul inns where they were fleeced; whipped his muleteers brutally, and parted from his client only to be thrown into the local jail.

The first organized tours began in the early 1850s: Catholic groups from Italy travelling by the Lloyd Triestino steamship line, and caravans organized by the order of St Vincent de Paul which set out twice yearly from Marseilles, at Easter and in August. The journey was a roundabout one, and nearly half the time was spent at sea. The French Messageries Maritimes was a commercial line designed to deliver and pick up cargo, not tourists, from a series of Levantine ports, and initially passengers had to change in Egypt to the Lloyd Triestino, which anchored off Haifa. The journey from France was prohibitively expensive; a contemporary French source calculated that it cost several years' savings of a curé's salary, and thus the travellers were mainly wealthy aristocrats or churchmen from moneyed foundations. Women were not admitted to these voyages until after 1868.

The first organized 'pleasure trip' to Palestine came, predictably, from the United States, part of a huge package deal; early in 1867, 150 Americans, organized by Henry Ward Beecher's Plymouth Church, planned to tour the continent of Europe and from there continue to the Holy Land and Egypt. This was the famous cruise of the 'Quaker City', described by Mark Twain – then a relatively unknown newspaper correspondent and professional humorist – in *The Innocents Abroad*. Sixty-seven thousand copies of this book were sold during the first year after publication alone, and a contemporary critic wrote of Twain's comments on Palestine: 'Dean Stanley is graphic and elaborate enough on Palestine, and Ernest Renan touches its past and present like a poet and philosopher, but anyone who wants to understand without going there exactly how it looks now had better read *The Innocents Abroad*.'

'Without going there', indeed; for Twain's account of Palestine was not designed to help the new travel firms attract clients. He maintained that both the romantic travellers and the scholars had conspired to give the reading public a totally false idea of the Holy Land, which was actually arid, squalid, boring and depressing. Twain was not the first writer to express disillusion with Palestine stripped of its biblical and literary glamour, but he was the first to reassure the ordinary traveller, as he stood bible in hand, looking around in bewilderment, that he could trust his own negative impressions, and not merely parrot scholarly literature: 'What the pilgrims said at Caesaria Philippi surprised me with its wisdom; I found it afterwards in Robinson. What they said when Gennaseret burst upon their vision charmed me with its grace. I find it in Mr Thompson's *Land and the Book*.' But most writers, he insisted, had conned their readers. What the visitor saw in Palestine was unworthy of Christianity, irremediably mired in the backward East, with no promise of a Western redemption from the primeval curse.

Authenticity meant squalor: 'Oriental scenes look best in steel engravings. I cannot be imposed upon anymore by that picture of the Queen of Sheba visiting Solomon. I shall say to myself, "you look fine, Madam, but your feet are not clean, and you smell like a camel".'

What Twain was proposing was to return the scenes of the Bible to the imagination, to the atmosphere of the Renaissance, where they belonged. He rejected Mount Tabor as the true site of the Transfiguration: instead, he suggested a more appropriate site, which he had recently visited: the garden of Count Pallavicini near Genoa: 'the faintest, softest, richest picture that ever graced the dream of a dying saint, since John saw the New Jerusalem glimmering above the clouds of heaven'.

Twain's book became as influential with readers as Chateaubriand's had been sixty years earlier. Within a few years almost every American travel writer was using the same tone: 'With the actual Jerusalem of today before our eyes, its naked desolation, its squalor, its vivid contradiction to what we conceive should be the City of our King, we find it easier to feel that Christ was born in New England than in Judea.' The first English writer to tour Palestine in a group informed his readers that the Jordan was 'not more than half the width of the Thames at London Bridge', that the water was muddy and dirty, and that the people of Jerusalem, lacking 'grandees', were 'of an inferior stamp'. The leader of a group of Mormons, after examining the city from various points of view, said that he could not imagine why King David had selected it for his capital; other visitors dismissed the fair-haired Jews they saw as 'inauthentic' and claimed that their tears at the Wailing Wall were put on for visitors.

Nevertheless, though the American Bayard Taylor was exaggerating in predicting that Jerusalem would soon become 'as familiar a station on the grand tour as Paris and Naples', the tourist trade to Palestine grew steadily, largely due to the efforts of Thomas Cook and the capacity for endurance which was to characterize tourists from this time forward.

*   *   *

Cook's 'Eastern Tours' were inaugurated shortly before the opening of the Suez Canal in 1869. He himself led the first party of ten travellers, whose adventures were recorded by one of the party, a Miss Riggs of Hampstead, in her diary.

All went well at disembarkation at Sidon, where they were welcomed by local dragomen, who introduced them to 'Tent Life': 'little iron bedsteads all put up with mattresses, bolster and Arab blanket . . . table in the centre and wash basin, and tents with linings and pocket to each bed'; the gong for breakfast sounded at five in the morning, and the tourists were expected to ride seven and eight hours a day. As the days passed a different and gloomier note crept in: 'Near Caesaria saw remains of the body of a white man; Alexander [the guide] said it had been there some time, killed by Bedouin; one of the mules shied at it' . . . 'water from a pond not good and yet obliged to drink it, so thirsty' . . . 'Mrs Rose off her horse again' . . . 'Poor Mrs Samuels', a fellow traveller, then dropped dead. 'Arabs have a great superstition with regard to the dead, and as she was to be taken to Jerusalem to be buried, the natives were told she was ill and she was packed up and carried there on a palanquin . . . a dead person could not be taken from convent without government permission so altogether it was thought advisable to act this deception. She died at three and was conveyed thither at six in the morning and buried that night . . . eastern burials are so awfully rapid.' On the way to the Dead Sea, Miss Riggs found 'the colour of sunset very peculiar. We knew that, if spared, we should soon be on the borders of that sulphureous and bituminous sepulcre steaming up death to all vegetation around.'

Camped outside the walls of Jerusalem, the party was robbed during the night. Though Cook insisted that the governor of Jerusalem was most helpful – he confiscated all the livestock of the suspected thieves as compensation – one wonders what Miss Riggs would have done with a flock of hennaed goats. Though the robbery was not repeated, the English papers were full of indignant letters and demands that Cook call off his Palestine tours. But he had not waited twenty years to realize his project in order to be defeated so quickly. He continued to promote the Palestine trip even though it was not good business, and was financed only by the profits Cook was making in Europe and America.

The fact that Cook soon cornered the market in travel to the Holy Land was not because he undercut competitors. Tours organized from Paris in 1870, for instance for English and Swiss

Protestants, by Ermete Pierotti, an Italian who had served as architectural engineer to Sureya Pasha in the 1850s, actually cost slightly less than Cook's. There was little difference between Cook's prices and those charged by the organizers of the Catholic caravans prior to 1882. But the middle-class Protestant clientele attracted by Cook's services, English and American, wanted the kind of tour and the kind of services that only he provided. He and his son John accompanied many of the parties themselves; almost everything was paid for in advance, reducing the risk of robbery; the dragomen were hand-picked.

Most of the established local dragomen were put out of business almost immediately. In May 1874 they complained bitterly in a letter to the London *Times* that their living had been taken by Cook. They argued that Cook's prices were higher than theirs, that the whole price had to be paid in advance, that Cook commandeered all the horses in the region, and that his agents did not provide fresh local food for their clients but preserves brought from England.

But this was exactly the point. Cook's tourists did not want local guides who might raise the stated price at will and whose patter reproduced what they regarded as 'pious frauds'. They were attracted by the portable accommodation, which was preferable to convent rooms or verminous khans. English travellers no longer had to plunge into the Jordan with half-naked Russian peasants, but had their own escorts employed by Cook. 'Both Ladies and Gentlemen, at their proper stations, bathe in the historic stream, and the superstitious and ritualistic fill phials of Jordan water for the christening of English and American babies,' promised Cook's brochure. It is impossible to imagine, on a Cook's tour, the scene described by the Swedish traveller Frederika von Bremer in which a well-born English-woman, having left her infant in Jerusalem, hired a Bedouin baby from a village near the Dead Sea to relieve the pressure of milk in her breasts.

Instead of suspect Oriental food, Cook's tourists had English ham and Yorkshire bacon, pickles, potted salmon and Liverpool sardines. Boatmen were engaged, under a Cook's flag, to row out to the tourists on the deck of the ship, 'relieve them of Arab rabble, and conduct them through Custom house annoyances'. In Jaffa, Cook's centre of operations by the mid-seventies was the Jerusalem Hotel 'high and dry above swamps and the decaying remains of dead Arabs' (the local cemetery).

Western susceptibilities were occasionally offended by the way the local workers – muleteers and porters – were treated, and by the state of the pack animals – but they soon got over it. Edwin Hodder, biographer of the great social reformer Lord Shaftesbury, and the first to publish a memoir recording a Cook's Tour, described how 'everything has to be packed up and fitted to the mule's back by the time we are ready to mount, a stupendous work which does not allow a moment's breathing time to the workers. The dragomen superintend this, and they do it with a whip in their hands, with which they mercilessly lash any of the muleteers who wish to argue, or who show a disinclination to work. This is a hateful practice, and called forth many protests, but before we had been a month in Syria we were used to it . . . and we were forced to confess that in the existing state of things it seemed so necessary, that we began to grow hardened and to look at it with indifference.' Thefts were dealt with summarily: a woman who tried to remove part of Hodder's luggage from his horse 'was whipped, thrown to the ground and kicked. "Better than sending her to prison," said the dragoman.' Cook, in his travel leaflets, wrote that he pitied the Syrian animals: 'Murray recommends camping [on Mount Hermon]. We most certainly do not, and think anyone who attempts to drive loaded mules up Mount Hermon ought to be punished for cruelty to animals.'

Despite all Cook tried to do for his clients, however, there were problems he could not solve. The middle class were poor riders. An American observer, the writer Charles Warner, noted: 'The Hotel Twelve Tribes in Jerusalem is now occupied principally by Cook's tribes, most of whom appear to be lost . . . excellent people from England and America, and most of them as unaccustomed to the back of a horse as to that of an ostrich. It is touching to see some of the pilgrims walk around the animals which have fallen to them, wondering how they are to get on, which side they are to mount, and how they are to stay on.' Cook did his best, providing English saddles, to spare the tourists the agony of the Arab saddle with its short stirrups (Twain had described the Americans riding with their knees near their elbows) and narrow seat. But the overloaded horses, shod with a flat plate rather than a horseshoe, Western style, regularly fell when attempting to cross flooded streams over slippery stones, and ladies like Mrs Rose were shot into the mud.

In 1874, Cook came to an arrangement with the Templars by which his parties were conveyed in the Germans' stagecoach from Jaffa to Jerusalem. Whether this was an improvement on riding is debatable. The coach was described as 'a compromise between the ancient ark, a modern dray and a threshing machine; if it were driven over smooth ground it would soon loosen all the teeth of the passengers and shatter their spinal columns.' The Turkish road was not smooth. This 'diligence', pulled by three horses abreast, and carrying a dozen passengers at a time, travelled at just over three miles an hour.

It was hard for the middle-aged travellers, awoken before dawn by gongs and whistles, to struggle into their clothes before the tent came down over their heads. One guide advised the tourists to sleep with their mouths shut, lest the local people steal their teeth; but sleep itself was hard to come by, for the grunting of camels and wailing of jackals.

Despite Cook's assurance that travel in Palestine was not dangerous, the tourists were not adequately protected from exposure to winter cold in the hills of Judea and Mount Lebanon. The winter of 1874/5 was a particularly hard one, storms blowing from Port Said to the Hermon, where tourists were penned up for three days and nights in an Arab village by snowstorms. The unpublished diary of George Jager tells the sad tale of Reverend Gale, who was fit enough in mid-November to baptize a fellow traveller in the Jordan, but back in chilly Jerusalem, a week later, was already 'in very poor condition'. Jager's diary goes on:

> November 20th: Poor Dr Gale succumbed, entirely losing his mind, and had to be left at a wayside place until a doctor could be sent to him.
> November 21st: Dr Gale brought in by wagon and carried in. He is quite childish – mind gone.

November 25th: Poor Dr Gale died about 5 this morning. Not been able to speak. Saw him last night and was recognized by him. His effects and burial left to Dr DeAss [De Haas] American consul. Melancholy thought to leave our friend dead and unburied. Got on steamer all right. All thankful to leave Holy Land.

*   *   *

Between 1868 and 1882, Cook brought about 4200 travellers to Palestine; he claimed that this accounted for about two-thirds of the total number of tourists arriving from the West. By comparison, the French Catholics organized thirty-five caravans between 1853 and 1873 – which carried only 618 pilgrims – still vastly outnumbered, of course, by the Eastern pilgrims from Russia, the Balkans and the Near East.

Among Cook's innovations there were 'Biblical Educational and General Tours', . . . 'designed specially for Ministers, Sunday school teachers and others engaged in promoting scriptural education', and 'educational tours for young gentlemen', later thrown open to others. Nobility and royalty eventually travelled under Cook's auspices, and so did a few working men, not to the entire approval of their fellow travellers.

In February 1877 some of the travellers complained of the presence of 'a working man, who had been dragged up from the lowest dregs of society, and who, it was feared, would prove a bore'. Fortunately for the man, one of the others in the group was C. E. Mudie, the famous Victorian proprietor of Mudie's Lending Library, who rebuked the critics. The man, he said, was 'a thorough Bible student, fully prepared to appreciate all the historic associations of the places visited', and had saved for thirty years for the journey. It was easier to be a working man travelling with Cook than an unbeliever, or worse, 'well up in classical matters, but ignorant of Scripture'. The tours combined visits to the Holy Places, the missions and their schools, and 'biblical excavations'; the parties carried not only maps and guide books but bibles and hymn books, and sang as they went. There was one stop, on the advertised schedule, at Miss Arnott's Mission School in Jaffa (a property which Cook had purchased for the mission), and another in Nablus, at the house of an Arab,

Selim el Karey, who had converted from the Greek Orthodox faith to Protestantism. El Karey had an English wife and had studied in a bible college at Pontypool, and he sang Arabic versions of the hymns to a Welsh melody. The guides used every opportunity to provide biblical illustrations, and the tourists could not pass through a wicket gate without hearing reflections on the strait gate of the Gospels.

Jerusalem, by this time, was assuming the more familiar aspect of a Levantine bazaar. 'If the traveller told the plain truth and spoke naturally,' wrote Hodder, 'he would say the first thing that struck him on entering Jerusalem was the number of coster-mongers selling pistachio and peanuts, the quantities of sherbert consumed at street stalls, the low row of cafés and cigar shops, and the knot of Englishmen (distinguishable anywhere by their hideous costumes) lounging outside the Mediterranean Hotel.'

There was a sharp trade in genuine and faked antiquities. 'In Jerusalem,' wrote Warner, 'copper coins of the Roman period abound, and are constantly turned up in the fields outside the city, most of them battered and defaced beyond recognition, and counterfeit silver shekel. The tourist is waited on at his hotel by a few patient and sleek sharks with cases of cheap jewellery and doubtful antiquities.'

Outside the Holy Sepulchre, the vendors ignored the poor Russian peasants and hurled themselves at the new tourists: 'Sharp-faced Greeks, impudent Jews, fair-faced women from Bethlehem, sleek Armenians thrust strings of olive beads and crosses into my face . . . as if I were the last man, and this were the last opportunity they would ever have of getting rid of their rubbish.' Now, the first word the tourists heard in Jerusalem was 'bakshish' and they were warned against being moved to Christian charity. A large Mormon group which visited Jerusalem in the mid-seventies was told that one near-naked beggar at the Jaffa Gate owned six hundred olive trees and four orchards.

The Reverend Hodder did the hornpipe and the Highland fling at Solomon's Pool. At Bethlehem, the tourists tossed away their uncomfortable paper collars; Arab girls picked them up and made elegant headdresses of them, entwined with wild flowers.

At the Jordan, where the Russian pilgrims soaked their winding sheets, tourists splashed and sang; in the Dead Sea, where Lynch had feared for his sailors' lives and Hunt sacrificed his scapegoat, 'stout gentlemen floundered in a struggle to keep their perpendicular'. In Jerusalem, they were hurried from one Holy Place to another; there was no time to sketch, no time 'to linger and reflect on the bible'; the sound of the dragoman's whistle summoned them all back into line.

*   *   *

But it was not good business for Cook. There was tension between Thomas, as head of the firm, and his son John, a hard-headed businessman who had disapproved from the start of his father's involvement with the missions everywhere on his travels, and of the Palestine venture in particular. Drought, famine and locusts in the Holy Land affected the tourists very little; but there were other problems. The sheikhs at Aqaba and Petra demanded 'a heavy blackmail' which was not included in the fare. In 1875 a cholera quarantine almost paralysed travel, and in 1877, with the Russo-Turkish war in the offing, Cook had to ask the British consul to provide military escorts when the Bedouin tribes near Petra suddenly turned nasty. Cook's were forced, for the first time, to advise against the trip. The American brochure turned away wrath: 'Don't blame us; we don't make the war.' By now, business was so unpredictable that Cook's were offering their chief guide, Rolla Floyd, a part interest in the Palestine takings in lieu of the higher salary he wanted.

In 1877, too, the crisis between father and son over Palestine came to a head. Two years earlier, Thomas had sent John to buy a large house and ground near Jerusalem, 'as a kind of wholesome threat to contractors and hotel proprietors, that if they do not treat our travellers and ourselves as they and we ought to be treated [another hint of trouble] we are prepared to open our own . . . headquarters on our own estate outside the walls of Jerusalem'. But by 1877 the house had become a liability, used only to store equipment or to lodge the guides, and John rounded on his father bitterly. Henceforth, both the Cooks tried to tighten expenditure in Palestine, though in effect this meant cutting

182

down on payments to the guides and refusing to take on extra staff. There was a lawsuit with one veteran guide, Alexander Howard, and a long and painful feud with Rolla Floyd.

Floyd was the most famous Western dragoman in Palestine over a period of more than thirty years. A hard-working handyman from Maine, Floyd had survived the collapse of the Adams colony by sheer resourcefulness. Despite the loss of his only child, an infant son, during the first difficult months, Floyd was among those who refused to give up; by 1867, before the Templars took over the route, he was driving an improvised stagecoach from Jaffa to Jerusalem, and when Cook met him in 1868, on the Jaffa quayside, he was already well known as a guide. He feared neither bad weather nor the Bedouin (on one occasion, though unarmed, he fought off an attack by a Turkish soldier in the street). Cook thought so highly of him that he advertised his services even before he had formally drawn up a contract with him, and in 1877, when the season failed, he paid for Floyd and his wife to travel to Philadelphia, to Paris, and to London to help advertise the firm. The Floyds sold olive wood souvenirs and mother-of-pearl work from Bethlehem at the Crystal Palace exhibition in London, and were taken up by a friendly Member of Parliament.

Ironically, however, the Floyds' world trip was the beginning of the end of their relationship with the Cooks. For Floyd, who had tried unsuccessfully for years to save enough money to return to the United States and 'spend the rest of my days where I can enjoy myself', now saw how well the Cooks were doing in Europe, and concluded that he was being grossly overworked and underpaid.

In 1881, when business was again beginning to look up in Palestine, Floyd refused to renew his contract with the firm, and the feud that followed did no credit to John Cook, who was by now running affairs in Palestine his way; Thomas being in his seventies and losing his sight.

In the event, Cook's were temporarily the losers. They were forced to employ a much larger staff – Floyd maintained that he was replaced by no fewer than nine men – and to pay higher salaries, while Floyd competed fiercely against Cook's new men for potential customers, even racing Cook's boatman to the ships in Jaffa port.

Floyd, however, missed the Cooks' greatest coup: in the spring of 1882, they were contracted to organize the journey of over a thousand French Catholic pilgrims on a round trip to the Holy Land and back – the largest pilgrimage to Palestine since the Crusades.

*   *   *

Until this time, France had seemed the most unlikely country to send so large a group to Palestine on an organized tour. Its visitors had long been outnumbered by those of England and America, and there were no French settlements. On 20 January 1882, *Le Figaro* commented: 'One sees princes of finance buying large estates in those desolate plains where their ancestors' cities once stood; the Russians send innumerable caravans between the Lebanon and Beyrouth every year. There are Germans on the Carmel and between Jaffa and Jerusalem. Schismatic Greeks flood the Holy Sepulchre. The English and Americans cover Palestine with their tweed ulsters and they make up the tourist groups. Not a Frenchman in sight!'

Nothing illustrated the different appeal of Palestine to the English and French better than the comparison between Cook's middle-class tourists and those who inaugurated the 'Pilgrimages of Penitence' in 1882 – the very name a deliberate archaism. Cook's tours had no political overtones; his internationalist and even his Evangelical sympathies meant nothing to his clients. The French 'pilgrimage' was a domestic political gesture, a protest, as one participant called it, against 'the unbelief and blasphemy of official France'.

Catholic France, which now regarded the Middle Ages as a Christian ideal, was increasingly identified with the monarchy, and in this sense the end of the Second Empire, in 1870, was a disturbing omen. The first republican president, Thiers, argued that pilgrimages 'were no longer a national custom', but a militant monastic order – one of many founded in France during the century – set out to prove him wrong.

The Assumptionist Fathers, an order founded in 1872,

distributed millions of tracts in an effort to save the souls of the working masses, and staged national pilgrimages to Rome, Lourdes and La Salette. It was their leader, Father Picard, who in 1882 led the Pilgrimage of Penitence to the Holy Land. Unlike Cook's tourists, the French pilgrims were mainly priests and aristocrats, with a sprinkling of *petits bourgeois* and peasants from Brittany and the Auvergne, economically backward regions of France where a somewhat primitive religious faith still existed.

The Assumptionists were not really happy about putting themselves in the hands of an English Baptist, and Picard only turned to Cook's when it became clear that there was no French or Catholic organization which could match Cook's price and organize facilities in Palestine. Picard explained to all applicants that this was to be no pleasure trip. In a mass ceremony, he swore the pilgrims to humility and obedience to himself, and told the married couples participating that they were to abstain from sexual intercourse throughout the journey.

At the Gare du Lyon, priests blessed the kneeling pilgrims amidst their heaps of luggage, and at Marseilles the local bishop consecrated the first of two specially chartered ships, the aptly named *Picardie*; a huge wooden cross was erected on the prow. The *Picardie* needed the blessing; it had been pawned by its first owner to meet his debts, its maiden voyage had been to Mecca, and its second to Algeria with a hold full of convicts.

During the journey the young society people, mindful of pilgrim humility, waited on table, and their elders bore their crowded conditions in the cabins 'perched like so many parrots' stoically, or hobnobbed with the peasants. One old peasant couple had sold their only cow to make the journey possible – a collection was arranged to enable them to replace it – and a Breton woman had drawn out all her savings.

In Palestine, the pilgrims looked anxiously for signs of French and Catholic prestige. They were gratified by the sight of the French flag flown by Latin priests everywhere and visited St Anne's church in Jerusalem, presented by the Sultan to Napoleon III after the Crimean War. But they bitterly resented the fact that at the Holy Sepulchre, Latin rites followed those of the Armenians and the 'schismatic Greeks'. They noted in consolation that the governor of Jerusalem, in their honour, had swept the streets for only the third time that century – the two previous occasions had been for Turkish dignitaries. Picard also adopted three Christian Arab boys whom he intended to place in monasteries in France.

But they were disappointed by their treatment by Cook's. Cook had seldom dealt with more than forty or fifty travellers at a time, and ten to twenty times that number strained the resources of the country to breaking point. There were long queues waiting to wash at the fountains in the courtyards of convents, and equally long queues of hungry, tired pilgrims checking out their Cook coupons at the entrance to their closely guarded encampments. The French pilgrims queued to say mass, queued to get their coffee, queued for their horses. The country had been scoured for every available mount, and the pilgrims complained that half the horses were lame, or strayed off to graze. The tents were as hot as ovens at midday, the food was below par, and Cook had provided no wine at all – a crowning insult. Though several pilgrims died on the return journey, none fell seriously ill in the Holy Land itself, perhaps due to precautions taken by the four doctors and 'one pharmacist of the third class' among their number. Their chroniclers concluded that the pilgrimage had been divinely protected 'as even the Protestant Cook's men acknowledged'.

'Personally,' wrote John Cook to his father, 'I have made up my mind never to have anything to do with another French pilgrimage, at any rate without seeing my way to a good profit.'

*   *   *

Privileged travellers were the subjects of paintings – the most accomplished of such studies was probably John Frederick Lewis's painting of Lord Castlereagh camped in Sinai in 1842. Cook's tourists were photographed. Photography evolved together with tourism. Yet it had not begun as a popular art. Where Palestine was concerned – and Palestine was one of the first Eastern countries where Europeans tried out the new technique – it began as a conscientious effort, against both technical and physical odds, to represent monuments and landscapes more precisely. By the 1880s, however, photography had produced not only important documentation, but the falsification which inevitably resulted from commercial demand and stereotyped observation.

The first photographs, from the 1840s, were rare specimens: the 'daguerreotypes' which could not be directly reprinted were processed like engravings, and had to be held up to the light in order to be seen. These were regarded primarily as a more accurate form of the preliminary artist's sketch. 'Views of Palestine' were among the first photographs of the East published in the 'Excursions Daguerriennes' commissioned by the Paris optician Lerebours, who wrote in his introduction that 'photographs are indisputably extensions of the engraving, making it possible to become acquainted with monuments and rare works of art'. Frédéric Goupil-Fesquet, who accompanied the painter Horace Vernet through Sinai to Jerusalem in 1841, was entirely preoccupied with problems of composition and light; the second photographer of Palestine, Girault de Pranjey, was interested primarily in the details of Moslem architecture; another, August Salzmann, produced magnificent and detailed studies of Jerusalem's walls, gates and stonework in 1852 in order to back up the (largely erroneous) antiquarian theories of Félicien de Saulcy.

Theirs was the Palestine of Chateaubriand and Lamartine, a Palestine of stones and relics, mosques, sanctuaries, Crusader remains: a romantic shell, a necropolis, without a single sign of contemporary life.

The earliest British photographer, George Keith, a Scottish doctor and one of the first amateurs of the art, produced the landscapes of Palestine which were to illustrate his father Alexander Keith's contribution to the debate on the authenticity of the Bible – 'Evidences of the Truth of Christian Religion' – apparently the first use of photography as documentation, evidence for use in polemic. All Keith's scenes were chosen with an eye to illustrating specific passages in the Bible, meant to show the biblical curse in its most graphic and literal form: the unploughed field, the desolate shores of the inland lakes, the treeless hillsides and the withered fig tree – not as emblems of the romantic or the picturesque, but as specimens of the evidence of prophecy.

Alexander Keith maintained that photography was 'a mode of documentation that could be neither questioned nor surpassed; as without the need of any testimony, or the aid of either pen or pencil, the rays of the sun could . . . depict what the prophets saw'.

Very soon, however, art critics were pointing out that precisely where light (and shade) were concerned photography could, more easily than other media, confuse shadow and substance. During the early years of photography, moreover, the necessity for long exposures – up to fifteen minutes – meant that the passing moment of an ideal light was just as elusive to the photographer as to the painter.

Painters like Roberts and Lear had confessed their inability to render the colouring of the mountains beyond the Dead Sea, or the valley around Petra, and Turner's water colour of Jericho, painted in England from a clergyman's sketch, captured late afternoon light in the Jordan valley more accurately than either, though Turner never reached Palestine and painted from his experience and imagination.

The photographers' problem was to capture the light of a moment; John Cramb described the distress of a fellow photographer who had not reckoned with the rapidity of Near East sunsets: 'he had just got his apparatus in position and plate prepared when he had the mortification of seeing the sun drop below the horizon.'

*   *   *

Technical progress soon meant that thousands of copies could be made of a single photograph – though they were still pasted into books by hand – and this led to commercial distribution. The result was thousands of photographs of Jerusalem from the Mount of Olives, the Dome of the Rock, the Pool of Bethesda, Rachel's Tomb and the Holy Sepulchre, which were easy assignments. Even the angle from which they were seen varied very little; Francis Frith, one of the first commercial photographers of Palestine, is remarkable for the fact that he appears actually to have chosen unusual viewpoints – the Holy Sepulchre from the drab alleys behind it, Mar Saba monastery seen through a gap in the mountains – and landscapes of deserted and dangerous roads where few photographers lingered, like his starkly gloomy picture of the road to Jericho.

But there is no sense in Frith's work, or in that of any of his contemporaries during the mid-century, of Palestine as a place where people lived, worked, or visibly worshipped. Though Marcel du Camp took photographs of Europeans climbing the Pyramids during the mid-century, and of archaeological excavations in progress, there were few photographs of Palestine with human figures until the late 1860s. While painters, both professional and amateur, had sketched scenes in the bazaars, Carl Haag had lived in a Bedouin encampment for his portraits, and local customs were portrayed in biblical illustrations, the commercial photographers stuck to their deserted landscapes: this, apparently, was what the market demanded.

When human figures finally appeared in Western commercial photography of the Holy Land, what survived was a very selective portrait of the people of the country.

When the British engineers who mapped Palestine arrived in the late 1860s, one of their tasks was to photograph all available evidence of ancient settlement; another was to document the character and customs of the local population. The scientific value of the first archaeological photographs was undeniable; the Orientalist Emmanuel Deutsch wrote that he found it easier to read an inscription carved on a ruined church near Nablus in the engineers' carefully focused photograph than when standing at the site itself, and when the Roman ruins of Jerash and Philadelphia were restored, years later, the landscape photographs by the French Bonfils were consulted. Photographs of the local people were another matter.

Just as the early photographers had preferred to focus on well-known sites in the cities rather than risk themselves and their equipment in isolated and dangerous parts of the countryside, so their successors preferred docile paid models to the unpredictable peasantry. The commercial photographers took very few shots of the peasants, however useful these might have been as biblical illustrations. Like the English engineers, whose ethnographic studies were taken for their scientific interest, the commercial photographers chose subjects chiefly from the non-Moslem communities. Rarest of all were portraits of Turkish officials and soldiers, or Moslem notables in the towns – though artisans and shopkeepers in the bazaars, anxious to please clients, were willing sitters.

Armenian priests, Samaritans, Bedouin, and Russian peasants were photographed frequently. The Samaritans were of particular interest because of their uninterrupted presence near Mount Gerizim since antiquity, and the ancient scrolls they had preserved. The Ta'amira Bedouin, tourist guides and semi-sedentary nomads, were more accessible than the Bedouin of the desert (the Petra Bedouin, when first captured on film by an American photographer in 1882, demanded thirty dollars a sitting).

The Jews of Jerusalem were also a captive subject, but a closer look at the small number of photographs of this community suggests some doubt as to how authentic were the photographs of any of the ethnic minorities. By the time of the tourist invasion of Palestine, the visit to see the Jews praying at the Wailing Wall had become part of the guided tour; but, unlike the romantic visitors of the early century, the tourists had little respect for the Jews' piety, knew nothing of their rituals, and often voiced anti-semitic or sceptical comments. The Jews, for their part, certainly did not enjoy being stared at by lounging, giggling foreigners. They objected to being the object of vicarious curiosity, as did many Moslems. Jews photographed with their backs to the camera – particulary blurred and unsaleable images showing them moving in prayer – are probably genuine. But Jews carefully lined up at the wall, men and women together, their faces turned slyly to the camera, are probably paid models.

One much reproduced portrait by the British army engineer Philipps shows seven 'Ashkenazi Jews' posed in two rows. Unfortunately for its credibility, two versions of this photograph exist, and in the second, the models have not only changed places, but also hats and kaftans; as these demonstrate the sect they belonged to, and their marital status, the exchange is inconceivable had the models really been 'Ashkenazi Jews', though they may have been converts or 'enquirers' supplied by the Mission, like Hunt's Jewish models.

Bonfils, the famous French photographer who arrived with the military expedition in 1860 and settled in Beirut, also used one handsome, distinguished-looking elderly man as his model for two supposedly Jewish portraits; in one version, the man holds an implement while in the other he holds a book. The same man is captioned, in different collections of Bonfils' work: 'Chief Rabbi of Jerusalem', 'Jewish cotton carder', 'Jew of Algiers' and 'Ashkenazi Jew'.

In his studio, Bonfils posed all the popular figures of Palestine as seen by tourists: the dragoman, the kavass, the artisan, groups of 'Syrian Bedouin' arranged in poses, the women often bare-breasted – *tableaux vivants* in which Bonfils intended, so he said, to preserve the local dress, appearance and habits of the people of a country whose visible past had been almost totally destroyed and whose present customs were fast disappearing under the influence of the West. What actually happened, therefore, was that the population, or that part of it which could be induced to pose for photographers, was presented as a museum exhibit.

Nevertheless, the immediacy of the live model, as compared to the idealized painted figure, did much to end the illusion of the 'authenticated' Bible. The Bedouin photographed by Bonfils – tattered, dirty and degenerate-looking – were obviously not models for the Patriarchs. And although Bonfils did stage a couple of biblical *tableaux vivants* – a Ruth and Boaz in the fields and a Raising of Lazarus – in his studio, these are exceptions in his repertory.

Although researchers have unearthed a couple of peasant Holy Families, the acceptable way to show Palestine as the Holy Land was to keep its Oriental aspect and its Christian significance separate. There were many series of photographs illustrating the Stations of the Cross, and the Sea of Galilee, with its anonymous fishermen seen through a flattering haze, was always a favourite site.

Hundreds of thousands of photographs of the Holy Land were

taken by the 1880s. Many came to resemble the 'phantasmagoria' and panoramas of the early years of the century; they were touched up, tinted and made into montages and lantern slides, and the stereographic techniques invented in the 1850s gave the illusion of three dimensions to photographs shown in Sunday schools in Europe and America from the 1860s onward; from the 1870s, card series were being sold from door to door.

Before long, the popular and selective view of Palestine had made its way over millions of front doorsteps. Ironically, the medium, which had promised truth and accuracy in the depiction of a country which more often than not defeated the descriptive skills of both painters and writers, had produced the most distorted image of all.

CHAPTER VII

———•◆•———

By Appointment to Palestine:
Soldiers and Scholars

'WE DID NOT BRING HOME THE ARK, or the salves of Dan, or Ahab's ivory house, or Joseph's mummy,' wrote Claude Conder of the Palestine Exploration Fund, the first archaeological mission to Palestine with public backing. The public wanted 'Jewish antiquities' as clearly identifiable as Egyptian pyramids or Greek temples: the tombs of the Patriarchs and the Kings of Judea, the remains of the First and Second Temples, the true site of the crucifixion and the burial place of Jesus. Edward Robinson challenged the traditional sites of the Holy Places; George Williams, Anglican chaplain at St Petersburg, defended them. Félicien de Saulcy attributed most of what he saw to the most glorious period of Jewish history, the reigns of David and Solomon. James Fergusson, a historian of architecture, insisted that the Holy Sepulchre was under the Dome of the Rock. Evengelicals wanted the Ark of the Covenant to be found, as Lord Shaftesbury said, 'as evidence in a day of trouble, of rebuke, and of blasphemy'. The directors of the Louvre, the British Museum, and the Imperial Library in Berlin competed savagely for stones and manuscripts. It was not an atmosphere calculated to produce objective, scientific enquiry.

The Scriptures were taught at schools as the earliest history of man. Though all the expeditions in Egypt, like Layard's dig at Nineveh in 1842, Schliemann's at Troy in 1873, indicated the existence of a wide network of Near East cultures, the public still wanted evidence of a specific and unique culture in the Holy Land, confirming the message of the Scriptures.

Though Palestine had passed through the hands of so many

conquerors, even scholars assumed that the relics of each age would be clearly distinguishable.

The scientific criteria on which modern archaeology is based had hardly been formulated. The principle of stratigraphy – that pottery and other remains could be dated by the depth at which they were found in the soil – though familiar from geology, and applied by Schliemann at Troy, was not adopted in Palestine until 1890. Robinson looked for visible ruins near the tels he thought were platforms for cities, not – as they were – the sign of settlements buried underground.

But Palestine yielded little on the surface. In the countryside, though practised eyes could detect wells, cisterns and aqueducts, the tels signalled their message to no purpose. In Jerusalem, whose ancient topography was still uncertain, the ruins of each age were embedded in those of its successor. Herodian engineers constructing the Second Temple had changed the very shape of the Temple Mount itself. So had deposits of centuries of rubbish in the valleys surrounding it. The Crusaders had used Moslem remains; the Moslems had used Crusader material – some visible, some hidden. The sixteenth-century Ottoman ruler Suleiman the Magnificent had built new walls to the city. In some places he had used older structures, in others he had bypassed them altogether.

Jerusalem stone was almost indestructible, which was the reason builders had used it again and again, rather than quarrying new. The fact that it was a holy city for three faiths meant that it had been preserved in this piecemeal fashion. But its monuments looked less impressive than those of Baalbeck, abandoned for lack of interest; and it was much more difficult to reconstruct than an undisturbed ruin like Troy.

Scholars arrived in Palestine with preconceived ideas of the shape of an ancient temple, synagogue or mosque; or what was Roman, Byzantine, or Crusader style. Jerusalem confused them. So throughout the nineteenth century the Al Aqsa mosque was believed to have been built on the ruins of a Byzantine church, just because its ground plan was laid out by Byzantine builders. Devout Christians found it difficult to accept that Moslem and Christian builders had influenced one another, just as they were amazed that Moslems respected Christian traditions. But what was most important was that most antiquarians came to Palestine to verify what they had read, or to prove a particular theory – not to document what they found.

Although archaeology, as a science, did not yet exist, there was however one skill in which great expertise had been acquired over a period of more than a hundred and fifty years, particularly in France. That was epigraphy, the deciphering of inscriptions. Hence the presence of a philologist, Ernest Renan, at the head of the French archaeological mission to Phoenicia in 1860. In the absence of other techniques, it was by inscriptions alone that explorers could date or classify their findings. Epigraphy was often the clue to an entire culture: the Abbé Berthelemy's deciphering of the Phoenician inscriptions in Malta in 1740; Rawlinson's, of the Accadian and Elamite (old Persian) lettering on the Behistun Stone – the key to which was his recognition of the repeated name of Cyrus – and the decoding of the Rosetta Stone by Champollion.

But, ironically enough, the culture richest in literary remains, that which had influenced the West most directly, had left least behind in the way of inscriptions. As one of the greatest epigraphers, Charles Clermont-Ganneau, said in 1890: 'Palestine has been almost the last to break its obstinate silence; it did so only a few years ago, and still speaks only at rare intervals, as if against its will, and only too often in a maddeningly laconic way.'

Two outstanding men were to overcome these difficulties, one to determine the real topography of ancient Jerusalem, the other to break Palestine's 'obstinate silence' for the first time. The first was Charles Warren, soldier and mining engineer, one of the officers of the Palestine Exploration Fund. The second was Charles Clermont-Ganneau, the Orientalist scholar and epigrapher.

Warren literally burrowed beneath Jerusalem to chart the original dimensions of the Temple Mount; his precise documentation of his work remains basic data for the archaeologists of today. Clermont-Ganneau located or deciphered the most important inscriptions found in Palestine, made the most brilliant contributions to the Fund's reports, and managed to unmask a number of archaeological forgeries which followed on his own discoveries.

Their letters and memoirs indicate that despite their very different backgrounds, qualifications and characters, Warren and Clermont Ganneau respected and admired one another's separate skills. In this they were unusual for their time. Both had to combat the chicanery and petty rivalries which made objective research so difficult at the time, as well as to face the inevitable physical and political problems involved in their work. The story of their careers in Palestine also illuminate the odd, and often uncomfortable, teaming of soldiers and scholars in that curious Victorian hybrid – the Palestine Exploration Fund.

* * *

Until the 1860s, the amateur antiquarians had Palestine to themselves. Such men were far from ignorant; but their studies, however encyclopaedic, were undirected, their methods haphazard. Ambitious researchers like Layard were wary of Palestine, where they doubted – correctly enough – that they would find the remains of a spectacular civilization. Thus the field was left to men like Félicien de Saulcy, the soldier explorer who was until the 1860s the best-known antiquarian of the century.

De Saulcy supplied the Louvre with the bulk of its 'Jewish antiquities' during the 1850s and 1860s. He located and transported a number of valuable finds: stone carvings, sarcophagi and Hellenistic sculptures, as well as smaller objects. But as he was no Orientalist scholar, he involved himself in a running battle with the French Academy. De Saulcy was, as his friend Prosper Mérimée remarked, a salty combination of artilleryman and academician, an early, if mediocre, graduate of the Polytechnique, the recently established school for military and civil engineers. He had studied geology, entymology and numismatics – the one field in which he was genuinely knowledgeable. He learned both Hebrew and Arabic in order to be able to decipher inscriptions, but this did not make him an epigrapher. He remained a wealthy adventurer of great charm who, as Renan observed, 'saw traces of a colossal antiquity everywhere'.

From his first journey to Palestine in 1850–1, he brought back a complete survey of the Dead Sea area, and located a number of important sites, among them the Hellenistic temple of a feudal ruler of the pre-Herodian era at Iraq el Amir, on the east bank of the Jordan. Unfortunately, de Saulcy was no Burckhardt, content to leave the interpretation of his finds to specialists. His fanciful account of his travels – he claimed to have seen the Cities of the Plain outlined beneath the Dead Sea – cause some scholars to argue that he had invented the whole journey. De Saulcy returned to Palestine in 1863, this time taking with him the photographer Salzmann.

On this second visit, de Saulcy revisited the Tombs of the Kings, a mausoleum beyond the Damascus Gate, to the north of Jerusalem. This site was almost too well known to antiquarians. All the details of its decorations had been recorded by historians, but by the nineteenth century little was left intact. Its Graeco-Roman frieze was battered, its doors shattered, its burial chambers ransacked. Lord Belmore's party, in 1816, had been detected trying to enter and ordered off; de Saulcy, who was a liberal distributor of bribes, was more successful. His workmen found two sarcophagi in one of the less accessible burial chambers, one of them with an inscription which he insisted was the name of King David's sister, Seruyah. This, and the fact that compared with other local tombs the mausoleum was exceptionally grand, convinced de Saulcy that these were indeed the tombs of David and Solomon.

De Saulcy's determination to remove the sarcophagi caused an uproar. The Jewish community protested that he was profaning the graves of their ancestors, and was backed up by the Prussian consul, Rosen. Though de Saulcy's foreman smeared clay on the inscriptions, a Jewish delegation detected the lettering, and it was only when the French consul Barrères, somewhat against his will, was dragged in to the dispute, that de Saulcy was able to carry off his prize. To the Jews, he continued to argue that these were the graves of Romans, the Jews' oppressors. But back in Paris, de Saulcy stuck to his original theory, though every scholar who could read the inscription identified the sarcophagus as that of Queen Saddan, or Helen of Adiabene, a convert to Judaism known to have died in the first century AD, and the mausoleum as belonging to her dynasty – about six hundred years later than the kings of Judah.

De Saulcy argued in vain that it was impossible to analyse ruins in Palestine from the libraries of Paris; the scholars knew better. The French government, moreover, showed no sign of wanting to back an expedition to Palestine on a grand scale, as de Saulcy suggested. French archaeologists either combined their researches with diplomatic postings, like Emile Botta, made use of military manpower, as Renan did in 1860, or went it alone, like Victor Guérin, who surveyed the biblical sites of Palestine single-handedly between 1853 and 1871, on behalf of the Ministry of Public Instruction.

Thus it was mortifying to the French scholars when a British organization announced that it was to carry out the first comprehensive survey of the country in history. Melchior de Vogüé, the French ambassador in Constantinople, wrote to de Saulcy in 1864: 'Have you read in the *Journal Officiel* that the English are carrying out *your idea* of a Palestine Commission? A group of scientists are going to explore, excavate and dig up the Holy Land in all directions and steal all your discoveries. Hang yourself, my fine antiquarian!'

*   *   *

The Palestine Exploration Fund was officially established a year later. It had Queen Victoria as patron, and archbishops and politicians sat on its committee with many of England's leading scholars and scientists. Its declared aims were, accordingly, a nice mixture of the ecclesiastical and the intellectual. The Fund was to uncover archaeological evidence of the 'political and domestic history of the Jews' and also 'to find remains in Palestine linking the arts of Egypt with those of Assyria'. It was also to collect information on the country's geology, ethnography and natural history.

However, the sponsors of the Fund, on both sides, were less enthusiastic, or optimistic, than its founders suggested, and the brief given its officers far less scientifically objective than might have appeared at first.

The Anglican Church's enthusiasm was tempered by concern lest the Fund's researches turn up material disturbing to a conservative view of the Scriptures. The passion for biblical illustration and Oriental authenticity was waning. A. P. Stanley, now Dean of Westminster, told the Fund that he would be pleased if its officers found nothing, for 'a negative result, important everywhere, is particularly interesting in regard to sacred history, because it there becomes a proof of the universal and divine character of the religion . . . independent of any local features or outward customs'.

Layard, England's most famous archaeologist, warned the Fund that 'nothing spectacular was to be expected from Palestine, first because of the Jewish prohibition of the representation of the human form . . . and also because the local stone was not soft or easily worked' – just that factor, as it happened, which had led to the survival of so many of the ruins of Jerusalem.

De Vogüé had been wrong in thinking that England was to send out its finest scientists. The Fund's work in Palestine was conducted in the main by soldiers: men of the Royal Engineers. This was coincidence. The PEF developed out of the expedition of Engineers sent out in 1864 to determine the water resources of Jerusalem for Lady Burdett-Coutts. They were the best-qualified men to carry out a topographical survey, and army officers had already provided the first accurate British map of Jerusalem in 1841.

The Royal Engineers who worked in Palestine, however, were not soldiers masquerading as antiquarians. They were all well versed in contemporary controversies, bible readers to a man, amateur students of Near Eastern history. To judge from their memoirs, they argued as feverishly about the origins of the ruins they came across as contemporary scholars, and published their views even more readily.

The maps they produced showed not only every natural feature of Palestine but every site of interest, which they worked hard to identify. These maps were important for future archaeological research, and were also used, later on, to draw up the frontiers of Mandatory Palestine.

Where the War Office was concerned, it was highly incongruous that when maps were wanting of the British colonies, and when the collection of basic information on the armies of foreign powers was entrusted to one harassed officer in the Ordnance Survey department of the War Office, that British army engineers loaned to the Fund (the War Office did not pay their expenses) should have been diligently noting every disused well and interesting ruin in Palestine.

It was the Palestine Exploration Fund, moreover, which continually tried to convince the War Office that at some future date its maps might be of vital interest to the nation; the War Office had other priorities. Though Palestine lay on the route to Suez and India, the main defences of that route, against Russia, lay in Asia Minor – maps of which did not exist; and in the provision of a coaling station and port for British battleships – which Palestine could not provide.

There was another problem for the Fund in having professional surveyors in the field, apart from trying to convince the War Office to put up money. The public was not going to be particularly excited by the production of one inch to a mile maps of the Nablus district, when what it really wanted was Joseph's mummy or the Ark of the Covenant. The Fund's first secretary, George Grove, was concerned above all with attracting wealthy donors; and donors wanted discoveries.

So when Charles Warren, a young captain in the Royal Engineers, was appointed to head the Fund's team in Palestine in 1867, for its second season, he was given more dramatic instructions. Surveying and map-making apart, he was to establish, once and for all, the location of the disputed areas of biblical Jerusalem: the course of the walls of the city in various biblical periods, and in particular the so-called Second Wall, that of Herod's time; the area originally forming the Temple Mount; and the true site of the Holy Sepulchre. All these questions were related.

The reason why the position of the Second Wall was so important was that the resolution of the bitterest controversy of the age depended on it: whether or not the existing Holy Sepulchre was really the site of Christ's burial. As no Jew could be buried, according to Jewish law, within the city limits, the original sepulchre must have lain outside the walls during the time of Herod. The existing Sepulchre, of course, was well within Suleiman's wall; but no one knew how this related to the earlier boundaries of the city.

It was a tribute to Victorian optimism that Grove believed that a small group of British army engineers, however thorough their knowledge of the Bible, with Josephus in one hand and an engineering manual in the other, could solve problems which had baffled scholars for centuries.

But Grove himself was no ordinary fund-raiser. An engineer by training, he was a self-taught musician who had been secretary to the Society of Arts and run the mammoth Crystal Palace, that momument to popular education, and was to write the famous *Dictionary of Music* which bears his name. In sending Warren off on this ambitious mission, he was also involving him, without his knowledge, in a gamble to save the fortunes of the Fund at the cost of its scientific integrity.

Only two years after its foundation, the Fund was almost out of funds. Its future appeared to depend on the support of one of its wealthiest and most influential members, James Fergusson. Fergusson had made a fortune in the indigo trade and he had devoted many years to perfecting his theory about the Holy Sepulchre lying under the Dome of the Rock; he also believed that Solomon's Temple had been built in the extreme southwest corner of the original Mount. This very peculiar theory had been worked up into two books and was also included in Dr Smith's *Dictionary of the Bible* in 1858, one of the standard ecclesiastical reference works of the period.

As far as Fergusson was concerned, Warren's expedition was designed to prove his theory and – as Warren was later to realize – Grove was, perhaps uneasily, committed to supporting Fergusson.

When Warren set out for Palestine he did not know the extent of Fergusson's influence on the committee and over Grove, though he was aware – as everyone was – of Fergusson's theory. Nor did he know that his initial payment of three hundred pounds was all the money in the Fund's possession. Grove gave him vague assurances that more would be despatched in due course, suggested that he wrap up warmly in Jerusalem in the winter, and assured him that his firman had been applied for and would duly reach him in Jerusalem.

There could have been no greater challenge to Warren's integrity, and his ingenuity, than the circumstances in which he was shortly to find himself in Jerusalem. When he arrived, there was no firman waiting for him, and he had a chilly welcome from the British consul – Noel Temple Moore, Finn's successor – who did not warm to the idea of a British soldier digging up the precincts of the third holiest site in Islam and ruining his relations with the governor, Izzet Pasha. No more money was forthcoming from Grove, and it gradually became clear to Warren that his increasingly complex labours in the Holy City were not appreciated by the Fund, which was waiting for him to find proof of Fergusson's theories and get them all out of debt.

*　　*　　*

The Temple Mount forms a rocky promontory at the southern-most extreme of the ancient city of Jerusalem. From near the village of Siloam, below, its walls rise sheer to the precincts of the Al Aqsa mosque. As it was clearly impossible to dig in the Sanctuary itself, Warren decided that if he wanted to find the original base of the Mount he would have to dig around its edges. Unlike de Saulcy, Warren rejected all idea of bribing the officials; instead, he explained his case to Izzet Pasha and obtained his permission, pending the arrival of the firman, to sink shafts round the southern periphery of the Mount.

However, when Warren tried to test the walls of a passage which he discovered leading under the Sanctuary itself, the sound of his sledgehammers was clearly audible to worshippers in the mosque. The Imam in charge of the mosque came to the conclusion that his neighbours were responsible for the disturb-ance, and, as Warren reported, 'mounted the battlements and summoned the Sheikh of Siloam to stand forth and answer for his misdeeds'. When the real source of the noise was identified, Warren's work was stopped until further instructions were received; these stipulated that he was not to dig near any religious shrine.

The firman from Constantinople finally arrived. As the result of some bureaucratic confusion, it referred not to the area of the Sanctuary but to that of the Machpela mosque in Hebron. Warren decided to work on regardless pending a new firman's arrival, and, with Izzet's tacit agreement, continued to sink shafts around the flanks of the Mount, continually shifting his ground when objections were raised, until he acquired the local nickname of 'the Mole'.

But when Izzet Pasha was replaced a few months later by the anti-Western Nazif Pasha, fresh limitations were placed on Warren's work; he was now not allowed to excavate on public property, or nearer than forty feet from the wall of the Sanctuary. Warren circumvented this ruling, too, by leasing private property and constructing tunnels like mining galleries which ran underground to the walls of the Sanctuary. Now, however, he was running out of money, which he needed for basic mining equipment such as ropes and the wooden planks to shore up his long galleries – wood being amongst the scarcest and most expensive commodities in Palestine. The only response he had from Grove, however, was (as Warren later put it), 'Give us results, and we will send you money'. Warren was reduced to covering the expedition's expenses from his own pocket.

Warren's great strength was that he understood the topography of Herod's Mount as one engineer contemplating another's work, just as he had a practical soldier's understanding of ancient Jerusalem's problems of defence. Within a few months he had reconstructed the topography of much of the Temple Mount as it was at the time of Herod, and the fact that he misdated many of his finds and assumed that he had located the lines of the walls described by Josephus was far less important. In fact the Third, Agrippan, Wall, was only discovered in the 1920s, and the lines of the all-important Second Wall have never been established.

What Warren did, however, by tunnelling through the accumulated debris of two thousand years, was to show that previous researchers had actually underestimated the height of the great retaining walls which had risen to as far as a hundred and twenty feet above bedrock. Warren located the Valley of the Cheesemakers, which had cut the city in two in biblical times, but was now no more than a depression between the Mount and the Upper City to its west; he also discovered that the platform on which the Second Temple had stood was not identical with the natural formation on which the First Temple had presumably rested, but had been extended by Herod's engineers. Beyond the southern wall of the city he discovered an ancient water conduit and parts of an early wall, indicating to later archaeologists that the first Jerusalem, David's city, lay outside the Herodian structure altogether. Beneath the Sanctuary he came on other conduits and giant cisterns which illuminated Jerusalem's legendary ability to withstand long sieges.

Once the newspapers of Europe took up his story, Warren became famous for the courage he had displayed by descending time after time into the shafts and tunnels which he could only afford to reinforce at their very weakest points. Loose gravel and earth threatened to collapse on him from above, and foul slime threatened to engulf him from below, together with his faithful second, Corporal Birtles. Warren said of Birtles that 'he endured all the dangers of a campaign without any of its rewards'. Conscious that only publicity could earn the Fund more donations, Warren arranged for tourists to be lowered carefully into some of the less dangerous shafts, a practice which became so common that an American journalist, Charles Warner, was able to write without explanation that 'Jerusalem is not a formidable city to the explorer who is content to remain above ground and is not too anxious about its substructure and buried walls, and has no taste, as some have, for crawling through its drains'.

Where the Fund was concerned, Warren's work scarcely received its proper recognition at first. The importance of his discoveries was not understood, and he had totally discredited Fergusson's theories. His underground probings had made it clear that the Holy Sepulchre could not possibly lie beneath the Dome of the Rock, and his discovery that the southwest corner of the platform had been artificially constructed showed that Fergusson's site for the First Temple had not even existed in Solomon's time.

Fergusson took this with a very bad grace; and the committee at first took its lead from Fergusson. Warren's reports were cut, and the book which he co-authored with Wilson describing the Fund's work in Jerusalem minimized his findings. To Warren's chagrin, Fergusson's theories continued to appear in reprints of the *Dictionary of the Bible*. However, after Warren appeared before the Fund's committee in April 1868 and argued his case, Grove was persuaded to resign his post in favour of a much more open-minded secretary, the novelist Walter Besant. It was clear now that the Fund could no longer rely on wealthy patrons with an antiquarian axe to grind; instead it followed Warren's lead in appealing to the general public. The artefacts Warren had found were put on public show, and the Fund's 'Quarterly Statement', a report on progress in the field, was issued to subscribers. Henceforth the Fund's activities were eagerly followed, and supported, by people all over Britain, and, as Warren later explained, 'it was through the public interest excited that I was enabled to proceed', rather than by the support of those he called 'the theorists'.

*   *   *

Warren returned to Palestine to continue his work. But while he had been in London, something had happened which was to affect the work of all the foreign researchers excavating in the Ottoman empire. The Porte had finally awakened to the fact that the provision or refusal of firmans was no longer an effective way of ensuring that the antiquities discovered remained under Turkish control. The Sultan had opened his own museum in Constantinople, and in March 1868 a law was promulgated prohibiting the export of all antiquities from the Ottoman dominions.

There was consternation in learned circles throughout the West. Many in the Fund were indignant that Moslems had objected to the engineers' excavations; only Layard asked Stanley, point blank, how he would feel if Moslem archaeologists were to start digging in the precincts of Westminster Abbey. The Foreign Office reacted immediately to the new Turkish law in its best schoolmaster fashion, instructing its ambassador at the

Porte to press the Sultan to repeal the prohibition. 'You will say', the ambassador was ordered, 'that Her Majesty's government cannot suppose that when all the pecuniary resources of the Turkish empire are insufficient to provide for the development of the material resources of the country, money would be applied for the erection and maintenance of Museums in Turkey.' He was also told to complain of 'the obstacles thrown in the way of science and . . . researches which excite so much interest among the educated and scientific classes in Europe'.

The law was not repealed. Henceforth the provincial governors were told, so far as it lay within their power, to prevent foreign researchers from removing their finds and to transfer anything of interest to Constantinople. Like most Ottoman laws, this was not applied consistently; but it did mean that the open removal of great chunks of masonry in the style of an Elgin or a de Saulcy was now impossible. Where the Palestine Exploration Fund was concerned, it meant that its officials had to break the law if they were to acquire antiquities to show its continually growing list of supporters.

The problem of funds remained acute. For a short time, an idea was floated of soliciting Turkish funds to subsidize the Fund's operations. Wilson actually drew up a memorandum for a joint survey of Palestine with the Turkish authorities. But fear of international repercussions, and the change of government when the strongly anti-Turkish Gladstone took over in December 1868, buried the idea.

Henceforth, moreover, all foreign archaeologists in Palestine had to operate very cautiously indeed, as Charles Clermont-Ganneau, probably the most gifted of his time, was to learn.

*　　*　　*

Clermont-Ganneau was only twenty-one when he arrived in Jerusalem, as dragoman to the French consulate, in 1867. A protégé of the poet Théophile Gautier, who had supervised Ganneau's education from the time of the early death of his father, he was one of the most outstanding pupils of Renan and other great Oriental scholars at the Collège de France. Unlike de Saulcy, Ganneau had neither the financial assets nor the social background which might have enabled him to pursue an independent career as an archaeologist. In order to support himself and his widowed mother, Ganneau sat for the French foreign ministry's examinations (unlike the British Foreign Office at this time, the French set rigorously high linguistic standards for its employees in the Orient) and was sent, on his first posting, to Jerusalem.

He had not been in the city long when, like other scholars in residence, he heard of the discovery of a huge block of black basalt, covered with inscriptions, in Bedouin territory in Dhiban on the eastern side of the Dead Sea. The stone was first seen by an Alsatian missionary named Klein, on one of his journeys to Christian outposts in the area. Klein managed to sketch a few of the letters and showed them to the Prussian consul in Jerusalem, Petermann, who thought he recognized the letters as a form of Phoenician script and immediately contacted the Imperial Library in Berlin. Despite the efforts of Klein and Petermann to keep the discovery secret until the Prussian government could buy the stone from the Bedouin, the news soon reached those who lived off the sale of biblical antiquities. One of the dealers, Selim el Qari, a Greek Christian Arab who had dealings with the Bedouin of Dhiban, made a clumsy copy of eight lines of the inscription and showed them to Ganneau.

Ganneau immediately recognized the great importance of the discovery. He himself could not leave the consulate, but he found a young helper to whom he taught the technique of applying squeeze paper to the stone to obtain an impression, and sent him off to Dhiban with two escorts. In the course of making the impression, the messengers were attacked by the Bedouin; but one of the escorts succeeded in stripping the still damp squeeze from the stone and returning with it to the consulate.

Ganneau now decided to make his own offer on behalf of the French government. But meanwhile, convinced by the interest of so many foreigners that the stone concealed hidden treasure, the Bedouin had smashed it to pieces. Ganneau managed to acquire the larger fragments of the stone – in which the Prussians had by now lost interest – and working partly from the original, and partly from the creased and torn squeeze, he managed to reconstruct the greater part of the inscription, which he sent, in instalments, to de Vogüé in Constantinople.

This inscription, henceforth known as the Moabite Stone, was and still is the only corroboration in writing ever found of the history of the Holy Land as related in the Old Testament, the recital, by Mesha, King of Moab, of the events which followed his victory over the Israelites, as told in the Second Book of Kings. 'I am Mesha, son of Kamosh, king of Moab, the Dibonite', the inscription began. It described the battles the king had fought, the fortresses, reservoirs and highways he had built, and the numbers of his subjects. Here, then, was the first voice from the soil of Palestine after its long silence.

Here, too, was the sensational discovery for which the public had been waiting, something to rival the inscriptions found in other parts of the Near East. Ironically enough, the Moabite Stone had been far easier to decipher, despite the physical difficulties, than the Behistun or the Rosetta stone. These had only been understood by comparing the familiar Persian or Greek lettering with the hermetic Accadian, Elawite or hiero-glyphic scripts – whereas ancient Hebrew and its semitic relations, of which the Moabite script was one, were known alphabets. Not only Petermann but Warren had tried to interest his colleagues in the stone fragments, of which he had acquired many smaller pieces. But they did not respond. Ganneau was fortunate to be the only scholar on the spot with the persistence to undertake the work of reconstruction, and his translation was published in the *Journal Officiel* at the beginning of 1870.

The Moabite Stone, and Ganneau, won instant fame. But the majestic voice of Mesha, King of Moab, was soon rendered inaudible by the sound of international squabbling as to who was to take credit for the discovery. Both the Prussians and the British Museum attacked Ganneau for his 'precipitate action' in acquiring the fragments. George Grove, who, though no longer secretary to the Palestine Exploration Fund, still regarded him-self as its spokesman, wrote a letter to *The Times* of London claiming the discovery as Warren's, with no mention either of the role of Klein or of Ganneau's part in its acquisition and translation.

When Warren learned of the letter he was horrified. He had no great love for the Prussians but he had refrained throughout from interfering with their negotiations with the Bedouin. Warren admired Ganneau's scholarship and had cooperated faithfully with the Frenchman in his attempts to piece the text together. He resigned forthwith from the Fund's employment in protest, and to underline his action, before leaving Jerusalem, handed over the remaining fragments to Ganneau. In 1875, the Moabite Stone, carefully reconstructed, went on display in the Louvre.

*   *   *

Clermont-Ganneau was already formulating a view of Jerusalem which was quite contrary to the view of his predecessors. 'Palestine has always lived,' he was to write later 'and in order to live, it has devoured itself.' It was misleading, therefore, to look for any one typical style of building in Jerusalem, and many scholars had erred in dating the remains for this very reason. The oldest visible period, to the modern eye, Ganneau wrote, was Crusader Jerusalem, for it was the Crusaders who had reused both Roman and Moslem stonework but had imposed on it their own characteristic style. The Crusaders were also the last systematically to sack Jerusalem, another reason why their characteristic architecture had survived.

Ganneau looked at each existing building in such a way as to analyse its separate components and even its separate stones. Many of the masons' marks he noted have still not been identified. In this way he made his second great discovery. In May 1871, surveying the ruins of an old Moslem seminary near the Sanctuary, he noticed, embedded in a wall, a Greek inscription on a plaque from the Herodian period, which he identified as the warning placed at the entrance to the Second Temple, forbidding entry to all Gentiles on pain of death. This inscription, relating to the Gospels, was as obviously important for the historical authentication of the New Testament as the Moabite Stone had been for that of the Old.

Whereas the Turks had originally agreed to the removal of the Moabite Stone by the Prussians – a special firman was issued to enable its transportation through Bedouin territory – the finding of the Temple Stone was a very different matter. The first reaction of the governor was to attempt to sell it to the highest bidder – who as it happened was a Rothschild – but eventually the stone was sent to Constantinople, a central feature of the Sultan's new collection.

Until now, the local traders in antiquities had dealt in coins, old lamps and other small objects, real and fake, to be passed off to gullible tourists. But now the presence of the Fund's officers, and Ganneau's discoveries, stimulated the talents of a number of local forgers. No sooner was the Temple Stone sent to Constantinople than a Christian Arab, a local stonemason named Martin Boulos, brought Ganneau a brand-new 'Temple Stone' engraved in Greek. Soon afterwards, Ganneau was offered the head of a statue 'recently dug up in Jerusalem' with pseudo-Moabite inscriptions; to his amusement he recognized in the statue's features those of Boulos himself.

These were only the first of a series of fake antiquities which now appeared in the Jerusalem market as if from an assembly line. A brick with fake cuneiform inscriptions, signed Nebuchadnezzar, was brought to Ganneau by the Bedouin from across the Jordan; another merchant blackened a newly carved statue of the Emperor Hadrian so that it should resemble basalt. One of the Samaritan sect, Jacob Shellaby, who posed for some time in England as a local 'prince', described to the Fund's officer his method of preparing 'ancient scrolls' by steeping skins in coffee grounds and keeping them for a month or two under the pillows of his divan. All this activity was so crude that, for a time, Ganneau scarcely took it seriously. But nothing had prepared him for the most impressive demonstration of the gullibility of the scholars of Europe – the appearance of the 'Moabite potteries'.

In 1872, hundreds of little terracotta figurines, horned female figures, phalluses, and other artefacts like vases full of clay coins, appeared in Jerusalem. Many were marked with what, to the untrained eye, appeared to be 'Moabite' lettering, and were said to have originated in the same territory as the famous stone.

All these objects had been purchased from their Bedouin sellers, it was said, by Moses Wilhelm Shapira, the best-known and most respectable merchant of antiquities in Jerusalem, a converted

Russian Jew married to a Lutheran German. The first batch of the potteries was bought up almost immediately by the Prussian government for its national museum; but before the potteries were shipped off to Germany, they were seen by the two officers of the Palestine Exploration Fund who had replaced Warren: Charles Tyrwhitt Drake, a Cambridge scholar, and Claude Conder, one of the Royal Engineers. Conder was allowed by Shapira to make water-colour sketches of the potteries and to copy some of the inscriptions, and these he sent back to the Fund's offices in London.

Conder and Drake had been in Palestine for some time working on the Survey of Western Palestine, the project which was to last, with interruptions, until 1878 and to include, besides the mapping, reports on archaeological remains, the natural history of the region, and its local customs. Drake's chief interest was the customs of the country, while Conder was in charge of the mapping. While Drake's academic training made him a far more critical observer than Conder, his reports were also coloured by the intense dislike he took to the local peasantry and his loathing of clericalism: he wrote back that all holy cities – Rome, Benares, Jerusalem – revolted him and he told Isabel Burton, whom he took round the city, that every time he revisited Jerusalem he began to feel ill.

Conder, on the other hand, had come out to Palestine, as his letters to his mother indicate, to make a name for himself at all costs in the newly fashionable field of archaeology and to learn, from scratch, all he could of Palestine's history. Almost immediately, Conder decided that excavations would not be necessary: 'Entre nous, there is hardly anything to be found in Palestine; all is smashed to powder,' he wrote to Besant in September 1872: 'You see in the last two hundred miles we have found only one ruin worth noticing.'

The appearance of several hundred totally intact artefacts at one fell swoop did not, however, arouse Conder's suspicions. Both Conder, who nicknamed the potteries 'the biblical abominations', and Drake were convinced that these were authentic examples of an early Palestinian civilization, evidence of an erotic and phallic cult.

The officers of the Fund in London were perplexed by Conder's sketches. They asked for a second opinion at the British Museum, where Emmanuel Deutsch, the eminent Oriental scholar, was sceptical as to their authenticity. As it happened, Clermont-Ganneau, who had not been shown the potteries in Jerusalem, was passing through London in the autumn of 1872, and as Besant respected the young man's reputation, he showed him the sketches. Ganneau immediately concluded that the potteries were not the work of antiquity, but of Selim el Qari, the Christian Arab who, three years earlier, had made the first copy for Ganneau of the lettering of the Moabite Stone. It was not the rough and grotesque style of the potteries that aroused Ganneau's suspicions – some had grimacing heads, and tongues stuck out in mockery – as he had seen very similar work which had been excavated in Cyprus. What alerted him to Qari's handwork was the fact that the letters incised on the pottery, copied by Conder, were 'palaeographic nonsense and philologically untranslatable'.

Ganneau held his peace, however, until such a time as he should be able to examine the originals; and in February 1873 he was posted as third dragoman to the French embassy in Constantinople.

In Jerusalem, Conder became increasingly restless at the Fund's continuing reluctance to publish his sketches. 'I hear you are all so anxious for something sensational to lay before the public,' he wrote to Besant. 'And here, with only the expense of a few lithographs, you might publish all the abominations of the bible idols and be even now the first in England to do so.' Prussian scholars were writing learned commentaries on the significance of the potteries.

The Fund meanwhile had another problem. The affair of the potteries was an uncomfortable reminder that they had no experienced Oriental scholar working in Palestine itself, and no one qualified to interpret findings made on the spot. Walter Besant, the Fund's secretary, thus decided, after consulting the committee, to approach the French foreign ministry – unofficially – for the services of Charles Clermont-Ganneau. Eventually, through the good offices of W. H. Waddington, a French statesman of English parentage, this was agreed, and in the autumn of 1873 Ganneau returned to Jerusalem.

*   *   *

From the outset of Ganneau's season with the Fund, Conder resented the presence on what he regarded as his turf of the brilliant French scholar. Ganneau was only two years older than Conder, but he was already world famous. As an amateur archaeologist, Conder was unhappy to be under Ganneau's critical eye, and as an army officer he resented the participation of a civilian, and a Frenchman, in a group made up mainly of British officers.

In public, Conder was civil enough to Ganneau, but behind his back he wrote bitterly jealous letters to Besant. In one of the frankest of these, he was to write:

> You must expect a considerable difference between Ganneau's reports and my own for several reasons. 1st) a man brought up as a simple soldier cannot fairly be expected to rival the productions of the eminent archaeologist in whose successful career you now rejoice; 2nd) Monsieur Ganneau had a different life seated here in his study surrounded with books and taking at least a week to write on two or three days' work from the said subaltern riding eight hours a day for 5 days out of the week. Thirdly, in our corps it is considered to be bad taste to blow one's own trumpet though that operation has the advantage of fattening the PEFQS [the Quarterly Statement] very much.

Conder's description of himself as a simple soldier did not prevent him frequently dismissing Ganneau's theories as 'nonsense' and describing his work as 'desultory attempts at archaeology'.

As soon as Ganneau returned to Palestine, he went with Drake to inspect a second batch of 'Moabite potteries' stored in Shapira's warehouse. By this time, Drake too was beginning to have his doubts about the potteries, but he hesitated to express them save privately, to Conder, and later in letters to the Fund. Ganneau, however, set out to find who was making them.

Within a short time, he had located the Jerusalem potter who admitted to having baked hundreds of statuettes for Selim el Qari. The potter's young apprentice told Ganneau that he had trotted back and forth between the pottery and Selim's house carrying the 'antiquities' hot from the oven, which he dipped into a cistern of saltpetre 'to make them grow old'. The potter accompanied Ganneau to the British consulate to make a sworn statement; and there, it seemed to him, the matter should have rested.

But far too much was at stake for the Prussians; everything was at stake for the forgers; and the young Englishmen had also been disconcerted by Ganneau's brisk dismissal of the theory to which they had already committed themselves. Drake's position was the most unfortunate. He believed – and over a century later his feeling was to be confirmed – that several of the early potteries did not resemble the second batch. But this was not enough to withstand Ganneau's argument and his effectiveness as a sleuth.

The German consul persuaded the potter to retract his statement; the Prussian scholars blustered; and Conder, who a few months earlier had been arguing that the Moabite potteries were 'unique specimens of ancient symbolic art', now wrote to Besant that 'Ganneau having had his innings, the Germans have still got to get theirs, and will return his bowling in furious style. I of course have nothing to do with such abstruse archaeological subjects, but will give you my private opinion that the affair is rather muddled – for what it is worth.'

Ganneau had now made bitter enemies both among the Germans and among the Christian Arab middlemen whose living depended on the continuing supply of ersatz antiquities to foreign buyers. But for the moment he had a more urgent problem: the Turks had still not sanctioned his work in Jerusalem with a firman.

*   *   *

Throughout the autumn of 1873 and the spring of 1874, the Foreign Office had badgered the Porte for Ganneau's firman, to no effect. All they could do was to remind him that Warren's firman had taken even longer to arrive. The Fund had given Ganneau a free hand; there was no repetition of the disastrous directives given to Warren. Anything he found had first to be offered to the Fund, but he could investigate whatever and wherever he chose.

Without the firman, however, he could not undertake any public investigations. Meanwhile, he despatched report after brilliant report on the archaeological features of different parts of the country, and even unearthed, discreetly, relics like early Christian sarcophagi with Hebrew inscriptions in caves near Jerusalem – though such aspects of his researches could not be immediately published.

He also used his good relations with the Moslem Kadi in charge of the Sanctuary to examine in detail the Dome of the Rock, where restoration work was under way. This was ideal for Ganneau's purposes, as he observed the underlying structure of the building as the ceramic tiling was peeled away, revealing the Crusader masonry put in when Abd'El Malik's seventh-century shrine was turned into the Crusaders' Templum Domini. He had even been promised that he would be allowed to see beneath the flagstone covering the crypt under the sacred rock – which Warren, despite his ingenuity, had just failed to do.

All this did not compensate Ganneau for the fact that he was limited to working on his own, and, without a firman, could scarcely hire workers in Jerusalem. In April 1874 he asked Conder for the loan of some of his soldiers. Ganneau was Conder's colleague and the soldiers had Turkish sanction to carry out research. Conder turned him down flat, giving as his reason that 'soldiers don't like working under a civilian'.

Thus Ganneau was to undertake, alone, the exploration which was to end in disaster and wreck all his chances of working in Palestine completely. In June 1874 he set out to locate the biblical city of Gezer, a problem which had occupied him for years.

Built in the fourth millenium BC, Gezer had flourished throughout Canaanite and biblical times. It had become one of Solomon's fortress cities, and during the Crusader period was rechristened Mont Gisart. Gezer became a Moslem fortress during the war against Richard Coeur de Lion. But since Crusader times the site had been abandoned, and eventually all traces of its existence disappeared.

In 1870, Ganneau had 'without moving from his study', as he said, concluded that the ancient city of Gezer was identical with an Arab site in the coastal plain – Tel el Djezzar. His argument

·was not based on a quick comparison of Hebrew and Arabic place names, in the style of a Robinson, but by a close comparison of Crusader and Arab sources, those of Guillaume de Tyr and the Moslem historian Moudjiv ed Din. Guillaume de Tyr had described the territory as the site of a great victory by the Crusaders over the Moslem leader Saladin in 1177; and a thirteenth-century Arab geographer, Yakout, had named Tel el Djezzar as the site of a great fortress – which had now disappeared. Ganneau had outlined his theory in a lecture to the French Academy, but physical proof was lacking, and the scholars were sceptical.

His interest reawakened when, in early 1874, a peasant from the Abu Ghosh village near Jerusalem showed him some Greek letters he had copied down from a stone in the vicinity of Tel el Djezzar. The letters were badly traced, and in themselves suggested no link with Gezer, but Ganneau decided to explore further, and in June he left Jerusalem and rode down to the coastal plain.

Tel el Djezzar was a grassy mound at the centre of an area of rich farmland, part of which was cultivated by peasants from the nearby village of Abu Shusheh. The lands of Abu Shusheh had recently been acquired, for the sum of the tax arrears owed to the government by the peasants, by a wealthy German family, the Bergheims of Jerusalem. Melville Bergheim, the head of the family, was a convert from Judaism to the Anglican Church, who had begun his career as pharmacist to the Mission to the Jews in Jerusalem. In 1851 he had set up the first bank in the city, and by 1874 he was a leading industrialist and experimental farmer. What was more important, in Ganneau's context, was that he was banker to the Palestine Exploration Fund. During the previous spring, Bergheim had helped ransom Canon Tristram, who was carrying out research in zoology for the Fund, when he was taken prisoner by the Sheikh of Kerak. So Ganneau had every reason to trust the Bergheims.

Melville Bergheim had built a large farmhouse with a closed courtyard on the tel itself, and when Ganneau arrived, Peter Bergheim, the eldest son of the family, was at the farm. Peter Bergheim ran a photographic studio in Jerusalem, and, like almost all the Protestants in Jerusalem, he was a keen amateur archaeologist, and an acquaintance of Ganneau.

Ganneau's careful examination of the area, step by step, in search of the stone the peasant had noticed, at first yielded nothing. But then he stooped to examine a rock protruding from the soil and made out lettering in Hebrew and Greek: the Hebrew read 'Boundary stone of Gezer', and the Greek 'property of Alkios'. Further examination revealed a second stone, and a third. Whatever the risk, Ganneau decided immediately, it was essential to save these stones 'from the thousand chances of destruction which they had so far escaped'. He quickly told Bergheim the news, and the photographer, who shared his excitement, told him that the farmhouse was at his disposal to store the 'boundary stones' safely until Ganneau could report his discovery to the Fund.

From Monday 28 June to Wednesday 30 June, the peasants on whose land the stones had been found, recruited as Ganneau's workmen, laboured to loosen the first stone from the soil without damaging the inscription, and on Wednesday evening it was lifted out and placed in the farmhouse.

During that day, a curious incident occurred. While supervising the threshing of his father's fields, Peter Bergheim suddenly complained that a grain of barley had lodged in one of his eyes and was hurting him; in the afternoon he left to consult the Mission doctor in Jerusalem. Thursday 1 July passed without incident, as the labourers slowly freed the second stone from the soil. But on the Friday morning – by which time Bergheim had returned from the city – a Turkish police officer, accompanied by horsemen, rode into Abu Shusheh and ordered the workmen, in the name of the Turkish government, to stop work immediately. He then insisted on entering the Bergheims' farmhouse and searching for the first stone, which he knew was concealed there.

The officer maintained that he had orders from the governor to sequester the stone. But when Ganneau and Bergheim demanded to see the written order, they were astonished. The order had been issued not by the governor, but by the German consulate; it was written in English; and it lacked the formal consular seal. It was signed, moreover, not by the German consul, the Baron von Munchausen, but by a mere dragoman – Serapion Murad, that same consular official who had been in the pay of the American consulate, seven years earlier, before he was discharged for 'contrivance'. Ganneau instantly remembered that it was Murad who had organized the Prussian consulate's enquiry into the authenticity of the potteries, the previous year, in an unsuccessful attempt to re-establish their reputation.

By now, Ganneau had begun to suspect Peter Bergheim himself. Bergheim was a Prussian citizen, and he was clearly on good terms with the Turkish officer, who, Ganneau had noticed, on entering the farmhouse took off his boots and sprawled on Bergheim's bed. Serapion Murad, it later emerged, was engaged to Bergheim's sister.

Ganneau wasted no more time at the farm. He hurried back to Jerusalem, where he gave a full description of the events at Abu Shusheh to the British consul, Noel Temple Moore. On the following day, Moore went to the governor of Jerusalem, Kiamil Pasha, to complain of interference with the work of the Fund, only to discover that the governor knew nothing of the affair, and had issued no order for the sequestration of the stones. Moore next approached the Baron von Munchausen; but he, too, said he had known nothing of the matter until he discovered the stones in the courtyard of the consulate. Serapion Murad had apparently acted on his own initiative, having asked the consul for a three-day leave that week.

It was now clear to everyone involved that Ganneau was the victim of a plot concocted by all his enemies in Jerusalem. Unfortunately, both he and Moore had miscalculated Kiamil Pasha's reaction. So, far from agreeing to restore the stones to the officials of the Fund, he immediately gave orders that they should be brought to his residence, where they would remain until he could ship them to the Turkish capital. Kiamil was now, understandably, highly suspicious of any further researches Ganneau might undertake.

Thus his work in the Noble Sanctuary precincts was prohibited. When he attempted to dig in the grounds of the Latin Patriarchate, he was immediately halted by Turkish soldiers; the same thing happened when he tried to work in the Armenian quarter.

Ganneau complained desperately to Besant that his work was at a standstill. He wanted the entire story published; he suggested that Queen Victoria appeal to the Sultan; he argued that it was essential, not only for his sake, but for that of all future researchers, that the matter should be 'fought out to a just conclusion'; and he insisted that he had not intended to export the stones, but merely to keep them safe from destruction in the Fund's premises.

Back in London, however, the Fund was in a quandary. Besant wrote to Ganneau that he sympathized with his 'annoyance' but that it was absolutely necessary to avoid any breach with the Turkish government 'which might not improbably lead to a total cessation of all systematic research'. To Moore, in a letter copied to Ganneau, Besant said that it was evident that Ganneau had infringed the law; and Ganneau, deeply hurt, sent in his resignation.

Though Besant assured Ganneau that the committee of the Fund did not intend to disavow his conduct or disapprove it – 'we have broken the law for six years at least, and we shall go on breaking it, until we are stopped, with every coin we bring away from the place' – he could not publicly defend Ganneau. He promised that both Moore and the committee would try to secure redress. But the months passed, Ganneau's tormentors were not punished, and no action was taken on Ganneau's behalf.

The Fund's committee was divided as to whether to accept Ganneau's resignation or to renew his contract, as had previously been their intention. Publicly, Conder commiserated with Ganneau, who, he reported, seemed to have regretted his resignation, had been ill, and had lost 'his usual energy'. Privately, he advised the Fund that 'in Mr Moore's opinion, M. Ganneau should be removed as soon as possible from Jerusalem, where it is no longer possible for him to work in peace.' 'I am always employed in defending him,' wrote Conder to Besant, 'but I am glad that it is not a Royal Engineer who is so spoken against.' He kept in with the Bergheims because 'the politics of the Survey require our being on good terms with the Germans, and so I mean to remain'. Grove, still a power in the Fund, agreed with Conder. Eventually the committee decided not to renew Ganneau's contract, and instead to replace Tyrwhitt Drake (who had died of malaria) with an assistant for Conder, another young Royal Engineer, called Horatio Herbert Kitchener, better known for his later role in Britain's Near East affairs than his early interest in Palestine.

Only Warren realized that the Fund's behaviour to its most gifted employee had been less than generous. After Ganneau had left Palestine, Warren wrote to Conder at the end of 1874 reminding him that the world regarded Ganneau as a great scholar, and that it was not for Conder to belittle his achievements. 'Army and navy men have no right to arrogate to themselves a term in use in civil life; I certainly consider Ganneau was an officer of the PEF just as was Drake.'

Conder was left king of the castle. He went on to become the greatest popularizer of biblical archaeology of the century, writing lively accounts of his adventures in Palestine, and theorizing about antiquity to the top of his bent.

Ganneau returned to Palestine in 1880 for a brief spell as consul in Jaffa; once more he was drawn to Gezer, where he identified another stone in 1881. He did not attempt to remove it, and though other indications of the boundary of Gezer were later discovered, this last discovery of Ganneau's was not seen again. Ganneau's explanation of the purpose of these strange stones, unusual as evidence of Jewish settlement, was that it was to mark the area, probably during the Hasmonean period, in which sabbath rituals were to be strictly observed. A modern Israeli archaeologist has argued that the area was marked off from that of Alkios, whose lands presumably lay outside the boundary of the town, so that the Jews of Gezer, surrounded by Gentile neighbours, and remote from Jerusalem, should pay their full complement of tithes to the Hasmonean rulers of the capital; the stones may have served as markers for the inspectors periodically sent out to gather the tithes.

The major part of the material gathered by the Fund's officers was published in 1878. Ganneau recognized that his reports were legally the Fund's property, but held out for separate publication; he also refused to allow his colleague Lecomte's illustrations to 'ornament Conder's prose'. His reports for the Fund were finally published as two separate volumes in 1896 and 1899, but even then the Fund's officers took it on themselves to eliminate the story of the Gezer incident, which Ganneau had told in some detail. Commenting in the text that 'it was deemed desirable to suppress this account', they put a row of asterisks in its place.

*   *   *

There were many repercussions to the season of Clermont-Ganneau with the PEF. The great archaeologist bore no grudge against the Fund, and continued to contribute to its *Quarterly Statement*; but he was perennially on the lookout for forgeries which might discredit the very practice of archaeology. The degree of complicity of Shapira in the Moabite forgeries was never established; neither the Royal Engineers, nor Ganneau himself, ever suggested that he was other than the dupe of his suppliers. In 1883, when the British Museum was about to purchase an ancient scroll found near the Dead Sea, from Shapira, for a million pounds, Ganneau once more discomfited the learned world by denying its authenticity. Disgraced for the second time, Shapira killed himself.

Over a hundred years later, excavations in the Negev, in the Edomite town of Kidmit, uncovered a handful of clay figurines which bore an astonishing resemblance to the 'Moabite' potteries – without bearing any lettering. There, perhaps, lay the explanation of Drake's contention that some of the original figurines bore genuine marks of age. The lesson of these finds was that only outside the area under Jewish rule were graven images to be found – Conder's 'biblical abominations'.

Palestine had indeed released its secrets in a 'maddeningly laconic way', calculated to confound all but archaeologists of the greatest detachment and scientific objectivity – whatever the techniques available to their age.

Now that Ganneau had gone, the Fund's officers in the field were all soldiers. Until this time, the Fund had used the services of the War Office; but now the situation was to be reversed. The War Office was to call on one of the Fund's leading scholars, Professor Edward Henry Palmer, who, because of his knowledge of Sinai and its Bedouin population, was asked to help the British war effort in Egypt in 1882. This adventure was ultimately to bring Warren back to Palestine for the last time.

The final years of the mapping of western Palestine under Conder and Kitchener coincided with the renewal of the Russian threat to British interests in the Near East. A memorandum of 1876 written by the British General Wolseley, who later headed the invasion forces in Egypt, indicates that one of Britain's concerns was that the Russians might occupy Syria under the pretext of protecting the Christians of the Holy Land.

'France,' Wolseley wrote, 'which was formerly always ready to fight for the "holy places" in the interests of the Latin Church, would not now do anything to prevent the permanent occupation of Syria by Russia; and to the other continental nations of Europe, it can be a matter of no moment whether the Sultan or the Czar is daily prayed for in Jerusalem as its lord and master. To us, however, it would be a most serious matter as the stepping stone to the Russian occupation of Egypt a little later on, and as an immediate menace to our communication with India via the Suez Canal.'

In 1878, with Russia and Turkey at war, there was a brief rumour that Britain might occupy Palestine, and Conder hoped that he would soon be joined by an army of occupation; but Britain's most urgent need, as Wolseley stressed in his report, was for a naval base in the eastern Mediterranean, and in that same year, at the Congress of Berlin, Britain was given that base at Cyprus.

The Fund's maps remained, for the moment, as they were advertised 'for the use of students and the elucidation of Biblical topography'. They were published in 1880 in hundreds of copies; and in February of that year they were presented to the Sultan by the British ambassador to the Porte as a token of British friendship.

In 1882, the Egyptian nationalist uprising under an army officer, Arabi Pasha, brought British armies back to the Near

East for the first time since 1841. Though the decision to invade Egypt was taken only at the last minute – General Wolseley occupied Ismaelia on 21 August – the War Office and the Admiralty had prepared contingency plans earlier in the year.

Late in June, a Captain Gill of the Intelligence department of the War Office contacted Professor Palmer with an invitation to breakfast the next morning with Lord Northbrook, First Lord of the Admiralty. There the professor was offered a heroic role; he was to travel into Sinai, east of the Suez Canal, to contact Bedouin tribesmen who might have been won over to Arabi's side and to ensure, with bribes, that they would not interfere with British army operations in the vicinity of the canal. The reason for the invitation was undoubtedly the experience Palmer had gained when he had travelled throughout Sinai with Tyrwhitt Drake, a decade earlier, for the Fund.

Palmer was flattered by the appeal to his expertise and his patriotism, and by the promise of state honours and ready cash. He was no Lawrence; his experience of the Bedouin had led him to see them as 'a simple and unmitigated nuisance', who, wherever they went, brought with them 'ruin, violence and neglect'. But he had unbounded confidence in his own capacities. A small, odd man in his forties, he was a juggler, mesmerist, mind reader and raconteur, as well as a distinguished Arabist who had translated the Koran into English and the New Testament into Arabic. He was also very hard up; he had recently married, and was supplementing his professorial salary by writing articles for the papers.

Palmer was not the last scholar to be flattered by an appeal to involve himself in public affairs; but he was certainly one of the vainest. He travelled into the Sinai from Gaza, meeting with the sheikhs of all the largest tribes, and it was enough for him to have recited Arabic poetry with a sheikh of the Haiwath Bedouin, and to have promised him £500 in gold, for him to be convinced that he had won the Bedouin's loyalty throughout the peninsula. Within a matter of days he was claiming that he had every Bedouin at his call 'from Suez to Gaza', and that a force of forty thousand pro-British Bedouin could be raised from among the Sinai tribesmen.

By the time he reached Suez, the British navy was about to take the town, which they did almost without opposition. Palmer joined the Admiral's flagship and was appointed interpreter-in-chief to the invasion forces. He was now, in his own estimation at least, 'one of the chief officers of the expedition, and an awful swell'.

The War Office placed twenty thousand pounds at his disposal, in gold, for the Bedouin troops he was to recruit. At first he wanted to take the entire sum with him into the desert; but the naval officers in charge insisted that he reduce the sum to about three thousand.

Until now, Palmer's 'cover' had been that of a journalist reporting the campaign for a London paper; now, however, it was put abroad that he was to buy camels for the British army. Accompanied by Captain Gill, whose task was to cut the telegraph wire linking Cairo and Turkey, a naval officer, and a Jewish cook, Palmer set out into Sinai under the guidance of a man he believed to be the sheikh of an important tribe, named Metter Sofia.

So incautious had Palmer been on his trip southwards, that the fact that he was carrying gold for the large Tiyyaha tribe further east in Sinai was at least shrewdly suspected by all the Bedouin of the region, and also by the Egyptian governor of Nakhl, a fort half way between Suez and Aqaba. Before they had gone more than a few miles, Palmer and his companions were intercepted, stripped, bound, and taken to Wadi es Sudr, a lonely valley in the southern Sinai. Metter Sofia had escaped with the gold and later seems to have refused to ransom the prisoners. The Bedouin led Palmer and his companions to the edge of a ravine, and there either shot them or pushed them over the edge, confident that the autumn rains would eventually wipe out all trace of the crime.

When Palmer and Gill failed to return, rumours of the real nature of his mission spread in London; questions were asked in Parliament, though the truth was stubbornly denied by government spokesmen in both Houses of Parliament.

Meanwhile, a search party of Royal Engineers was sent out to Sinai under the command of Charles Warren. Warren was now a military instructor at the Engineers' barracks at Chatham.

Though he had not visited Palestine since his resignation from the Fund a dozen years earlier, he had proposed a plan of his own for the pacification of the Bedouin of Sinai – which had been rejected in favour of the Palmer mission.

Throughout September 1882, and most of October, Warren travelled through the desert, retracing Palmer's movements. He eventually came upon the remains of the party at the bottom of the narrow ravine. The bodies had been savaged by wild animals, but Warren retrieved such objects as a portable sponge bath, a tattered copy of Byron's *Don Juan*, a Bradshaw travelling guide, 'the truss of a very small man' – presumably Palmer – and Gill's socks with his feet still in them. Later, he was to recover more evidence among the local tribespeople; the naval officer's tobacco pouch was spotted on the belt of a Bedouin, and his wife wore, among her head ornaments, a silver pencil case. A few days after Warren's discoveries, the desert rains fell which might have swept away the evidence.

Eventually, by taking hostages among the Bedouin in Cairo, Warren succeeded in tracking down the murderers. Metter Sofia, an elderly man, died in prison before he could be sentenced; three Howeytat Bedouin were hanged.

The opposition in the House of Commons lambasted the Palmer mission and termed the execution of the Bedouin 'judicial murder'. They argued that Palmer's killing was part of the national resistance of Egypt against the Christian invaders.

Whatever view was taken of the mission, or indeed of the invasion of Egypt, it was clearly a spectacular failure for British intelligence. Besant, the secretary of the Fund, argued that a soldier, not a scholar, should have been sent on the mission. Warren agreed with him. His official summing up for the War Office was devastating: Palmer, he said, had made his first mistake in deciding to enter Sinai through Syria, thus publicizing his presence throughout the area; he subsequently should have avoided Fort Nakhl, with its pro-Arab governor, altogether; and he would have been more able to judge the Bedouin's intentions had he spoken to them through an interpreter. Warren ascertained, moreover, that Palmer's estimate of available Bedouin forces was grossly inflated, and, in any case, the early collapse of the Egyptian army had made the entire mission unnecessary. Palmer's expedition, and murder, had actually made further relations with the Bedouin all the more difficult.

*   *   *

The teaming of scholars and soldiers was to be tried by the Fund once more, on the eve of the First World War, when two archaeologists (one of whom was T. E. Lawrence) joined the Engineers in surveying the Wilderness of Zin – or the Negev. Only at this date could it be said that the Fund was now genuinely involved in the work of military intelligence. But this was in a very different age.

The Fund had been established at the height of the passion for the biblical geography of Palestine which was already on the wane by the 1880s. In 1885, Walter Besant, summing up the first twenty years of the Fund's operations, wrote that the circumstances which were so favourable to the establishment of the Fund no longer existed: 'We have ceased, for instance, in a large measure, to hear sermons on the teachings of certain episodes in the Old Testament. Those who applied every episode in the life of David, say, to the conduct of our daily life are gone; the expounders of prophecy are nearly all gone; the . . . admiration of the ancient Jew, which used to be combined with an unreasoning hatred of the modern Jew, is gone – with, one hopes, the hatred.' Besant concluded that 'were we to begin, today, the Survey of the Holy Land, we should have a very much smaller support, in proportion to our wealth and numbers, than we had in the year 1865'.

By the 1880s, too, there was a different breed of archaeologists. The climate that had produced army officers prepared to dig for Solomon's Temple had changed, and the evolution of scientific method was eliminating the antiquarians. What was to remain, for many years, was the reluctance to understand that the great monuments on the Temple Mount had actually been constructed by a small and poor relation in the ancient Near East, to accept the thought that their spiritual legacy apart, as Clermont-Ganneau observed, 'the tiny kingdoms of Juda and Israel cut a poor figure beside the great monarchies of the Orient, of which they were, for most of their history, only the humble vassals', and to see the archaeology of Palestine in its widest context.

CHAPTER VIII

'Till the Conversion of the Jews'

> Had we but World enough, and Time,
> This coyness 'Lady' were no crime.
> We would sit down, and think which way
> To Walk, and pass our long Love's Day.
> Thou by the Indian Ganges' side
> Shouldst Rubies find; I by the Tide
> Of Humber would complain. I would
> Love you ten years before the Flood;
> And you should if you please refuse
> Till the Conversion of the Jews.
>
> ANDREW MARVELL, *To His Coy Mistris*

MARVELL, LIVING IN an earlier period of political upheaval and eschatological speculation, believed that England had a central part to play in the advent of the Millenium and Christ's Second Coming. An integral part of this belief, in theological tradition, was the prophecy of the Return of the remnant of Israel from exile, as Christians: a vast theory constructed on a minuscule textual base, Romans, 9, xxvii: 'Esaias also crieth concerning Israel, Though the number of the children of Israel be as the sand of the sea, a remnant shall be saved.'

In the seventeenth century the identity of Israel itself was debatable – some regarded the English as the Chosen People and the Jews stiff-necked outcasts whose conversion, according to the belief Marvell invoked in his poem, was impossible.

Millenarian beliefs revived at the end of the eighteenth century, but this time the Jews played a central part. The missions to the Jews were now vital to the fulfilment of prophecy, and no subject was more eagerly debated, in pamphlets and journals, in sermons in the churches, and in Evangelical society, than their return to Jerusalem. While the probable date of this interesting event varied, according to the interpretation of the prophetic books and apocrypha, it was also calculated by reference to contemporary political events.

But it was confined to Evangelical circles in England and Protestant groups in America, and had no direct political importance. At international conferences Palestine was discussed in the context of the protection of the Holy Places, without any mention of a future role for the Jews. Speculation about the country's eventual destiny revived with each challenge to Turkish rule, but most proposals for a Western role in the Holy Land were linked not to a Jewish, but a Christian revival: the 'peaceful Crusade', the penetration of the Orient by Western Christianity and its ultimate victory, by persuasion and commerce, over Islam.

There was romantic speculation in Europe about a Jewish renaissance of some kind, as the Jews' emancipation progressed and their talents were recognized. Disraeli's Oriental novels suggested that Jewish financiers in the West and Arabs in the East, 'Jews on horseback' as he called them, would control the destinies of empires; Lamartine wrote of a Palestine 'repeopled with a young and Jewish nation, cultivated and watered by intelligent industry'.

But those who actively campaigned for the idea of a Jewish return were not literary statesmen like Disraeli or Lamartine, or those who supported the emancipation of the Jews in their native countries, but the men and women whose chief interest in the Jews was to see them turned into Christians. These were Evangelical leaders like Lord Ashley and his circle in England, the missionaries (many of whom were recent converts from Judaism) and the Christian settlers in Palestine, particularly American Protestants. All these saw the future 'Hebrew Christians' as playing a central part in a regenerated Holy Land.

The Evangelicals preached the Jewish Return in England. The missionaries descended on Palestine with their bibles and medicine chests; the American Millenarians and the German

Templars (who though they believed themselves the Chosen People greatly influenced the local Jews by their example) with their modern ploughs and fertilizers. They set up the first Western hospitals, schools, and welfare schemes for the Jewish poor; and built the first religious institutions and farming settlements outside the protection of the city walls.

Fear of their influence sent the orthodox Jews of Palestine with pleas for help to the Jewish philanthropists in the West, who set up rival hospitals, schools and farms for the Jews. The attempt to convert the Jews of Palestine failed; but it was the catalyst which, perhaps, more than any other single factor, hastened the involvement of emancipated Western Jews with Palestine.

The Christian idea of the Jewish Return had nothing to do with the modern concept of political independence for the Jews. The motive force for Jewish nationalism was to come not from the West, but from Eastern Europe, where continuing persecution, and disillusion with the promise of emancipation, created a political and secular constituency for Zionism. The Return of which the Evangelicals dreamed came about, therefore, in a way that no interpretation of Scriptures, however ingenious, might have predicted.

*   *   *

The London Society for the Promotion of Christianity among the Jews was founded at the height of Evangelical popularity in 1809. Other societies appearing at that time were the Climbing Boys (for chimney sweeps), the Degraded Females and the Foreigners in Distress. The London Jews' Society, as it was known for short, was to save the Jews from Judaism as the climbing boys were to be saved from asphyxiation and the degraded females from a fate worse than death. Unlike the other societies, however, the London Society had ramifications throughout Europe, and its agents functioned everywhere save where rival churches (for instance, the Catholics in Poland) were hostile to their presence.

At first, the London Society took little interest in Palestine. Its founders believed the conversion of the Jews to be a worldwide and gradual process, and that the Jews would eventually return to Palestine as converts, in accordance with the Protestant interpretation of prophecy. While Europe endured revolution and war, and street-corner preachers daily predicted apocalyptic events – of which the Return of the Jews was only one – the Society prudently disassociated itself from prophetic 'enthusiasm'.

In 1810, the committee announced that it 'wished to distinguish between the restoration of Israel to their own country and the conversion of Israel to Christianity'. In 1823, the Society's leaders 'disclaimed all intention of promulgating any particular views as to the nature of the Millenium, their object being the conversion of the Jews to Christianity'.

But in the late 1830s, the Society acquired some powerful supporters, and a new conjunction of political events in the Near East appeared to favour the extension of the mission in Palestine. Chief among its supporters on the lay side was the great reformer, Lord Ashley, stepson to Palmerston, the Foreign Secretary, and on the ecclesiastical side, most of the Anglican episcopate, who became official patrons of the Society.

At this period there was still only a handful of missionaries in the Levant. When representatives of the Scottish church visited Jerusalem in 1839, they were warned by John Nicolayson, the Danish lay preacher who had been in Jerusalem on and off since 1824, that it was a rabbinical stronghold; that missionaries could neither circulate tracts nor address the Jews at public assemblies – as they did elsewhere – and that any potential convert would not only be rejected by the entire community, but deprived of his share in the charitable funds from Europe on which most of the Jews subsisted.

Jerusalem was indeed a stronghold of orthodoxy. It was the desire to escape the secular influences spreading throughout central Europe which drove many Jews to Palestine during this period. Rabbi Akiva Schlesinger of Pressburg, one of those who urged migration on the Jews, argued that Palestine promised the only refuge from 'the culture of corruption'. This did not discourage the missionaries; when the Scottish envoys came to write their report on the Jews of Europe and the Near East, they concluded that the Holy Land was 'the most important and interesting of all fields of labour amongst the Jews'. The fact that the Jews of Palestine were very poor meant that they were suitably 'humbled'; and they were 'untainted by the infidelity of France or the neology of Germany'. Though in England many of the converts had been made from the poor immigrant Jews who had little education of any kind, including that in their own religion, the belief persisted that it was among deeply religious Jews whose faith had been shaken by events that the missionaries could make converts. This belief was encouraged by the better known of the converts, like Moses Margoliouth, and the fact that among them –two hundred and fifty converts became Anglican clergymen – were many former rabbinical scholars.

The crux of all missionary debate with the Jews was the identity of the Messiah and the Jews' refusal to recognize that he had appeared in the person of Jesus. Thus it was with some excitement that missionaries sent out by the Society in all directions, from Eastern Europe to North Africa, reported that many orthodox Jews believed that redemption was close at hand. The origin of these rumours was certainly the fact that, according to the kabbalists' interpretation of the mystical book of Zohar, the year 5600 in the Jewish calendar – or 1840 – was one of the 'favourable periods' in which God would 'raise up the nation of Israel from the dust of its exile'. This was not the first time that Jewish scholars had calculated a date for redemption; they had done so before 1096 and 1648. However, most orthodox Jews were wary of calculations of this kind, since predicting the advent of the redemption was in a sense a Jewish heresy; most rabbinical teaching rejected attempts by man to anticipate the wishes of God. But the ultra-orthodox sect, called the Perushim, strongly represented in the little Jewish community of Jerusalem, believed fervently in the kabbalist predictions.

The missionaries, however, had little understanding of these complexities. It was enough for them, and their patrons, that the prediction had been made, and it set off a fresh outburst of 'enthusiasm' among the Evangelists and even, by an extraordinary chain of circumstances, a political proposal by Lord Palmerston to the Porte.

The kabbalists' prediction was conveyed to Lord Ashley 'by a convert recently returned from Warsaw' (probably the missionary Pieritz) and to the British public by Ashley in an article in the *Quarterly Review* in 1838, in which he informed England that 'the Jews were convinced that the turning of the captivity was at hand'.

There were two promising features for the Evangelicals in Lord Ashley's news: firstly, the possibility that when the Messiah failed to appear, the Jews would be particularly malleable to Christian persuasion; and secondly, that the Jewish people as a whole were probably, at that moment, inclined to answer a call to return to Jerusalem, preferably under British protection. The Evangelists were worldly people and the calculation of how the Jews were to return to Palestine was as important as the timing.

Ashley therefore told Lord Palmerston of his discovery, and tried to convince him that Britain should attempt the immediate restoration of the Jews to Palestine as part of the eventual fulfilment of Christian destiny.

It was said of Palmerston that he 'did not know Moses from Sir Sidney Smith' and he was certainly unconcerned with the fulfilment of prophecy. However, Ashley's proposal fitted his own interest in having a community of protégés in Jerusalem (the first British consul had taken office only a year earlier) and he incorporated Ashley's news about the Jews into a series of proposals made to the Sultan through the British ambassador at the Porte.

'There exists at present, among the Jews dispersed over Europe,' wrote Palmerston authoritatively in August 1840, 'a strong notion that the time is approaching when their nation is to return to Palestine.' He argued that it would be greatly to the advantage of the Ottoman empire should Palestine be settled with wealthy foreign Jews who constituted, as he thought, 'a sort of Free Mason fraternity' (not Lord Ashley's terminology) as a British protectorate.

The reference to wealthy foreign Jews and a Freemason fraternity suggests that the Jews Lord Palmerston had in mind were the great financiers of Western Europe and not the poor Talmudic scholars of Vilna or Biserta. Ashley had made it clear to his stepfather that the candidates for the Return were 'not the English Jews, or the rich, or the reformed or infidel Jews of Germany . . . But throughout the whole world, the rabbinical Hebrews would joyfully accept it. The early immigrants will come from Poland, Russia proper and the shores of north Africa' – all those places where the missionaries had heard the kabbalists' prediction.

It was ironical that Ashley and his informants in the Mission, with Palmerston tagging on, should have been encouraged by these reverberations of an ancient Jewish debate to believe that a national revival was near. The entire burden of Evangelist polemic against Judaism was that the Jews were no longer the people of the Old Testament, but slaves of 'Rabbinism' and of the study of the Talmud and the Kabbala, which – in the Christian view – distorted the message of the Scriptures and confirmed the Jews in their resistance to Christianity.

Moreover, Palmerston's unexpected proposal of a wholesale packing of Jewish bags and removal to the Orient, had it been public at the time, would have amazed the emancipated Jews of the West, who certainly had no knowledge of the messianic fervour attributed to them by the British Foreign Secretary.

*   *   *

Western Jews had been told often enough, during the early years of their emancipation, that they must abandon the kind of separate national consciousness which Palmerston was now attributing to them and which later polemicists were to urge on them. The French Constituent Assembly in 1789 had applauded the revolutionary Clermont-Tonnerre's famous proposal to 'give the Jews everything as individuals, nothing as a nation'. Macaulay, arguing in favour of civil rights for the Jews of England in 1833, had assumed that the Jews' faith in an Ingathering was mystical, and would not influence their behaviour as British citizens. When challenged by German philosophers on the specifically Jewish content of many of the laws of the Talmud, German Jewish apologists stressed the universal ethical message of Jewish teaching and played down its particular historical and social context. Reform Judaism, from the beginning of the nineteenth century, interpreted Jewish sources in such a way that Messianism meant the benefits of enlightenment and the Promised Land had a purely symbolic meaning.

The Jews of Europe played no part in the bible scholars' and scientists' rediscovery of Palestine in the century, as the explorer MacGregor noted in 1869: 'I wonder how with all their love of their people and their land they leave it to us Christians to search for their records among the rubbish – how they never ask the world for what the world would give them free, their own beloved Palestine.' A pioneering Jewish geographer of the mid-century, Yehosaf Schwartz, whose study of Palestine appeared in 1845, had made the same criticism: 'I cannot avoid blaming my fellow Israelites for their neglect of this beautiful science [geography] since they display no interest in our country in the scientific point of view.' But as an orthodox Jew himself, for whom all Gentile sources were suspect, Schwartz either did not read, or refused to quote, contemporary researches.

For assimilated Western Jews, Palestine was of no real interest; and for the orthodox, Jewish history and learning, not its geography, was of importance. When they returned to Palestine, it was the better to observe Jewish law as interpreted in the Talmud, not to revisit the sites of the battles of antiquity.

Emancipated Jews were prominent among Orientalist scholars, but it was no accident that, like the Jewish philosophers and historians of the time, their interest was in the general historical and cultural context of the texts they studied in a secular spirit, rather than in their territorial or national connotation. Nor were they favourably disposed to the Eastern European Jewish orthodoxy preserved intact in the holy cities of Palestine.

But if most emancipated Western Jews were uninterested in Palestine, there was a small group which felt a paternalist responsibility for the poverty-stricken and remote community. Moses Montefiore is the most celebrated example.

Born into a family of middle-class merchants, Montefiore married into the Jewish banking aristocracy and retired early from a career as a stockbroker to devote himself to philanthropy and public service on behalf of persecuted Jews all over the world. He visited Palestine seven times between 1827 and 1875 and attempted to alleviate the community's sufferings in a number of ways. But like most emancipated Jews, Montefiore was very remote from the community whose piety he respected as much as he deplored their backwardness (in European terms) and dependence on charity.

In the English context, Montefiore was a conservative among Jewish leaders. He opposed the Reform movement, did not believe in lobbying too fervently for radical changes in Jewish status, kept a sternly patriarchal grip on the community, and tried to ensure that the English legal system should accept rabbinical rulings as the sole law binding on Jewish marriage and divorce. But in Palestine, his lack of Jewish learning was obvious. He spoke no Hebrew – the lingua franca among the Jews of the different communities there – and needed the assistance of the learned Dr Louis Loewe, his amanuensis and an Oriental scholar, to decipher the petitions addressed to him and communicate with the Jews of Jerusalem. As a Sefardi, he knew no Yiddish – the language spoken among Ashkenazi Jews.

In Palestine there was no division between the secular and the religious life. The community was a theocratic one in which rabbis administered charity, and punished those who strayed from strict orthodoxy by withholding their allowance, excluding them from the synagogues, imprisonment, and in extreme cases excommunication and the refusal of Jewish burial. Although Loewe tells of encounters with a few Palestine Jews possessing secular learning – a Rabbi Moshe Meisil in Hebron with whom he discussed Schiller, Lessing and Herder – these were exceptions. For most of the Jews of Palestine all secular knowledge was forbidden, and even the teaching of foreign languages; there was no education but the *heder*, where the Bible was studied, and the *yeshiva* or Talmudic seminary, from both of which girls were excluded.

Montefiore had little formal education, but he admired learning, was put up for both the Athenaeum and the Royal Society, and apart from his attendance at synagogue led the life of an English gentleman. The belief he shared with his fellow philanthropists that the Jews of Palestine should be made productive citizens, taken out of their overcrowded and squalid ghettos in the cities, and properly educated – girls as well as boys – meant nothing to the rabbis, who suspected that such foreign utilitarian ideas would be disruptive of their way of life.

The leaders of the Palestine community were not passive objects of philanthropy. They saw themselves as an elite, entitled to live on the charity of the wealthy; Jewish scholars were traditionally supported by the merchant class. Moreover, the Montefiores and the Rothschilds, like the Guedallas and the Mocattas, were not the only foreign Jews dispensing charity. A far more powerful family, in terms of its links with the Jews of Palestine, was the strictly orthodox Lehren family of Amsterdam and The Hague, who since 1824 had controlled the flow of charitable funds from orthodox Jewry all over Europe to Palestine. Their central organization, the Clerks and Treasurers of Amsterdam, had a close relationship with the Palestine rabbis and saw to it that the allocation of charity remained dependent on the orthodoxy of the recipients. This family was, on many occasions, a formidable opponent to the 'enlightened' Jews of England, Germany and France.

*   *   *

Montefiore's first visit to Palestine in 1827 was part of a Grand Tour through the Mediterranean during which he and his wife also visited Rome, sightseeing on the Jewish Sabbath in ancient sites and churches, with only a brief glance at the Jewish ghetto. In Palestine itself the couple stayed at a Greek Orthodox convent (the Jews' deadliest enemies in the Holy Land were the Greeks) where they ate meat, and drank wine not prepared according to Jewish custom – both heinous sins in orthodox eyes. All this without any sign of awareness – according to Judith Montefiore's journal, the only undoctored part of the Montefiore's voluminous diaries which has survived – of any impropriety.

After Montefiore took on an official role in Anglo-Jewish life and became head of the English community, in the early 1830s, he made a point of observing every Sabbath and the main dietary laws. Nevertheless, on each of his successive visits he managed to offend orthodox feeling. His efforts to make an accurate census of the Jewish population as the first step towards organizing welfare projects infuriated Lehren and the rabbis of Jerusalem, who believed that counting Jewish heads brought misfortune. When the Noble Sanctuary was opened to foreigners after the Crimean War, Sir Moses horrified the Jews of Jerusalem by ascending the Mount on an official visit – no Jew was allowed to set foot there before the coming of the Messiah lest he tread the forbidden ground of the Holy of Holies – though they stopped short of an actual excommunication.

Nevertheless, at the outset of his activities in Palestine, Montefiore found that not all the Jews of Palestine were confined to their seminaries in the four Holy Cities. When he and Loewe set out to collect all the information they could on the lives of the Jews of Palestine, he found that numbers of Jews had lived in smaller towns in the north earlier in the century, where they had lent money to the Arab Moslem peasants to buy seeds or equipment, and taken part of the produce in return. This was not because they intended to become farmers themselves. Many of the Perushim, the ultra-orthodox sect which had arrived in Palestine from Lithuania during the first decade of the century, had bought vines and orchards during the period of Egyptian rule for a very specific religious purpose.

Many of the religious commandments or *mitzvot* specified in the Bible could only be carried out in the Land of Israel; they were laws which had long been in abeyance in the Diaspora. They detailed, for instance, which seeds should be planted by Jews, and the distance between them; the prescribed intervals after which fruit could be eaten from certain trees; and the law which ordered that the soil should lie fallow every seventh year, as well as many laws regarding tithes. It was to implement these laws that the Perushim leased land from its owners, complete with the peasant farmers.

There was also another reason why the Perushim were prepared to use Montefiore's good offices with the Turks; during the 1830s the original core of devout Talmudic scholars who made up the Ashkenazi community of Palestine had been swelled by thousands more who had left Eastern Europe to avoid the conscription of their sons, from as early as the age of twelve, for a quarter century of military service, or simply from poverty. Not all were scholars; so the Perushim rabbi Mordechai Tsoref proposed that groups of 'those less gifted at study' should lend a hand on the farms where the peasants would sow and plough the land.

It was with these requests in mind that Montefiore set out for Egypt in 1839 to make what was by far his most ambitious proposal on behalf of the Jews of Palestine: the suggestion that the Egyptian ruler should grant land in Palestine for hundreds of Jewish villages, the rent to be paid annually in Alexandria, but the land itself to be tax-free. 'By degrees,' Montefiore wrote, 'I hope to induce the return of thousands of our brethren to the land of Israel. I am sure they would be happy in the enjoyment of the observance of our religion in a manner which is impossible in Europe.'

So the first Western proposal for Jewish settlement in Palestine was a commercial proposition by a visionary businessman, grafted on to the traditional rituals of Eastern European rabbis. It had nothing to do with early nationalism or a Jewish return to the land. In any case, Mohammed Ali turned down the proposal; and a year later he lost control of Syria.

By far the most important event linking the Jews of West and East followed immediately on Montefiore's return to England. In Mohammed Ali's province of Damascus the ancient blood libel against the Jews had been revived, and several Jews had been imprisoned and tortured, falsely accused of murdering a French priest.

Now, for the first time, the emancipated Jews of the West took a public stand on behalf of their less privileged brothers. Palmerston witnessed the rallying of international Jewry after the blood libel, and it is possible that this too affected his view of an imminent Jewish Return supported by the 'Freemason fraternity'. With Montefiore in July 1840, when he set out for Constantinople to have the charge against the Jews annulled, was Adolphe Crémieux, the Franco-Jewish Minister of Justice. The mission was successful. Henceforth Montefiore's activities all over the world were part of his campaign for assistance against persecution and discrimination for the Jews of Eastern Europe,

North Africa and the Levant. His many journeys were undertaken as a British Jew representing not only Jewish solidarity but the humanitarian conscience of his country.

Where Palestine was concerned, however, there was an embarrassing anomaly. On the one hand, the Jews of Palestine were protected from persecution by the activities of the foreign consuls whose protégés they were – among them the British consul. On the other, the Jews of Palestine were now to be the chief objects of the conversionist attentions of the London Society, a highly respectable English institution and one which was shortly to achieve political backing.

There were several 'medical missionaries', chiefly converted Jews, to counter whose influence Montefiore despatched a Jewish doctor to Jerusalem; Loewe records that in 1838, Montefiore considered backing a proposal for a railway from Jaffa to Jerusalem, but was deterred by the thought that the missionaries might use it to expand their presence in Palestine. Yet the Mission was not yet identified with British policy in the region.

The whole situation changed with the creation of the Jerusalem bishopric.

*   *   *

Palmerston's proposals to the Sultan for the encouragement of a Jewish Return, at Ashley's urging, had come to nothing. But another ecclesiastical and political project which was backed by the Evangelists was the establishment of the Anglican bishopric in Jerusalem in 1841.

The original proposal for the bishopric had come from the Prussians, and it was largely a consequence of Prussian disappointment that their proposal for an European protectorate in Jerusalem had been rejected. The suggestion that the Anglican and Lutheran bishops should alternate in office gave the Prussians, and the Lutheran Church, a new status in the Holy City, and it was thus controversial in England both on political and on ecclesiastical grounds. The bishopric was an indication of how powerful the Evangelicals had become in the Anglican Church, and how important the idea of the conversion of the Jews had become to the Evangelicals.

For the duties of the bishop were 'to superintend the English clergy and congregations in Syria, Chaldea (Iraq), Egypt and Abyssinia and such other protestant bodies as may hereafter place themselves under his episcopal care . . . to direct the efforts now making in those countries for the conversion of the Jews; and to enter into relations of amity with the . . . Ancient Churches of the East'. As there were no English congregations in this enormous diocese worth mentioning, and the best guarantee of 'amity' with the Eastern bishops was staying out of their way, the conversion of the Jews was the bishopric's *raison d'être*.

It was also constitutionally awkward from the English point of view, being the only bishopric to be set up outside the British dominions; a special act of parliament had to be passed before the first bishop could be consecrated, as he was not an Englishman.

Michael Solomon Alexander, the first Anglican bishop of Jerusalem, was a Polish Jew of German birth who had been rabbi of a congregation in Plymouth before his conversion, chosen as much for his origins as his accomplishments. He seems to have been an amiable, not very clever man, with less animus against his fellow Jews than many other clergymen converts; he had headed the 'Hebrew Christian' protest against the Damascus blood libel in 1840.

Alexander set sail for the Holy Land in a British battleship, the *Devastation*, in the winter of 1841/2. After a difficult journey – Mrs Alexander was in the last stages of one of her many pregnancies – the family arrived in Jaffa and set out for the Holy City in the company of the British consul in Beirut, Hugh Rose.

'Our entry into Jerusalem was most honourable,' the bishop wrote later to a colleague in Leamington. 'The chief officers of the Pasha with a troop of soldiers conducted us through the gate into the City under the firing of Salutes headed by Arab music; the Jews here are greatly interested in our coming and say I am sent to build up the Jerusalem [sic]; . . . willing to come to us if we had the means of giving them substinence, which, as you know, they immediately lose on showing a Disposition to come to us.'

The bishop was wrong about the welcome, on all counts. The second-in-command of the governor's soldiers had been sent out to welcome Colonel Rose, not Alexander, and the guns were fired to celebrate the eve of the Moslem Feast of the Sacrifice, Corban Beiram. 'Thus, by an odd chance,' wrote the Jewish convert missionary F. C. Ewald, whose account was used by *The Times*, 'the Protestant Bishop made his public entry into one of the four holy cities of Israel . . . on the occasion of one of the greatest festivals of the Mahometan religion.' He was welcomed neither by Turks nor Jews; and the celibate churchmen of Jerusalem mocked the 'bishopess' and all the little 'bishoplings'. The Turks refused Alexander a firman to build a Protestant church, and the Jews pronounced anathemas.

When news of the indignities suffered by the bishop reached England, *The Times* castigated the adventure as 'precipitate' . . . 'undertaken by one or two of our own prelates because the King of Prussia gave money to improve . . . various Christian sects and to convert Jews (we forget whether the Turks also) in Jerusalem'. In a poorly attended debate in the House of Commons, the Liberal opposition called on the Prime Minister, Peel, to produce the correspondence with the Porte on the bishopric; the affair was a diplomatic fiasco, it was said, and if the Tory government really wished to improve the lot of the Jews, all they had to do was to remove their remaining civil disabilities in England itself – a barb aimed at Lord Ashley, who had steadily opposed the admission of Jews to parliament.

There is no indication in Montefiore's diaries of how he felt about the bishopric or the boost it gave to the missionaries. But the arrival of the bishop intensified the violence of the new confrontation between the London Society and the Jews of Jerusalem which was soon to involve Montefiore, and other European philanthropists, in the affairs of Palestine far more deeply than before.

With the approach of the year 1840 the Mission had stepped up its efforts at conversion. Part of the London Society's creed was the insistence that converted Jews made the best missionaries. In one sense this was a mistake, for no Jew was more hated than the convert, called by the orthodox a *meshummad* or destroyed one. But missionaries with a Talmudic background had great advantages and skill at working their way into Jewish circles, entering Jewish synagogues as worshippers and initially winning the Jews' confidence. Nor were they all as naive as Alexander. Among those who had proselytized among the Jews of the Levant since the 1820s was the legendary Joseph Wolff, who 'could conciliate a pasha, or confute a patriarch, travels without a guide, speaks without an interpreter, can live without food or pay without money'; F. C. Ewald, who in conversation with the Jews was evasive about his Jewish origins; Ridley Herschell, a nonconformist who had his own congregation in England and who debated fiercely with the rabbis of the Galilee; Moses Margoliouth, author of a vitriolic and encyclopaedic 'guide' to the Talmud, who entered a synagogue in Biserta, asked to participate in the service as a rabbi, and suddenly began preaching Christian doctrines; and the medical missionaries like Behrens and Bergheim, who were so important in the community during the period of epidemics in the mid-century that the rabbis hesitated to pronounce anathemas against them.

Among the most vulnerable to the missionary's message, as the year 1840 came and went, were the Perushim, the first of the Ashkenazi Jews to have settled in Jerusalem. Disciples of the spiritual leader, the Gaon of Vilna, they had been deeply involved in the messianic expectations of the period through their addiction to kabbala, and had even made changes in the liturgy in expectation of the miraculous event.

*   *   *

Three rabbis, one of them a member of one of the founding families of the Perushim, entered into discussions with the missionaries; in October 1842 they became 'enquirers' and began receiving instruction in the Christian religion. Nicolayson, in the missionary bulletin, was exultant: 'The apparently impenetrable phalanx of Rabbinism in Jerusalem has actually been broken into.'

For a year and a half Jews and missionaries fought over the souls of the three rabbis; families were separated, children sent abroad, back to Eastern Europe, for spiritual safety; copies of the New Testament were seized and publicly burned. Bishop Alexander and Rabbi Moses Maggid Rivlin, one of the heads of the Jewish community, confronted each other at the home of an 'enquiring rabbi', Eliezer Luria. Finally, in May 1843, two of the rabbis, Luria and Goldberg, with three other converts, were baptized; the third, Abraham Wolpin, changed his mind at the last moment, apparently so that he should not be parted from his wife.

It was a pyrrhic victory where the Mission was concerned, for the crisis strengthened those among the rabbis who opposed all attempts to interpret or hasten the process of redemption; there were to be no more rabbinical conversions. But it had shaken the community badly, and sent them to the Jews of the West for help to prevent all future contact between the Jews and the London Society's missionaries.

The most frequent form of contact was by sick Jews seeking the help of the medical missionaries. From 1839 the Society had provided a dispensary which handed out free medicines and medical advice, and its records indicate that the entire community consulted the Mission's doctors regularly. This was not surprising, given the appalling conditions in which the Jews lived. Dr Edward MacGowan, the Mission's physician, wrote: 'Their dwellings are in dark vaulted caves, the roof dropping with damp from above and the bare earth underneath, and often without a door or window to keep out the wind and rain. It is in these dark and dismal abodes that the descendants of God's chosen people drag out a miserable existence, and present a striking fulfilment of that utter desolation which was to fall on His city and nation.' Hyperbole apart, the fact that the water sources were badly contaminated, that most of the Jewish population was undernourished, and that the Jewish quarter was hopelessly overcrowded, ensured that, as MacGowan noted, no sooner had he cured a patient than he or she would relapse and again seek treatment at Christian hands.

Frantic appeals were launched, in the early 1840s, to the Jews in the West to provide an alternative to the Mission's medical services. The Rothschilds were prepared to contribute to the main expense of constructing a Jewish hospital; but they attached a condition, which was that adjoining the hospital a secular school was to be set up on the European pattern. The rabbis, prompted by Lehren, turned the proposal down. They dreaded the influence of European emancipation more than they feared the cholera or the Mission.

Montefiore financed the despatch of a German doctor, Fränkel, to Jerusalem, paid his salary and expenses and a rival dispensary was set up. But this was totally insufficient for the growing community, as the Mission realized. At the end of 1844, Nicolayson and MacGowan opened a well-staffed hospital. The New Testament, in Hebrew, was placed in every ward and there were daily prayers to which all were invited. 'All the officers and agents connected with the medical department avail themselves of every suitable opportunity to convey to the minds of those receiving benefit . . . that it is to the principles of Christianity alone, and not to being a mere philanthropic effort, that they are indebted.'

The rabbis proclaimed an anathema against anyone using the hospital, set guards to watch the access to the building, and refused to bury a Jew who died there a month later. Subsequently, the Mission bought a plot for a special cemetery which was neither Jewish nor Christian consecrated ground, but was used for those Jews who died in the hospital without having been converted – a kind of perpetual limbo.

Despite the bans, threats and warnings, the Jews of Jerusalem, who had no other alternative, continued to patronize the hospital in their thousands for another ten years. Surprisingly few were converted there. According to the Society's records, the first convert was made only when Montefiore arrived for his third visit in 1849, after a cholera epidemic. The response to the rabbis' renewed pleas for a hospital came in 1853, when they were suddenly courted by both Montefiore and the Rothschilds, each with elaborate plans and promises.

During this period, the Jews of Jerusalem, cut off from their main source of funds in Eastern Europe by the Crimean War, became nearly destitute. One of the Rothschilds paid a secret visit to Jerusalem to assess the community's needs, while an American Jew, Judah Touro, left a substantial sum to the 'indigent Jews of Jerusalem' to be used by Montefiore. Franco-British rivalry played as great a part in what followed as Jewish charity. While Montefiore commissioned an architect to design an ambitious building, the Rothschilds leased local premises and formally opened their hospital in July 1854 in the presence of the consuls and city dignitaries. Albert Cohn, the Rothschilds' agent, in his inaugural speech – which to the chagrin of James Finn mentioned neither the mission hospital nor Montefiore's previous help to the Jews – announced: 'Today we witness the first fruit in the East of European civilisation.' As if to underline the point, while the hospital itself admitted only Jews, and was still inadequate for the community, its clinic provided free medical help to Christians and Moslems as well.

*   *   *

Before long, the failure of the Mission to make significant numbers of converts was well known all over Europe. Thackeray, who visited Jerusalem in 1843, wrote: 'The English mission has been very unsuccessful with these religionists. I don't believe the Episcopal apparatus . . . has succeeded in converting a dozen of them; and a sort of martyrdom is in store for the luckless Hebrew in Jerusalem who shall secede from his faith . . . we could not but feel a pity for them, as they sat there on their benches in the church conspicuous, and thought of the scorn and contumely which attended them without, as they passed in their European dresses and shaven beards, among their grisly, scowling, long-robed countrymen.' The French consul Jorelle seeing, as most of the other consuls did, a machiavellian English plot behind the establishment of the bishopric, reported in March 1847: 'England must attribute huge importance in converting a few Jews to Protestantism, for the tiny number and zero value of their successes of the English mission do not at all justify the huge expense its proselytising costs in Palestine.'

Alexander died on a journey to Egypt in 1845 and was succeeded by Samuel Gobat, the Prussian nominee; Bishop Gobat was, according to Mrs Finn, the tallest man in the city – taller even than the German consul von Munchausen. He was an experienced missionary who had worked for the Church Missionary Society for years in Abyssinia and from the outset expressed his scepticism about converting Jews. All his energies, and those of the Church Missionary Society's rival missionaries who joined him in Jerusalem, were directed to the Arab Christians of Palestine. His bishopric was characterized by an increase of Protestant institutions in Jerusalem, most of them schools and orphanages set up by German missionaries and patronized by Arabs, converts from the Greek Orthodox community. But all the mission schools also attracted a small number of Jewish pupils, and once more the philanthropists in the Jewish communities abroad were goaded into action.

The London Society, meanwhile, had realized that it could not hope to encourage 'enquirers' if these were to be immediately deprived of their share in Jewish charity, and that some form of alternative employment had to be provided. From the early 1840s they provided workshops where the poorer Jews could learn a trade while receiving instruction, and at the end of 1848, the Mission set up a 'House of Industry', an 'enquirers' home' on the lines of a similar project in London where potential converts could study bookbinding, or carpentry; this organization, too, very expensive to run, attracted only a handful of Jews. Its main importance was that the rabbis almost instantly asked for a Jewish equivalent: in the case of the 'House of Industry', they approached Montefiore in the following month.

But the trouble was that the rabbis wanted only practical help – at the most an extension of those artisan facilities which already existed; while Western Jewry wanted to give them a secular education. The Jews also wanted more investment in the country, on their own terms, than the philanthropists could raise abroad. Virtually every scheme of Montefiore's collapsed: a weaving school, set up in 1844, with antiquated machinery, was abandoned; a school for girls was rapidly deserted after the Ashkenazi rabbis menaced families who dared send their daughters there; attempts to settle Jews on the land in the Galilee and on the coast, with no preparation or training, were total failures.

Both Austrian and French philanthropists who tried to set up schools teaching secular subjects, with the help of the consuls in Jerusalem, suffered setbacks. Ludwig August Frankl, a poet and Jewish functionary from Vienna, arrived in Jerusalem in 1858 to set up a Jewish school on behalf of a wealthy Austrian Jewish family, the von Laemels. Although Frankl disapproved strongly

·of the missions, their enticement of Jews into what he called the 'golden net', their 'demoralisation' of entire families, he could not help admiring their hospital, schools, and the orderly and pious convert congregation. While the local Sefardi Jews applauded his efforts, the Perushim proscribed the Laemel school and Frankl found himself suspected of spreading Christian influence; before the opening ceremony, held under the school portraits of the Austrian Emperor and Simon von Laemel, Frankl had feverishly to scrape the Grand Cross off the Emperor's breast with a penknife and erase a Christian-looking lamb, part of the coat of arms of his Jewish patron.

'Were I to express an opinion on the subject,' wrote MacGowan to the Society in 1856, 'I would say that the views of Sir Moses Montefiore, though highly rational and enlightened in the abstract, are not altogether suited to the subjects for whose benefit they are designed.' The Jews, MacGowan explained, did not want to return to the world of commerce, something the English Jew 'with his businesslike habits and utilitarian views, did not comprehend'. The Jews of Jerusalem lived according to a religious system: 'This system may be destroyed, but cannot be secularised.'

But the Mission itself was already deep in trouble. If the problem of the Jewish philanthropists was that they could not change the way of life of the orthodox Jews who were so resistant to the missionaries' blandishments, the London Society's missionaries were to discover that the converts they did succeed in making were attracted to the Western way of life, with all its material satisfactions, and did not afford the missionaries the spiritual satisfaction they were seeking – the conviction that they had made good Christians of bad Jews.

While the Society wanted to give the Jews enough support to maintain them as 'enquirers', they did not seek to make them independent of the Mission. When in the early 1850s the Finns tried to obtain more than a token contribution from the London Society for the employment of indigent Jews, they ran into trouble: James Graham, the lay treasurer, wrote to London explaining that the Society in Jerusalem in no way supported Finn's agricultural schemes 'on behalf of 150 to 200 squalid wretches'.

The Society repeatedly announced, in its official publications, that it did not undertake to provide employment for proselytes. Initially, the missionaries had handed out money to the needy. When the numbers of patients at the Mission hospital ran into thousands, MacGowan reported that 'it was gratifying to be able to make them a small weekly allowance either in provisions or money'. By 1861, the heads of the Society deplored anything 'which tends to keep up a permanent connection in their minds between their profession of Christianity and the collection of money' and opposed a converts' welfare fund run on an independent basis.

The irony was that, in Jerusalem, it was not poverty alone that had driven the Jews into the arms of the missionaries. By 1858, on the contrary, the convert community in Jerusalem was a reasonably prosperous group of tradesmen, artisans and hotel keepers. Many had been converted outside the borders of Palestine itself: others clearly regarded their conversion as a passport to the West. It was initially believed in the community that conversion increased the chances of acquiring foreign nationality, just as many thought that to become a protégé of a Western state automatically entitled one to that state's nationality. It was not the poor and humble, who were all the more vulnerable to the rabbis' harassment, who converted, but the more successful members of the Jerusalem community, who could afford to ignore them. Moreover, as August Frankl and others noted, many of the poor Sefardi Jews – whose charitable funds were in any case more meagre – played off the Jewish philanthropists against the Christians, playing the 'enquirers' for temporary benefit and then scurrying back into the rabbinical fold.

The records of the Mission confirm the impression that the converts were not motivated by strong religious beliefs, or driven out of the community by spiritual conflicts like those of 1840. Careful notes were made of the converts' economic situation and moral character, revealing that very few met the Society's standards where their religious beliefs were concerned, though most were 'industrious and respectable'. Mr Hauser, manager of the Mediterranean Hotel, was hard-working, but 'his religious knowledge was small'. Rosenthal, dragoman at the British consulate, was 'unsatisfactory in the religious point of view', as were the Meshullams of Artas. Some converts, like Wiseman the hospital steward, were reformed characters; others, like Nahman, 'partly maintained by the mission', wanted 'energy of character'. Even the Bergheims, bankers and industrialists, and the wealthiest converts in the city, and Moses Shapira, the owner of Jerusalem's most successful antiquities shop until his downfall, did not satisfy the missionaries. 'Of Shapira, we cannot say more than that he sincerely and enthusiastically believes the truth.'

During the next couple of years, disaster struck the convert community, and the London Society's Mission. The English newspapers were full of the Rosenthal case; accused by Gobat of dishonesty (in his role of building contractor – like most consular officials he had another occupation), Rosenthal was defended by Finn, who accused Gobat in turn of libel. All Protestant Jerusalem was in an uproar. A watchmaker named Cinianki, a father of ten, baptized only a few years earlier, 'a waving, wavering, unsatisfactory character . . . toying with the RCs', insisted on having his daughter's tent pitched near that of the Crawfords, among the Society's leading figures, when the community went on a trip to the Jordan. During the night the girl gave birth to an illegitimate baby, which she drowned in the river. Neither the Prussians nor the British consul wanted to handle the case. Miss Cooper, the head of the girls' school, returned to England after a tug of war with Bishop Gobat over pupils – of whom there were all too few; a missionary named Miss Creasy, a 'poor misguided firebrand', was murdered in a field near Jerusalem, and worst of all for the missionary cause as a whole were the scandals connected with the bishopric: accusations of homosexual practices among convert boys in Gobat's school, and the Hanna Hadoub case.

Hanna Hadoub was an Arab from a Latin family known to have lived off the prostitution of a number of women, including two wives. In the hope of keeping Hadoub Protestant – he was threatening to become a Greek Orthodox Christian – Gobat connived at his marriage to a fourteen-year-old girl. Barely a year later, he was convicted of armed robbery and sentenced to life imprisonment.

Crawford wrote despairingly to the London Society that despite the hopes aroused by the bishopric, 'for some reason or other it has pleased God to abuse these lofty expectations, to disappoint them in every respect.' Where the converts were concerned, they were 'thorns in our side'; he thought that in the entire community, there were not more than two or three who present 'evidence of abiding impression'. The painter Edward Lear, visiting Jerusalem in this year, wrote to his friend Lady Waldegrave: 'One word about the Jews: the idea of converting them to Xtianity at Jerusalem is to the sober observer fully as absurd as that you should institute a society to convert all the cabbages & strawberries in Covent Garden into pigeon-pies & Turkey carpets.'

*   *   *

While the missionaries grew increasingly disillusioned with their Jewish protégés, Jewish philanthropists in the West were taking a far more critical attitude towards the orthodox leadership in Jerusalem and the charitable policies of men like Montefiore.

In 1860 the Alliance Israelite Universelle was founded, centred in Paris. It signalled a move towards Jewish action not dependent on a few charitable individuals. It also favoured not merely the distribution of charity but the promotion of secular education. While the Alliance rapidly became an instrument for the dissemination of French culture in the East, the Jewish press in England and America, and to a lesser extent in Germany, urged reforms on the Palestine community and tried to wean them from their dependence on charity.

Deputations went out to Palestine at the end of the 1860s, sent both by the Alliance and the Anglo-Jewish community, and reported that living on charity bred corruption and idleness – a criticism of the orthodox community unthinkable in an earlier period. The Sefardi Jews were signalled out for praise because they constituted the main source of Jewish artisan labour and did not share the Ashkenazi fear of foreign culture. Heinrich Graetz, the great historian of the Jews, among the few Jewish intellectuals in the West who actually visited Palestine during the nineteenth century, regarded the orthodox sects like the Hassidim and the Perushim, with their kabbalistic interests, as an anachronism in the age of enlightenment. He visited Palestine in 1872 and proposed that Jewish charity be withheld from parents unwilling to send their children to schools where a general education was provided, and to those who married their children off before puberty; he also recommended that no funds be sent to those who entrusted their children to the care of the missions.

Anglo-Jewry was well aware of the fact that Protestant visitors to Palestine who knew little of Jewish tradition saw the Talmudic scholars as lazy paupers. One of the sharpest critics of the system of charity to the orthodox was Henry Lumley, secretary to the Poor Law Committee, who, visiting Palestine in 1875, branded Jewish life there as an example of 'corruption, demoralisation and mendicancy'. The English Poor Law had long since ended the support of 'able-bodied paupers' and their families, and Lumley was particularly critical of the tradition of child marriage, which swelled the rolls of those eligible for funds at the price of high infant mortality.

Montefiore, by now an old man, and his conservative supporters in Jewry, resented criticism of the orthodox whether from Jews or Protestants. Haim Guedalla argued that the Jews of Jerusalem 'have as yet escaped Stock Exchanges, syndicates and dancing rooms and may as well permanently continue without them'. As it happened, no European Jew was as yet suggesting that Jerusalem be turned into a branch of the Stock Exchange; instead, they were looking at the example of the Protestant settlers in Palestine and proposals to turn Talmudic students into farmers, proposals which came from men with Evangelical sympathies.

Montefiore's last visit to Palestine, at the age of ninety, in 1875, was undertaken to refute his critics. He urged his fellow philanthropists to learn from 'the munificent endowments and institutions of the non-Israelites', and suggested that the Jews create garden suburbs, 'houses with olive trees, vine and necessary vegetables . . . so as to give the occupiers a taste for agriculture'.

Some of the Jews of Palestine were already learning from the Protestant settlers, and from the establishment of the Hebrew press in Jerusalem in 1863 reported their activities faithfully. At first they warned their fellow Jews against farming ventures, pointing to Finn's bankruptcy, the failure of Montefiore's farms at Jaffa and Tiberias, and the hostility of local peasants and Bedouin. When Meshullam's neighbours flooded his lands, the Jaffa settlers were murdered, and Arabs pastured their flocks on Templars' fields, the warnings seemed justified. But by the 1870s, the Hebrew press was holding up the Protestant settlers as models. One of Finn's Jewish protégés, Joshua Yellin, tried to set up in partnership with Arab tenant farmers. Joel Moses Salomon, a Jerusalem printer, was sent to investigate the process of grafting (in accordance with Jewish law) in the Templar settlements. Queries about the Templars' work, and the equipment necessary to begin farming in Palestine, arrived from traditional Jewish communities as far afield as Ponevetz in the Russian Pale of Settlement.

The idea of putting Jews back on the land appeared less threatening to the local community than Christian hospitals and schools, and Protestant models were the original inspiration for the first Jewish settlement of Petah Tikva, founded by observant Jews from Jerusalem in 1878. The Protestants who laid down the blueprints for such villages were colonialist patrons, used to dealing with difficult settler material; it was not accidental that the idea of experimental farms had first been put to Montefiore by Lieutenant-Colonel George Gawler, an ex-Governor-General of Australia, who had strong Millenarian views on the Jewish Return. In the 1870s, his son, John, late of the British army in South Africa and India and later Keeper of her Majesty's Regalia at the Tower of London, proposed that as the Jews of Palestine were demonstrably unused either to farming or manual labour, they should be employed on the lines familiar to him from India: 'piecework for fair remuneration'. His actual ambition, it later became clear, was to encourage Protestant settlement in Palestine with Jewish labour, and ultimately thus to achieve the Jews' conversion. Laurence Oliphant, the other leading English backer of agricultural settlement schemes for the Jews, was playing for larger political stakes, seeing Palestine as a field for the kind of political and diplomatic intrigue in which he revelled. His schemes proposed the settlement of those Jews who fled Rumania during the persecutions and pogroms of 1882 on the east bank of the Jordan, the thin end of the wedge of an ultimate British protectorate in Palestine. Though brought up in Evangelical circles, and related to Lord Shaftesbury, Oliphant professed to share none of their eschatological views. But he was very well aware of the financial resources available to those Protestant and conversionist organizations involved with Palestine, and even promised to the politically naive and desperate Jews of Eastern Europe that their Christian friends in the West would contribute hundreds of thousands of pounds to assist their settlement.

In fact Oliphant was in no position to fulfil the expectations he had aroused, and his interference in Jewish affairs led to a confrontation with the Alliance. Their experience in trying to run the first educational agricultural school in Palestine, Mikve Israel, near Jaffa, and the opposition it had encountered from the orthodox community, as well as the problems of settling Jews on the land, had convinced them that were thousands of destitute Jews to flee to Palestine, the missions would spring back to life to prey on them: 'that which the promotors of the movement [for mass settlement] have sown,' insisted Charles Netter, the dedicated founder of Mikve Israel, in 1882, 'the buyers of souls will reap.'

The last battle between the missionaries and the orthodox Jews of Palestine was indeed fought over the bodies and souls of a few hundred Russian Jews who managed to emigrate to Palestine towards the end of 1882. These people, though members of observant families, had come to Palestine expecting to find work and homes. Neither, as Netter had predicted, was ready for them. Nor were they eligible for a share of the charitable funds of the established Ashkenazi residents. A few found work at Mikve Israel under Moslem overseers – which they resented, and the Ashkenazi rabbis advised them to make their own appeal to charity from Western Jewry.

This galvanized the half-dead Mission into action. Under an energetic convert missionary, Moses Friedlander, the Mission offered living quarters, a regular salary and an education for their young to the new immigrants. They were assured that they were free to worship as they pleased and to observe their Sabbath. All the anathemas, threats and warnings pronounced by the rabbis initially had no effect. The newcomers founded a separate community of their own, with the Mission's help, and they were even promised land.

Friedlander had appealed to the London headquarters of the Society, and money to buy land in the plain – now very expensive –was raised by the 'Jewish Refugees Fund' headed by Lord Aberdeen. Lord Shaftesbury bought the community a set of Scrolls of the Law. But it soon became apparent to the settlers that they were not to be left to go their own way where worship was concerned. Many of the children were separated from their families in mission schools and began receiving instruction in Christian doctrine; and those employed by the Mission found that they could only earn high wages if they were prepared to listen to sermons – forbidden by the rabbis under pain of total excommunication. Once again, appeals were sent out to Western Jewry; the money received by the Ashkenazi rabbis, on the immigrants' behalf, was used to send many of them back to Russia. The Jewish settlement of Artuf, with forty families, was sponsored by the Society and set up in early 1883. But no settlement patronized by those determined to change their faith could survive. The colony lasted only three years.

*   *   *

During the two decades following the scandals of 1858, the number of Jews converted dropped dramatically. While from the time of the Mission's revival until the period of the scandals, some ninety-six adult 'Israelites' were baptized in Jerusalem, according to the Society's records, between this period and the dissolution of the Joint Bishopric, in 1883, only twenty-six adult Jews were baptized; the others, a hundred and twenty-five in number, were infants. So by 1883, with the Jewish community in Jerusalem grown to eighteen thousand souls, only some two hundred and fifty, more than half of them unwittingly, had become Christians.

Not only had the missions failed to convert the Jews; in so far as they had any influence at all over Jewish opinion, they had actually discouraged a Jewish Return. The rabbis of Jerusalem sent Jews back to Eastern Europe to escape the blandishments of the Mission, and leading Jews in both England and France argued against mass emigration to Palestine lest destitute Jews fall into missionary hands.

The Church *Quarterly Review* pronounced the bishopric 'entirely barren of results, good or bad' in 1883, when the partnership with Germany came to an end. This was not quite true from the political point of view. What the bishopric had done, especially during Gobat's term of office, was to strengthen the German presence in Palestine. When the German ambassador in London wrote to the Archbishop of Canterbury in 1883 dissolving the agreement, he remarked that as German Protestants now outnumbered the English in Jerusalem, and had now created all their own institutions there, 'the growth of the German community made Anglican patronism [sic] unnecessary'.

*   *   *

The Evangelical vision faded. From the time of Palmerston's brief flirtation with the idea in 1840 until late in the First World War, there was no serious political interest, in European circles, in the Return of the Jews. If some of the British officers of the Palestine Exploration Fund supported the idea of Jewish settlement in the interests of British imperialism (Wilson, Warren, Kitchener, and – after initial misgivings – Conder), it was because they thought the Jews more reliable protégés than the local Moslems, and not in the hope of fulfilling prophecy.

It was British political interests, as perceived in 1917, which prompted the Balfour Declaration, not dormant hopes for the Millenium – whatever the sentimental gloss given their backing for the Zionists by bible-reading politicians like Balfour and Lloyd George.

The orthodox Jews of Palestine never received their historical due for having resisted the subtle and benevolent advances of the London Society and its supporters. They remained vigorous opponents to Western Jews' attempts to enlighten and secularize them. The nature of Zionism as a secular and revolutionary movement was hard to reconcile with Jewish orthodoxy. Yet it was this battle which brought the almost forgotten Jews of Palestine to the attention of the emancipated Jews of the West, at the period when the Damascus blood libel, the Mortara case – the kidnapping and forced conversion of a Jewish child by Italian Catholics – and renewed persecution in Eastern Europe revived international Jewish solidarity.

Even the most imaginative of philo-semitic writers in the West did not wholly comprehend Jewish opposition to the idea of conversion. Browning, in his poem 'Holy Cross Day', published in 1855, put the following lines in the mouth of his archetypal medieval rabbi, Ibn Ezra:

> God spoke and gave us the word to keep
> Bade never fold the hands nor sleep
> Mid a faithless world at watch and ward
> Till Christ at the end relieve our guard.

The real voice of Jewry sounded different. A fifteenth-century Spanish Jew, Moses Remos, wrote on the eve of his execution for refusal to convert:

> The Arch enemy offered to save my head if I would exchange my glory for the worship of his God. I answered him: it is better for my body to die than my soul. My portion is the living God: let the dead one be his.

BIBLIOGRAPHY

The sources consulted for this book are listed in two sections. All sources from the period itself are given under chapter headings in the first section. This is followed by a general bibliography, in which the historical, biographical and other works produced later (mostly in the last two decades) are to be found.

Chapter I   The Rediscovery of Palestine, 1799–1831

'The Siege of Acre', or Descriptive Collections related to the late scene of combat, etc. Companion to the 'Great Historical Picture' painted by Robert Ker Porter at the Lyceum (London, 1801).

Berthier, L. A., *Relations des Campagnes du Général Bonaparte en Egypte et en Syrie* (Paris, 1800).

Bourienne L. F. de, *Mémoire de M. de Bourienne sur Napoléon* (Paris, 1801).

Heeren, A. H. L., *Essai sur l'influence des Croisades*, tr. Charles Villiers (Paris, 1808).

Clarke, Edward, *Travels in various countries of Europe, Asia and Africa*, Vols. II, III, (London, 1810–23).

Conder, Josiah, *The Modern Traveller: Vol. I – Palestine* (London, 1825).

Volney, F. C. Comte de, *Travels Through Syria and Egypt, 1783–85* (London, 1788).

Wittman, William, *Travels in Turkey, Asia Minor, Syria, etc. with the British Military Mission* (London, 1803).

Damoiseau, Louis, *Voyage en Syrie, etc.* (Paris, 1833).

Forbin, M. le Comte de, *Voyage dans le Levant en 1817 et 1818* (Paris, 1819).

Neophitus, Diary of, 1821–1841, English translation by Spyridon. *Journal of the Palestine Oriental Society*, Volume XVIII (Jerusalem, 1938).

Joliffe, T. R., *Letters from Palestine, Syria and Egypt* (London, 1819).

Carne, John, *Letters from the East* (London, 1826).

Carne, John, *Recollections of Travels in the East* (1830).

Carne, John, *Syria and the Holy Land* (London, 1836–8).

Madden, R. R., *Travels in Turkey, Egypt, etc.* (London, 1829).

Henniker, Sir F., *Notes during a visit to Egypt, Nubia, etc.* (London, 1824).

Light, Henry, *Travels in Egypt, etc.* (London, 1818).

Didot, Ambroise Firmin, *Notes d'un voyage fait dans le Levant* (Paris, 1826).

Turner, William, *Journal of a Tour in the Levant, Vol. II* (London, 1820).

Curzon, Robert, *Visits to Monasteries in the Levant* (London, 1844).

Chateaubriand, F. R. Vicomte de, *Itinéraire de Paris à Jérusalem* (Paris, 1811). See also: *Itinéraire de Pantin au Mont Calvaire en passant par la rue Mouffetard, etc.* (Paris, 1811) and *Itinéraire à Jérusalem de Julien, domestique de M. de Chateaubriand*, ed., Charpin (Paris, 1904).

Chateaubriand, F. R. Vicomte de, *Journal de Jérusalem; notes inédites publiées par G. Moulinier et A. Outry* (Paris, 1950).

Leblich, Domingo Badia y (Ali Bey el Abbasi), *Travels of Ali Bey, Vol. III* (London, 1816).

Richardson, Robert, *Travels along the Mediterranean and ports adjacent in company with the Earl of Belmore, 1816–17–18* (London, 1822).

Belzoni, G., Narrative of the operations and recent discoveries in Egypt (Mrs Belzoni's narrative on p. 285ff) (London, 1822).

Dumont, Louise, *Journal of the Visit of H.M. the Queen to Tunis, Greece and Palestine* (London, 1821). See also: 'The New Pilgrim's Progress, or a Journey to Jerusalem' in *Political Satires* (London, 1821).

Jowett, Rev. William, *Christian Researches in the Mediterranean from 1815 to 1820* (London, 1822).

Jowett, Rev. William, *Researches in Syria & Palestine, 1823–4* (London, 1825).

Fisk, Pliny, *Memoir of the Rev. Pliny Fisk* (Boston, 1828; reprinted Arno Press, NY, 1977).

Fisk, Pliny, Sermon preached in the Old Church, Boston, before the departure of the Palestine Mission (Boston, 1819; reprinted Arno Press, NY, 1977).

D'Beth Hillel, Rabbi David, *Travels, 1824–32*. Revised edition under the title *Unknown Jews in Unknown Lands*, ed., Walter J. Fischel (NY, 1973).

Löwinsohn, Solomon, *Lexicon of the Land of Israel* (Hebrew) (Vienna, 1819; reprinted, with an introduction by George Kressel, Tel Aviv, 1945).

Michaud, Joseph and Poujoulat, J. F., *Correspondance d'Orient 1830–33*, Vols. IV, V (Paris, 1833–5).

Chapter II   The Baroque in the Desert

Seetzen, Ulrich J., *A Brief Account of the Countries Adjoining Lake Tiberias, the Jordan and the Dead Sea* (London, 1813).

Seetzen, Ulrich, J., *Reisen dürch Syrien, Palästina, etc.* (Berlin, 1854–9).

Burckhardt, Jean Louis, *Travels in Syria and the Holy Land* (London, 1822).

Burckhardt, Jean Louis, *Notes on the Bedouins and Wahabis* (London, 1831).

Otter, W., *Life and Remains of the Reverend E. D. Clarke* (for Burckhardt's letters to Clarke (London, 1824).

Buckingham, James Silk, *Travels in Palestine through the Countries of Bashan and Gilead* (London, 1821). *Travels among the Arab Tribes* (London, 1825).

McMichael, W., *Journey from Moscow to Constantinople and Jerusalem* for Legh's memoir (London, 1819).

Verbatim Report of the Actions for Libel in the case of Buckingham *v.* Bankes, tried in the court of the King's Bench, 19 October 1826 (London, 1826).

Irby, Charles, and Mangles, J., *Travels through Nubia, Palestine and Syria* (London, 1823).

Marcellus, Vicomte de, *Souvenirs de l'Orient* (Paris, 1839).

Chapter III   Palestine and the Authentication of the Bible

Géramb, Marie-Joseph de, *Pelérinage à Jérusalem et au Mont Sinai en 1831–3* (Paris, 1848).

Hogg, Edward, *Visit to Alexandria, Damascus and Jerusalem during the successful campaign of Ibrahim Pasha* (London, 1835).

Blondel, Edouard, *Deux Ans en Syrie, 1838–9* (Paris, 1840).

Poujoulat, B. P., *Voyage dans l'Asie Mineure*, Vol. II (Paris, 1841).

Palestine Exploration Fund Quarterly Statement 1879 (p. 51), (henceforth PEFQS) 'The visit of Bonomi, Catherwood & Arundale to the Haram esh Sharif at Jerusalem in 1833'.

Bartlett, W. H., *Walks about the City and Environs of Jerusalem* (for 'Mr Catherwood's adventure', pp. 148–65) (London, 1842).

Finden, William, *The Biblical Keepsake* (London, 1835). *Landscape Illustrations of the Bible*, 2 vols. (London, 1836).

Burford, Robert, *Description of the View of the City of Jerusalem and the surrounding country, now exhibiting at the Panorama, Leicester*

Square (London, 1835).

MacEnery, Robert, *Eastern Manners and Customs* (London, 1857).

Munk, Solomon, *La Palestine; Description Géographique Historique et Archéologique* (Paris, 1845).

Clarke, Adam, ed., *Observations on various passages of Scriptures, etc. compiled by the Rev. Thomas Harmer* (London, 1816).

Robinson, Edward, *Biblical Researches in Palestine, Mt Sinai and Arabia Petraea* (London, 1842).

Robinson, Edward, *Later Biblical Researches in Palestine* (London, 1856). See also: Smith, H. B. and Hitchcock, R. D., *The Life, Writings and Character of Edward Robinson* (New York, 1863).

Lynch, William Francis, *Narrative of the US Expedition to the River Jordan and the Dead Sea* (London, 1849).

Lynch, William Francis, *Official Report of the US Expedition to explore the Dead Sea and the River Jordan* (Baltimore, 1852).

Montague, P., *Narrative of the Late Expedition to the Dead Sea* (Philadelphia, 1849).

Allen, W., *A New Route to India* (London, 1844). See also: in PEFQS, 1886 (p. 145), Professor Hull; 'Did the Waters of the Jordan Originally Flow into the Gulf of Aqaba?'

Thomson, William McLure, *The Land and the Book* (London, 1859).

Thomson, William McLure, *The Land of Promise* (London, 1865).

Tristram, Henry Baker, *The Land of Israel; journal of Travels in Palestine* (London, 1865).

Tristram, Henry Baker, *A Natural History of the Bible* (1867); *The Land of Moab* (1863).

Tristram, Henry Baker, *Fauna & Flora of Palestine in the Western Survey of Palestine* (1884).

Stanley, A. P., *Sinai and Palestine in Connection with their History* (London, 1856). See also: Prothero, R. E. and Bradley, G. G., *The Life and Correspondence of A. P. Stanley* (London, 1893).

Keith, Alexander, *Evidence of the Truth of Christian Religion* (with a refutation of the Rev. A. P. Stanley's Poetical illustrations) (London, 1844).

Gadsby, Rev. J. D., *A Visit to Mt Sinai and the Holy Land* (London, 1864).

Gadsby, Rev. J. D., *The Biblical and Oriental Warrior* (London, 1888).

Martineau, Harriet, *Providence as Manifested through Israel* (London, 1832).

Martineau, Harriet, *Traditions of Palestine* (London, 1830).

Martineau, Harriet, *Eastern Life, Present and Past* (London, 1848).

Renan, Ernest, *La Vie de Jésus* (Paris, 1863).

Jésus (14th edition of the same work) (Paris, 1864).

Correspondance, vol. I (1846–71) (Paris, 1926).

Kitto's Family Bible (London, 1871).

Cassell's Family Bible (London, 1870–4).

Doré, Gustave, *Illustrated Bible* (London, 1872–6).

Roberts, David, *The Holy Land, from Drawings made on the spot* (London, 1842–9). See also: Ballantine, James, *The Life of David Roberts*, RA compiled from his journals and other sources (Edinburgh, 1866).

Lear, Edward, 'A Leaf from the Journals of a Landscape Painter' (The Journey to Petra), *Macmillan's Magazine* (April, 1897).

Goupil-Fesquet, F., *Voyage en Orient fait avec Horace Vernet en 1839 et 1840* (Paris, 1840).

Fromentin, Eugène *Un Eté dans le Sahara* (Paris, 1855).

Holman-Hunt, William, *Pre-Raphaelitism and the Pre-Raphaelite Brotherhood* (London, 1905). See also: Unpublished Letters, Bodleian Library, Oxford MS Eng. Let. 296, and Farrar, Archdeacon & Meynell, Mrs Alice: W. Holman-Hunt, *His Life and Work* (London, 1893).

Chapter IV   'King Consul'

UNPUBLISHED SOURCES

Public Record Office, Kew, London: Consular Records from Jerusalem and Beirut in FO 78 (Turkey) and FO 195 (Consular), 1839–82.

Ministère de l'Extérieur, Paris. Correspondance Consulaire et Commerciale, Jerusalem, Tomes I–IV, 1842–82.

National Archives of the United States, Washington (microfilm; Hebrew University of Jerusalem, Mt Scopus). Despatches from US Consuls in Jerusalem, 1856–82.

PUBLISHED SOURCES

Blondel, Edouard, *Deux Ans en Syrie et en Palestine 1838–9* (Paris, 1840).

Poujade, Eugène, *Le Liban et la Syrie, 1845–1860* (Paris, 1861).

de Nerval, Gérard, *Voyage en Orient* (Paris, 1851).

Finn, James, *Stirring Times; or Records from Jerusalem Consular chronicles of 1853 to 1856*, 2 vols. (London, 1878).

Finn, Elizabeth, *Reminiscences of Mrs Finn* (London, 1929).

Finn, Elizabeth, *Home in the Holy Land* (fiction) (1886).

Finn, Elizabeth, *A Third Year in Jerusalem* (fiction) (1869).

Thackeray, W. M., *Notes of a Journey from Cornhill to Jerusalem* (London, 1845).

Saulcy, Félicien de, *Carnets de Voyage en Orient (Voyage de 1850)* ed., Bassan (Paris, 1955).

Flaubert, Gustave, *Journals* (Paris, 1925).

Malherbe, Raoul de, *L'Orient, 1818–45, Vol II* (Paris, 1846).

Minor, Clorinda, *Meshullam: or Tidings from Jerusalem* (Philadelphia, 1851).

Lortet, Paul, *La Syrie d'Aujourd'Hui, 1825–80* (Paris, 1888).

Oliphant, Laurence, *Haifa, or Life in Modern Palestine* (London, 1887).

Chapter V   Feudal Palestine; Akil Aga

UNPUBLISHED SOURCES

Public Record Office, Kew, London: Consular despatches from Finn in Jerusalem and Moore in Beyrouth, 1856–61.

Ministère de l'Extérieur, Paris: Correspondance Politique des Consuls, Turquie, Beyrouth (vols. 11–14), 1856–63.

PUBLISHED SOURCES

MacAlister, R. A. S., and Masterman, E. W. G., 'A History of the Doings of the Fellahin during the First Half of the 19th century from Native Sources', PEFQS, 1906, pp. 221–5 and pp. 286–91.

Thomson, W. M., *The Land and the Book*, op. cit.

Holman-Hunt, W., *Letters*, op cit. Letter to Mr Combe, 21 August 1864.

Cornille, Henri, *Souvenirs d'Orient* (Paris, 1836).

Lynch, William Francis, *Narrative of the US Expedition, etc*. op. cit.

Finn, James, *Stirring Times*, op. cit.

Rogers, Eliza Mary, *Domestic Life in Palestine* (London, 1863).

Stanley, A. P., *Sermons Preached before HRH The Prince of Wales during His Tour in the East in the spring of 1862* (London, 1863).

HRH The Prince of Wales, *Memoir of, from Birth to Convalescence, etc.*, (London, 1872).

Tristram, Henry, *The Land of Israel*, op. cit.

HaLevanon, Jerusalem: Report dated 13 Shvat (January) 1865.

HaLevanon, Jerusalem: Report dated 20 Tammuz (June) 1865 (Hebrew).

HaMevaser, Lemberg, Report no 26. dated Tammuz 1865 (Hebrew).

Dixon, W. Hepworth, *The Holy Land* (London, 1864).

Chapter VI   Popular Palestine

UNPUBLISHED SOURCES

Cook's Archives, London: Holograph letters between Thomas & John Cook.

Diary of Miss Riggs (1869).
D7. Diary of George Jager: Palestine and Egypt, 1875–80.

PUBLISHED SOURCES

Cook, Thomas, 'A Brief History of our Eastern Tours' in *Cook's Excursionist and Tourist Advertiser*, 8 December 1873 (henceforth CETA).

Buckingham, J. S., 'An Earnest Plea for the Reign of Temperance and Peace, as Conducive to the Prosperity of Nations – submitted to the visitors of the Great Exhibition in 1851'.

Holthaus, David, *Wanderings of a Journeyman Tailor, etc.* (London, 1841).

Morot, Jean-Baptiste, *Journal de Voyage, Paris à Jerusalem 1839/40* (Paris, 1841).

Galton, W., *Vacation Tourists and Notes of Travel* (1860).

Perinaldo, Padre da Francesco Cassini, *La Terra Santa* (Genoa, 1855).

Christ, Tommaso, *Aventure d'un Viaggio a Gerusalemme di Tomasso Christ, 1865* (Milano, 1883).

Bernardi, Jacopo, *Viaggio in Terra Santa* (Treviso, 1878).

Porter, Josias Leslie, *Handbook for Syria and Palestine* (London, 1858).

Ross Browne, John, *Yussuf or the Journey of the Franji (A Crusade in the East)* (New York, 1853).

Taylor, W. Bayard, *In the Lands of the Saracen* (New York, 1854).

Stephens, J. L., *Incidents of Travel in Egypt, Arabia and the Holy Land*, Vol. II (New York, 1837).

Twain, Mark, *The Innocents Abroad* (Connecticut, 1869).

CETA, 1869–82.

Burns, Jabez, *A Help Book for Eastern Travellers* (London, 1871).

Hodder, Edwin, *On Holy Ground* (London, 1874).

Bremer, Frederika, *Travels in the Holy Land*, tr., Mary Howitt (2 vols.) (London, 1862).

Warner, Charles Dudley, *In the Levant* (New York, 1875).

Jenner, Thomas, *That Goodly Mount and Lebanon, being the Narrative of a ride through the country of Judea, Samaria, Galilee etc. in the company of Youhamel el Karey of Nablus* (London, 1873).

Manning, S., *Those Holy Fields* (London, 1874).

Smith, G. A., Snow, L. etc., *Correspondence of Palestine Tourists 1872–3* (Salt Lake City, 1875; reprinted Arno Press, NY, 1977).

Floyd, Rolla, *Letters from Palestine 1868–1912*, ed., Helen Palmer-Parsons (Maine, 1981).

Mourot, M. l'Abbé V., *La Terre Sainte et le Pélérinage de Pénitence en 1882. Impressions et Souvenirs* (Paris, 1882).

265

Coupigny de Louverval, M. le Comte de, *Souvenirs du Pélérinage de Pénitence à Jérusalem* (Cambrai, 1882).

Salzmann, Auguste, *Jérusalem, Etude et Reproduction Photographique des Monuments de la Ville Sainte* (Paris, 1856).

Goupil-Fesquet, F., *Voyage en Orient, etc.*, op. cit.

Frith, Francis, *Egypt, Sinai and Palestine* (London, 1862).

Chapter VII   By Appointment to Palestine; Scholars and Soldiers

UNPUBLISHED SOURCES

Palestine Exploration Fund Archives, London: Letters sent from Palestine by Charles Wilson, Charles Warren, Claude Conder, Tyrwhitt Drake and Charles Clermont-Ganneau. Also correspondence between the Fund and the War Office.

Institut de France, Paris. Fonds Clermont-Ganneau (4112), Vol. V. Papers relating to Clermont-Ganneau's work for the PEF, including letters exchanged between Ganneau and Walter Besant during 1873/4.

Public Record Office, Kew, London. Consular despatches relating to the PEF in FO 78 (Turkey) and FO 195 (consular).
War Office papers (WO).

Private Letters of Claude Conder. Hebrew University, Jerusalem, MS Varia V 1209.

PUBLISHED SOURCES

Palestine Exploration Fund, ed., *The Survey of Western Palestine* (7 vols.).

See in particular: Vol. II Memoirs of Conder; Vol. IV Jerusalem: Warren and Conder; Vol. VI Fauna & Flora; Vol. VII Special Papers (Mrs Finn, Drake, Ganneau on the population of Palestine).

Committee of the PEF, *Our Work in Palestine* (London, 1873).

PEF Proceedings and notes, 1865–9.

PEFQS 'On the Survey': 1872, p. 1ff; 'The Shapira Collection', 1874, pp. 114–124; 'The Gezer Stone' 1874, pp. 148, 276; 'The Moabite Stone', 1871, pp. 135–9; 'The Original Discovery of the Moabite Stone', (1870) p. 281–3; Letter from Selim el Qari, 1878, p. 100; 'Moabite Potteries', 1878, pp. 41, 95.

Conder, Claude Reignier, *Tent Life in Palestine* (London, 1878). *Heth and Moab* (London, 1883). *Palestine* (London, 1889).

Saulcy, Félicien, de, *Voyage autour de la Mer Morte* (Paris, 1853). *Voyage en Terre Sainte* (Paris, 1865). *Carnets de Voyage en Orient, 1845–1869*, ed., Bassan, (Paris, 1855).

Fergusson, James, *An Essay on the Ancient Topography of Jerusalem* (London, 1847). *The Holy Sepulchre and the Temple at Jerusalem* (London, 1865).

Williams, the Rev. George, *The Holy City; or Historical and Topographical Notices of Jerusalem* (London, 1845).

Wilson, Charles, *Picturesque Palestine, Sinai and Egypt* (4 vols.) (London, 1878).

Wilson, Charles, and Warren, Charles, *The Recovery of Jerusalem* (London, 1871).

Warren, Charles, *Underground Jerusalem* (London, 1875).

Ganneau, Charles Clermont, *Archaeological Researches in Palestine, 1873/4*, Vol. II (London, 1896); Vol. I (London, 1899).

Ganneau, Charles Clermont, *Les Fraudes Archaéologiques en Palestine* (Paris, 1885).

Ganneau, Charles Clermont, *La Palestine Inconnue* (Paris, 1876).

Ganneau, Charles Clermont, 'Mont Gisart et Tell el Djezer' in *Récueil d'Archéologie Orientale*, pp. 351–91 (Paris, 1888).

Drake, Charles Tyrwhitt, *The Literary Remains* ed., with a memoir by Walter Besant (London, 1877).

Palmer, E. H., and Drake, C. T., *The Desert of the Exodus* (London, 1871).

Besant, Walter, *The Life and Achievements of Edward Henry Palmer* (London, 1883).

Haynes, A. E., *Manhunting in the Desert, being the Narrative of the Palmer Search Operation* (London, 1894).

Blunt, Wilfrid Scawn, *The Secret History of the English Occupation of Egypt* (London, 1907), pp. 399–415.

Besant, Walter, *Twenty-one Years' Work in the Holy Land* (London, 1886).

Ganneau, Charles Clermont, 'Les Antiquités Sémitiques', inaugural lecture, Chair of Epigraphy and Semitic Antiquities, Collège de France (Paris, 21 May 1890).

Chapter VIII   'Till the Conversion of the Jews'

UNPUBLISHED SOURCES

Papers of the London Society for Promoting Christianity among the Jews (Church Mission to the Jews).

CMJ Papers. New Bodleian Library, Oxford.

St Anthony's College, Oxford, Middle East Centre: Letters of Bishop Alexander. DS 125.3.A5.

Diary of John Nicolayson, 1826–9. Copy in Jerusalem Municipal Archives.

PUBLISHED SOURCES

Gidney, W. T., *Missions to Jews: a Handbook of Reasons, Facts and Figures* (London, 1897).

Gidney, W. T., *History of the London Jewish Society, 1809–1908* (London, 1908).

Halsted, T. J., *Our Missions* (London, 1886).

Stock, E., *The History of the Church Missionary Society* (London, 1899).

Salle, Eusèbe de, *Pérégrinations en Orient, 1837–39* (Paris, 1840).

Michon, M. l'abbé J. H., *Voyage Réligieux en Orient* (Paris, 1853).

Disraeli, Benjamin, *Tancred, or the New Crusade* (London, 1847).

Lamartine, Alphonse de, *Souvenirs, Impressions et Paysages pendant un voyage en Orient*, 4 vols. (Paris, 1835).

Schwartz, Yehosaf, *Descriptive Geography of the Holy Land*, tr., Isaac Leeser (Philadelphia, 1850).

McCaul, Alexander, *The Old Paths* (London, 1837).

McCaul, Alexander, *The Duty of and Method of Bringing Good Tidings to Jerusalem. Sermon etc.* (London, 21 April 1841).

Wolff, Rev. Joseph, *Missionary Journal and Memoir* (London, 1824).

Herschell, Rev. Ridley, *A Visit to my Fatherland* (London, 1844).

Margoliouth, Rev. Moses, *A Pilgrimage to the Land of my Fathers* (London, 1850).

Margoliouth, Rev. Moses, *The Fundamental Principles of Modern Judaism Investigated* (London, 1853).

Ewald, F. C., *A Journal of Missionary Labours, 1842–44* (London, 1846).

Bonar, A. R., and M'Cheyne, A., *Narrative of a Mission of Enquiry to the Jews from the Church of Scotland in 1839–1846* (London, 1846).

Neil, Rev. James, *Palestine Repeopled or Scattered Israel's Gathering* (London, 1877).

Loewe, Dr Louis, ed., *Diaries of Sir Moses and Lady Montefiore* (London, 1890).

Montefiore, Judith, *Private Journal of a visit to Egypt and Palestine in 1827* (privately printed in 1836; selection published, Jerusalem, 1975, with an introduction by Y. Bartal).

Pupils of the Gaon of Vilna, from Safed, 1810, in *Ya'ari*, ed., *Letters from the Land of Israel* (Hebrew) (see General Bibliography).

Frankl, Ludwig, *The Jews of the East*, tr. Beaton (London, 1859).

Oliphant, Laurence, *The Land of Gilead* (London, 1881).

Oliphant, Laurence, 'Jewish Tales and Jewish Reform' in *Blackwood's Magazine* (November, 1882).

GENERAL BIBLIOGRAPHY

UNPUBLISHED SOURCES

Bensinger, G., Palestine in German Thought and Action, 1871–1914. Ph.D. thesis, (University of Michigan, 1971).

Cohen, Amnon, Jezzar Ahmed Pasha (Hebrew). M. A. thesis, (Hebrew University of Jerusalem, 1965).

Morgenstern, Arieh: The Clerks and Treasurers of Amsterdam and the Jewish Community in Palestine (Hebrew). Ph.D. thesis, Hebrew University of Jerusalem, 1981.

Sharon, Moshe, The Bedouin in Palestine in the 18th and 19th centuries (Hebrew). M.A. thesis (Hebrew University of Jerusalem, 1964).

PUBLISHED WORKS

Albright, W. F., The Archaeology of Palestine (London, 1949).

Albright, W. F., Yahweh and the Gods of Canaan (London, 1968).

Albright, W. F., Proto-Sinaitic Inscriptions and their Decipherment (Oxford, 1966).

Albright, W. F., Archaeology and the Religion of Israel (Baltimore, 1942).

Anderson, M. S., The Eastern Question, 1774–1923 (London, 1966).

Aref el Aref, History of Gaza (Arabic) (Jerusalem, 1943).

Aref el Aref, Bedouin Love Law and Legend (Jerusalem, 1944).

Ashkenazi, Tuvia, Tribes Semi-Nomadiques de la Palestine du Nord (Paris, 1938).

Avigad, Nahman, Discovering Jerusalem (Jerusalem and Nashville, Tennessee, 1980).

Avissar, Oded, Book of Tiberias (Hebrew) (Jerusalem, 1973).

Avitsur, Shmuel, Daily Life in Palestine in the 19th century (Hebrew) (Tel Aviv, 1972).

Bahat, Dan, 'Warrens' digs in Jerusalem' in Broshi, ed., Beyn Hermon le Sinai (Hebrew) (Jerusalem, 1977).

Bailey, Clinton, 'The Negev in the 19th Century; Reconstructing history from Bedouin oral traditions' in Asian and African Studies, XIV, pp. 35–80, (Jerusalem, 1980).

Bartal, Israel, 'Moses Montefiore and the Land of Israel' in Cathedra (Hebrew) no. 33 (Jerusalem, 1984).

Bassan, Fernande, *Chateaubriand et la Terre Sainte* (Paris, 1959).

Ben Arieh, Yehoshua, *Jerusalem in the 19th Century; The Old City* (Jerusalem and New York, 1984).

Ben Arieh, Yehoshua, *The Rediscovery of the Holy Land in the 19th century* (Jerusalem and New York, 1978).

Ben Arieh, Yehoshua with Bartal, Israel, ed., *The History of Palestine in the 19th Century*, Vol. 8, 1799–1917 (Hebrew) (Jerusalem, 1983)

Bliss, F. J., *The Development of Palestine Exploration* (New York, 1903).

Blumberg, Arnold, *A View from Jerusalem, 1849–1858. The Consular Diary of James and Elizabeth Ann Finn* (New York, 1980).

Canaan, Tewfik, *Mohammedan Saints and Sanctuaries in Palestine* (Jerusalem, 1927).

Carmel, Alex, *German Settlement in Palestine at the end of the Ottoman Period* (Hebrew) (Jerusalem, 1973).

Carmi, T., ed., *The Penguin Book of Hebrew Verse* (London, 1981).

Chadwick, Owen, *The Victorian Church*, parts I, II (London, 1966/70).

Chelini, Jean and Branthomme, Henri, *Les Chemins de Dieu; Histoire des Pélérinages Chrétiens des Origines à Nos Jours*, pp. 314–43 (Paris, 1982).

Chouraqui, André, *L'Alliance Israélite Universelle et la Renaissance juive contémporaine; Cent Ans d'Histoire* (Paris, 1960).

Cohen, Amnon, *Palestine in the 18th century* (Jerusalem, 1973).

Cohen, Richard I., Ed., *Vision and Conflict in the Holy Land* (Jerusalem and New York, 1985).

Corey, M. W., *From Rabbi to Bishop. The Life of Michael S. Alexander* (London, 1957).

Davies, Moshe, ed., *With Eyes toward Zion, Vol I* (New York, 1977); *Vol II* (New York, 1986).

Dupont-Sommer, André, 'Un Dépisteur de Fraudes Archaéologiques: Charles Clermont-Ganneau, 1846–1923' in *Comptes Rendus de l'Académie des Inscriptions et Belles Lettres*, pp. 591–610 (Paris, 1974).

Dussaud, René, 'Les Travaux et les découvertes archaéologiques de Clermont-Ganneau' in *Comptes Rendus de l'Académie des Inscriptions et Belles Lettres*, pp. 140–241 (Paris, 1974).

Eliav, Mordechai, *Palestine and its settlement in the 19th century* (Hebrew) (Jerusalem, 1978).

Eliav, Mordechai, *Under Imperial Austrian Protection, 1849–1917* (Hebrew); selected documents from the Austrian Consulate in Jerusalem (Jerusalem, 1985).

Eliav, Mordechai, ed., 'Shorashei Ha Yishuv Hehadash' in *Sefer HaAliya HaRishona* (Aleph), Jerusalem.

Field, James A., *America and the Mediterranean World* (Princeton, 1969).

Finnie, David, *Pioneers East; the Early American Experience in the Middle East* (Cambridge, Mass., 1967).

Fraser Rae, Sir William, *The Business of Travel* (London, 1891).

Gilbert, Martin, *Jerusalem, Rebirth of a City* (London, 1985).

Gillespie, C. C., *Genesis and Geology* (New York, 1962).

Gissing, A. C., *William Holman-Hunt* (London, 1936).

Hagen, Victor von, *Frederick Catherwood* (London, 1967).

Hardy, R. T., ed., *The Holy Land in American Protestant Life. 1800–1948* (New York, 1981).

Holman-Hunt, Diana, *My Grandfather, His Wives and Loves* (London, 1969).

Hoskins, H. L., *British Routes to India* (New York, 1928).

Hourani, Albert, *Europe and the Middle East* (California, 1980).

Hourani, Albert, 'Ottoman Reform and the Politics of Notables' in Polk, Chambers, ed., *The Beginnings of Modernisation in the Middle East* (Chicago, 1968).

Hourani, Albert, 'The Changing Face of the Fertile Crescent in the 18th Century' in *Studia Islamica*, vii, pp. 89–122 (1957).

Hyamson, Albert M., *The British Consulate in Jerusalem in Relation to the Jews of Palestine 1838–1914*, 2 vols. (London, 1939–41).

Hyamson, Albert M., 'British Projects for the Restoration of the Jews to Palestine' in *Publications of the American Jewish Historical Society*, no. 26.

Iseminger, G. L., 'The Old Turkish Hands; the British Levantine Consuls' in *Middle East Journal*, XXII, p. 298 (1968).

Jaussen, Antonin, *Coutumes des Arabes au Pays de Moab* (Paris, 1908).

Jaussen, Antonin, *Coutumes des Arabes; Naplouse* (Paris, 1908).

Jullian, Philippe, *The Orientalists: European Painters of Eastern Scenes* (Oxford, 1977).

Kark, Ruth, 'Millenarism and Agricultural Settlement in the Holy Land in the 19th century' in *Journal of Historical Geography*, 9, pp. 47–62 (1983).

Kark, Ruth, *Jaffa, A City in Evolution, 1799–1917* (Jerusalem, 1986).

Kark, Ruth, 'Changing Patterns of Land Ownership in 19th century Palestine: the European influence' in *Journal of Historical Geography* 10, 4 pp. 357–84 (1984). 'The Importance of Reports of the US Consuls in the Holy Land for the study of 19th century Palestine' in Davies, ed., *With Eyes toward Zion, Vol II*, op. cit.

Kedem, Menachem, *The Endeavours of George Gawler to Establish Jewish Colonies in Eretz Israel. Cathedra* (Hebrew) 33, pp. 93–107 (Jerusalem, October 1984).

Kedourie, E., and Haim, S. G., ed., *Palestine and Israel in the 19th and 20th centuries* (London, 1982).

Kelner, Jacob, *For Zion's Sake; World Jewry's Efforts to Relieve Distress in the Yishuv, 1869–1882* (Hebrew) (Jerusalem, 1976).

Kenyon, Kathleen, *Archaeology in the Holy Land* (London, 1965).

Klausner, Israel, *A Nation Awakes. The Movement from Russia to Zion* (Hebrew) pp. 307–20, missionary activity (Jerusalem, 1962).

Kon, Maximilian, *The Tombs of the Kings* (Hebrew) (Tel Aviv, 1947).

Lipman, Sonia, and V. D., ed., *The Century of Moses Montefiore* (Oxford, 1985).

Lipman, V. D., ed., *Sir Moses Montefiore: A Symposium* (Oxford, 1982).

McAlister, R. A. S., *A Century of Excavation in Palestine* (London, 1925).

Mansur, A., *History of Nazareth* (Arabic) (Cairo, 1924).

Ma'oz Moshe, *Ottoman Reform in Palestine and Syria* (Oxford, 1968).

Ma'oz Moshe, ed., *Studies in Palestine during the Ottoman Period* (Jerusalem, 1975).

Marmorstein, Emile, *Heaven at Bay* (Oxford, 1969).

Migdal, J. S., ed., *Palestine Society and Politics* (Princeton, 1980).

Moorey, Roger, *Excavation in Palestine* (Guildford, 1981).

Neuville, René de, 'Heures et Malheurs des Consuls de France à Jérusalem au XVII, XVIII et XIX siècles', *Journal of the Middle East Society*, 1, 2 (Jerusalem, 1947).

Nir, Yeshayahu, *The Bible as Image; The History of Photography in the Holy Land, 1839–1899* (Philadelphia, 1985).

Notes et Documents des Musées de France, 5. *Félicien de Saulcy et la Terre Sainte* (Paris, 1982).

Onne, Eyal, *Photographic Heritage of the Holy Land, 1839–1914* (Manchester Polytechnic Institute of Advanced Studies, 1980).

Oppenheim, Max Freiherr von, *Die Beduinen, Vol. II*, p. 30ff – Akil Aga (Leipzig, 1943).

Parfitt, Tudor, 'The French Consulate and the Jewish Community in Palestine in the 19th Century' in *Cathedra* (Hebrew), 5 (Jerusalem, 1977).

Ponko, Vincent, Jr, *Ships, Seas and Scientists: US Naval Exploration and Discovery in the 19th century* (Annapolis, 1974).

Pudney, John, *The Story of Thomas Cook* (London, 1936).

Reardon, Bernard M. G., *Religious Thought in the Victorian Age* (London, 1980).

Reich, Ronni, 'The Boundary of Gezer; on the Jewish settlement of Gezer in Hasmonean times' in *Eretz Israel: Archaeological, Histor-*

ical and Geographical Studies (Hebrew) Vol. 18, pp. 167–80 (Jerusalem, 1985).

Russell of Liverpool, Lord, *Knight of the Sword* (biography of Sir Sidney Smith) (London, 1964).

Schama, Simon, *Two Rothschilds and the Land of Israel* (London, 1978).

Schölch, Alexander, 'European Penetration and the Economic Development of Palestine, 1856–1882' in Owen, Roger (ed.), *Studies of the Economic and Social History of Palestine in the 19th and 20th centuries*, pp. 10–87 (London, 1982).

Silberman, Neil Asher, *Digging for God and Country* (New York, 1982).

Simmons, Jack, 'Thomas Cook of Leicester', lecture to the Leicester Archaeological and Historical Society (1 June 1932).

Sims, Katharine, *Desert Traveller; the Life of Jean Louis Burckhardt* (London, 1969).

Stevens, Mary Anne, ed., *The Orientalists: Delacroix to Matisse; European Painters in North Africa and the Near East* (London, 1984).

Swinglehurst, Edmund, *Cooks' Tours, the Story of Popular Travel* (London, 1982).

Swinglehurst, Edmund, *The Romantic Journey* (London, 1984).

Taylor, Anne, *Laurence Oliphant* (Oxford, 1982).

Tibawi, A. L., *British Interests in Palestine, 1800–1901* (London, 1961).

Tibawi, A. L., *American Interests in Syria, 1800–1901* (Oxford, 1966).

Tidrick, Kathryn, *Heart Beguiling Araby* (Cambridge, 1981).

Tuchman, Barbara, *Bible and Sword* (London, 1957).

Turner, Ralph, E., *James Silk Buckingham, 1786–1855. A Social Biography* (London, 1934).

Vaczek, L. and Buckland, G., *Travellers in Ancient Lands; a portrait of the Middle East* (New York, 1981).

Vereté, Mayir, 'Palmerston and the Levant Crisis, 1832' in *Journal of Modern History* XXIV, pp. 143–51, (1952).

Vereté, Mayir, 'Why was a British Consulate established in Jerusalem?' in *English Historical Review*, p. 316 (1970).

Vereté, Mayir, 'The Idea of the Restoration of the Jews in English Protestant Thought 1790–1840' in *Middle Eastern Studies* 8/1, pp. 3–50 (1972).

Vincent, Père, L. H., 'Charles Clermont-Ganneau et l'Archéologie Palestinienne' in *Journal of the Palestine Oriental Society*, III, pp. 88–92 (1923).

Vital, David, *The Origins of Zionism* (Oxford, 1975).

INDEX